Fashion as Photograph

for my father

Fashion as Photograph

Viewing and Reviewing Images of Fashion

Edited by Eugénie Shinkle

I.B. TAURIS

LONDON · NEW YORK

Published in 2008 by I.B. Tauris & Co Ltd
6 Salem Road, London W2 4BU
175 Fifth Avenue, New York NY 10010
www.ibtauris.com

In the United States and Canada distributed by Palgrave Macmillan,
a division of St. Martin's Press, 175 Fifth Avenue, New York NY 10010

ISBN hardback: 978 1 84511 516 6
ISBN paperback: 978 1 84511 517 3

A full CIP record for this book is available from the British Library
A full CIP record for this book is available from the Library of Congress
Library of Congress catalog card: available

Typeset in Caslon by Dexter Haven Associates Ltd, London
Printed and bound in Great Britain by TJ International, Padstow, Cornwall

Contents

Figures

Plates

8. Hans Feurer, *Pick Yourself a Winner*, fashion feature for *Sunday Times* Magazine, 11 July 1971.

9. Richard Burbridge. Stella Tennant models for the cover of *i-D*, London, April 2001. Bruce Weber, *United States Olympic Special*, cover of Andy Warhol's *Interview*, New York, January–February 1984.

10. Toni Frissell, 'United we Stand', cover of American *Vogue*, July 1942. Zanna, *England Rules OK*, feature on stylist Katy England for *ES* magazine, London, 28 September 1997.

11. Terry Richardson, *Nancy, What's for Dinner?*, catalogue for Sisley, 2002.

12. Laurence Le Guay, 'Untitled (Fashion Queue with Masked Child)', 1960. Gelatin silver photograph, vintage 32.0 x 56.3 cm. Purchased 1978.
Collection Art Gallery of New South Wales. Copyright Candy Le Guay.

13. Mary McCartney, Stella McCartney, Spring/Summer 2004.
Image courtesy of Stella McCartney.

14. *Dress Me Up, Dress Me Down*, SHOWstudio interactive featuring Liberty Ross, 2005.
Courtesy of SHOWstudio.

15. Nick Knight, 'It's a Jungle Out There', Alexander McQueen show invitation, 1997.
Courtesy of Nick Knight.

16. Nick Knight, 'Laura de Palma', *Visionaire*, 1997.
Courtesy of Nick Knight.

17. Cover, *Street* 165, May 2005.
Courtesy of *Street*.

18. Martin Parr, 'Junk Space', *Fashion Magazine* 1, Summer 2005.

19. Juergen Teller, 'Kristen Lifting Skirt', London, 2005.
Courtesy of the artist.

Acknowledgements

I owe a great deal to the following people and organizations; without their help and support, this book simply could not have happened.

I am very grateful to the Arts and Humanities Research Council for a generous grant to cover the cost of colour illustrations. Additional financial support was provided by the University of Westminster; in particular I'd like to extend thanks to Stevie Bezencenet, and to Rosie Thomas at the Centre for Research and Education in Art and Media.

For their cheerful and efficient help in locating images, I'd like to thank Zoe Tomlinson at Rankin Studios, Laura Bradley at SHOWstudio, Kaylie Mountford at Nick Knight, and Ayse Arf, April Day and Angela Espinosa at Icon International. For their invaluable technical support with image files, I'm very grateful to Rachel Cunningham and Dave Freeman at the University of Westminster. Very special thanks to digital wizard Keith Moodie – I could not have navigated my way through the arcane world of tiffs, jpegs, drop shadows and file conversions without his assistance.

Heartfelt thanks to Philippa Brewster, my editor at I.B. Tauris, for her support and advice, and for making the process as smooth as possible. I'm very grateful to Peter Saville for his time and his interest in the project. My colleagues in the Department of Photography and Digital Media at the University of Westminster also deserve special mention for being outstandingly supportive and understanding, particularly during the final preparation stages of the manuscript.

The original idea for the book came out of a conference held at London's National Portrait Gallery in May 2004. The conference was organized by myself, my colleague Neil Matheson, and Stephen Allen and Roger Hargreaves at the NPG, with the support and assistance of Andy Golding and Sally Feldman at the University of Westminster's School of Media, Arts and

Design. I owe them all a great deal.

Finally, I'd like to extend heartfelt thanks to everyone who contributed to *Fashion as Photograph*. Many of those who gave their time to the project did so in the face of incredibly demanding schedules. All of the contributors to this volume were a pleasure to work with, and I thank them for their generosity and kindness, as well as their interest and belief in the project.

Introduction

Photographic images play a key role in defining global fashion culture and in charting its discursive space. They are seen by many as the driving force behind the fashion system, with cultural pundits and industry creatives heralding the photograph as fashion's 'ultimate signifier' (Saville in Burgoyne 2002: 36). Since the early 1990s, fashion photography has commanded an increasing share of public consciousness, as well as a growing amount of wall space in museums, galleries and auction houses. It has engaged with new technologies and challenged ideals of beauty, it has proved politically and aesthetically provocative, economically lucrative, and ideologically potent. Despite this, fashion photography has been paid little attention by the scholarly and critical community.

Printed media on fashion photography are everywhere these days: accounts of photographers, designers and trends, volumes of portraiture and street chic, magazines and themed collections, exhibition catalogues, monographs, limited-edition folios and bookworks. Critical accounts of fashion photography are much less easy to find. The limited number that exist are scattered throughout exhibition catalogues, magazines, journals, anthologies, newspapers and other media. For its part, photographic criticism has yet to engage with fashion photography in a sustained way, sharing with other forms of cultural criticism a kind of unspoken aversion to the medium. Fashion photography's coupling with industry and commerce, its flirtation with the frivolous and the ephemeral, its role in the marketing and selling of garments, the questionable part it plays in the construction of feminine identity — none of these have helped it to gain status in the eyes of visual and cultural studies. Lumped in with other forms of advertising, fashion images have too often been subjected to a limited range of analytical tools, most of them inherited from other discourses.

Fashion photography comprises a wide array of practices (editorial and advertising, beauty, portraiture and documentary photography, to name a few) and involves a range of skilled creatives and businesspeople (stylists, photographers, models, advertisers, artists, designers, hairstylists, creative and artistic directors, makeup artists, set builders and so on), brought together by shared goals and contexts. The field of fashion photography is capricious and hugely diverse, and the following chapters make no attempt to fix its boundaries or to confine it to a specific genre or practice. If there is one characteristic that is shared by all fashion photographs, however, it is their simultaneous placement within the artistic and commercial realms. 'Creativity versus commerce' debates have preoccupied critical assessments of fashion photography for some years. Important as this unique position is to the very identity of fashion imagery, art and commerce don't necessarily exist in a relationship of opposition, and the following chapters show the boundary between the two to be a shifting and highly permeable one. Presenting the voices and concerns of current cultural and photographic criticism alongside those of industry professionals, they explore the fashion photograph as visual image, material object, process, artwork and commodity form. *Fashion as Photograph* engages with the complexity of fashion photography, charting a path through its discursive space, identifying some of its key concerns, and making space for new critical languages to emerge.

*   *   *

The history of fashion photography is inseparable from that of fashion itself. Both are linked to the growth of capitalist economies and the development of mass markets. As a measure of social standing, fashion has been a part of Western culture since the Renaissance. It was not until the early nineteenth century, however, that it emerged as a widespread cultural and commercial phenomenon. Part of industrialized Europe's new individualist mentality, mass fashion emerged into a burgeoning culture of spectacle, self-development and material enjoyment, gaining a social and cultural significance that had previously been available only to society's elite. As part of the 'democratic revolution', fashion was a metaphor for the advent of modern democratic society and its growing cult of individuality, personal freedom and choice (Lipovetsky 1994). In an environment obsessed with appearance and novelty, the fashion designer was able to exercise considerable creative freedom. The modern couturier was no mere dressmaker, but was celebrated as an artist and a creative genius, despite the tacit knowledge that he or she was bound to the vagaries of consumer desire in a way that other artists were not.

As well as creative talent, however, modern fashion also depended upon image and advertising spectacles, and the visual presentation of fashion quickly became as important as the production of garments. The first couturier to open his doors to the public did so within 20 years of the birth of photography: Paris's first haute-couture salon was set up by Charles Frederick Worth in 1858. An innovator in the marketing of fashion, Worth knew that the commercial success of his designs was linked to their perceived exclusivity, and put considerable effort into promoting himself as an arbiter of style. Aware that the garment gained meaning and relevance for the consumer through its reproduction and circulation as an image, Worth also made sure that his designs were featured regularly in the elite fashion press (Breward 2003).

Illustrated fashion magazines first appeared at the end of the eighteenth century, but photographs of garments did not feature widely in the fashion press until early in the twentieth century. Thomas Condé Nast was one of the first publishers to replace fashion illustrations with photographs – a decision intended to satisfy readers who were 'so literally interested in fashion that they wanted to see the mode thoroughly and faithfully reported – rather than rendered as a form of decorative art' (Condé Nast in Craik 1993: 98). Early on, photographs functioned primarily in a documentary capacity, as an objective means of recording the latest styles. Within a short time, however, Condé Nast turned to the aesthetic and conceptual devices of artistic modernism for inspiration, engaging photographers like Baron Adolf de Meyer and Edward Steichen to bring their innovative photographic vision to the pages of *Vogue*.

Though it drew its visual inspiration from modern art, the fashion image was also concerned with the creation of consumer desire, and it is worth noting that, alongside the growing circulation of fashion photographs, the first two decades of the twentieth century also saw the emergence of modern advertising techniques. Advertising, as Robert Goldman describes it, is a 'mass mediated semiotic process' – a vehicle for the production of signs. Advertising images are visual frameworks 'within which meanings are rearranged so that exchanges of meaning can take place' (1992: 5). Understanding advertisements – revealing their meanings and their hidden ideological agendas – involves turning their semiotic structure back on itself in order to 'decode' them. Reading images in this way was also the dominant *modus operandi* of postmodernist photographic criticism, and a good deal of critical writing on fashion photography is still caught up, in one way or another, with these methodological habits. When critical theory engages fashion photography, it still tends to operate on the tacit – if rarely stated – assumption that fashion images communicate coded meanings in a more or less straightforward way. However, fashion photography's placement within the combined context of the traditional artistic avant garde and the more tightly circumscribed demands of corporate capitalism suggest that its means and methods are not necessarily those of other forms of advertising.

It might seem absurd to conceive of a discourse of photography that does not concern itself at some level with the reading of images, and it is not my intention here to argue for the wholesale rejection of semiotics as a method. In fact, many of the following essays draw, in one way or another, on two seminal texts by Roland Barthes – *Myth Today* and *The Fashion System* – in order to address the way that language, naming and rhetoric operate in the fashion image. In the latter text, Barthes treats fashion photography as a genre with its own unique set of codes:

> The Fashion photograph is not just any photograph, it bears little relation to the news photograph or to the snapshot, for example; it has its own units and rules; within photographic communication, it forms a specific language which no doubt has its own lexicon and syntax, its own banned or approved 'turns of phrase'. (1985: 5)

However, Barthes wrote *The Fashion System* between 1957 and 1963, at a time when it was still possible to characterize fashion photography as a relatively homogeneous field with a clearly defined lexicon and syntax. More recently, however, it has become obvious that there is no single and easily described genre of 'fashion photography'. Equally, there is no single methodology which is best suited to its analysis – examining fashion imagery through the lens of advertising overlooks the specificity of its form of address, not to mention the growing sophistication of its intended audience. Fashion images call into question many of the domain assumptions on which semiotic analysis depends, and the following chapters move away from straightforward semiological approaches in order to examine the relationship between fashion photography and signification in more nuanced ways.

While it would be a mistake to confine developments in recent fashion photography to a single decade, there is little doubt that the 1990s were a pivotal period in the recent history of fashion photography, and the following chapters focus primarily, though not exclusively, on fashion photography post-1990. This decade marks the beginning of a complex period in the culture of contemporary fashion and fashion image-making. Up until the mid-1980s, argues fashion-industry creative Peter Saville, identity was still being brokered through the medium of fashion:

> You actually still [had] people believing in something, and doing some-thing regardless of its profitability… Within that, there [were] other ways, and other lines, and other silhouettes; there [were] still gender issues, there [were] still political issues, [there was] still a stance to make for the individual. (2006)

By some accounts, the end of this period marked the beginning of a steady decline in fashion culture. There is little doubt, however, that the fifteen or so years that followed the end of the eighties were also marked by a wave of creative and professional freedom in both the alternative and mainstream fashion press. Less than five years ago, magazines like *Creative Review* were celebrating the 'golden age' of fashion photography, and the aesthetic choices it offered to contemporary image-makers (Derrick 2002: 63). These days, however, the high-fashion industry is dominated by a handful of massive companies – among them the French luxury goods group LVMH, PPR (owners of the Gucci Group), Prada and Dior – who tend to be more con-servative in their advertising and less willing to gamble on wild ideas and lesser-known talents.

Many of the essays in the collection highlight the spontaneity and creative freedom that typified fashion photography in the nineties and earlier, while others lament the control that advertisers now have over the content of advertising and editorial. Yet creative pathways exist even through this tightly controlled system. Since its launch in 2001, online fashion resource SHOWstudio has been funded by photographer and founder Nick Knight, allowing it to develop a content and direction that were led by its audience and participants rather than by advertisers. Shortly before this book went to press, however, SHOWstudio made the decision to include advertising on its site. The best ad campaigns, as Knight points out (2006), are intelligently constructed and socially engaged productions involving substantial research and effort by talented creative teams. SHOWstudio's decision to present fashion advertisements in the interactive critical context of its website is a tacit acknowledgement of the increasing media literacy of its audience, and of the finesse with which many fashion images combine visual seduction and social or political commentary. The following texts explore some of this content, focusing on the ways that representation contributes to changing definitions of gender and sexuality, drawing from fields like cultural politics and phenomenology to examine fashion photography as a situated practice. These and other ideas are developed in the chapters that follow, which are loosely grouped into four broad sections. There is considerable room for overlap between sections, however, and readers are encouraged to pay attention to the multiple and often conflicting viewpoints that chart the complex political, creative and ideological landscape of contemporary fashion photography.

*   *   *

The first section, 'Critical Contexts', examines some of the different institutions and ideologies that shape the meaning of the fashion image. For most fashion consumers, media images constitute their only point of contact with haute-couture garments. Caroline Evans examines the way that such images function as both signs and commodities within the context of capital to mediate and structure desires and social relations. Focusing on the linked phenomena of the catwalk show and the magazine page, Evans draws upon Guy Debord's notion of the 'society of the spectacle' to show how contemporary fashion circulates as both a situated practice and an image or idea.

Eva Respini and Susan Kismaric discuss fashion imagery in the context of the public art institution. In an edited excerpt from the catalogue essay for *Fashioning Fiction*, an exhibition of fashion photography held at New York's Museum of Modern Art in 2004, they examine the influence of art photography on the sensibility of recent fashion imagery. Focusing on the 1990s as a key decade in the development of contemporary fashion photography, they chart the movement of such imagery away from notions of idealized beauty towards a new vernacular allied with youth culture and street style, identifying the snapshot and cinema as its two dominant narrative modes. Presented to the gallery-going public as an art form in its own right, the expressive possibilities of fashion photography are considered independently from its commercial circumstances. In this context, the perceived value of the image has little to do with its success or failure as a piece of advertising. Instead, it is linked to the status of the photographer as artist, and in many cases to the quality or uniqueness of the image itself.

While the vast number of fashion images are as fleeting and accessible as the magazine page, a relatively small number go on to enjoy a lucrative afterlife on the collectors' market. Philippe Garner has been involved in the marketing of fine and rare photographic prints for over thirty years. Aware of the power that a small number of iconic images have on the shape (both critical and historical) of the field as a whole, Garner suggests that the photographic print may not necessarily be the most appropriate vehicle through which to read the story of fashion photography. Drawing on a selection of work from the sixties through to the present, Garner examines the magazine as the original point of interface between the photographers and their intended audience, pointing up the unique possibilities it offers for the study and appreciation of fashion photographs.

For Margaret Maynard, the meaning of the fashion photograph is dependent upon a network of influences. Maynard uses the metaphor of an ecology to examine how the look and meaning of a fashion image are less the result of an individual vision than the product of a set of dynamically interacting internal and external variables surrounding the production, publication and circulation of images. Here, the fashion photograph is considered not as a stand-alone artwork but as an 'incomplete utterance': a representation which is continually reframed by outside factors such as editorial policy, technical apparatus and the often conflicting opinions of the various creatives involved in its production. Maynard's approach suggests that fashion photography is best understood neither in terms of the photographer as auteur, nor in terms of the fixed formal rules that constitute an established genre, but as a set of shifting practices without consistent rules or straightforward histories.

The career of photographer Lee Miller was far from straightforward. Artist, model and muse, fashion photographer, and later war correspondent for *Vogue*, Miller appeared as both model and photographer in the pages of inter-war *Vogue*. Many of her fashion images are also self-portraits, and, as Becky Conekin writes, Miller's awareness of her own aesthetic presence, and the role she played in her own representation, problematizes notions of the active (male) photographer and the passive (female) model that underlie many narratives of fashion photography. Miller spent more than twenty years exploring the aesthetic, and later the political, potential of photography as a medium, and her fashion images must be seen in the context of her career as a whole.

The second section, 'Processes and Politics', looks at the day-to-day business of creating fashion images. Here, three fashion-industry creatives talk about fashion image-making as an industry with its own set of commercial strictures and internal politics. Despite these apparent restrictions, as they demonstrate, the fashion-photography industry provides no shortage of opportunities for creative and artistic development.

London photographer and publisher Rankin is a key figure in the 'second wave' of the alternative style press. Emerging from the rarefied critical environment of the London College of Printing in the late 1980s, Rankin, along with Katie Grand and classmate Jefferson Hack, launched *Dazed & Confused* in 1991, at a time when established titles like *i-D* and *The Face* had started to lose touch with their younger audience. Though he is often described as a fashion photographer, Rankin doesn't think of himself in this way. In fact, the bulk of his work consists of portraits and beauty photography commissioned for the fashion and lifestyle press, and he feels most at home in this critically under-represented sector of the industry, which is still free of many of the creative constraints that exist in editorial and advertising work. For Rankin, fashion photography has always been a relatively small part of wider business and artistic concerns. Unabashedly entrepreneurial, he's aware that he's become something of a brand himself. At the same time, he is deeply committed to the process of photography, and regards the fashion magazine as both a commercial concern and a creative medium.

Sascha Behrendt has also been working in the fashion photography industry for over twenty years. After entering the field as a model in the 1980s, she went on to work as a photographer and model booker, opening her own fashion-photography agency in 1996. In 2000, she moved into the world of advertising, working as an art buyer for agencies like St Luke's and Saatchi, and later as a freelance art director for fashion client Stella McCartney. Her article offers a glimpse of the complex amalgam of the creative, commercial and political factors that go into the creation of a fashion image. Like Rankin, Behrendt has embraced the creative potential of the fashion-photography industry, and her account charts a career spent exploring its various possibilities.

SHOWstudio is a London-based online fashion broadcasting company dedicated to showcasing the creative process and examining fashion image-making from within the industry. Originally the brainchild of Nick Knight and Peter Saville, now headed up by Knight and Editor-in-Chief Penny Martin, SHOWstudio pioneers new forms of interactive and motion imagery, broadcasting unique art and fashion collaborations, as well as films, interviews, articles, images and other media forms, on its website, www.showstudio.com. The recent decision to open up the site to selected advertisers is not just a consequence of the growing financial resources demanded by the industry, but also reflects a growing awareness of, and interest in, fashion advertising as a creative medium. Perhaps more importantly, SHOWstudio's commitment to moving imagery takes the field of fashion photography beyond the confines of the single image and the magazine form, exploring fashion and fashion image-making as situated processes.

Images of dress play an important role in the construction of identities. The chapters in the third section, 'Image and Identity', explore some of the ways that fashion images – and the circumstances of their production – participate in charting the boundaries of femininity, race, age and gender.

Bärbel Sill examines the recent popularity of the 'actress-model', and the role of fashion imagery in supporting the identification process between the star and the public. The star's 'fashion image' is constituted by elements such as clothes, makeup and hairstyle, which work together to define a star's individual look. Fashion photography is a way of both developing the star's fashion image and linking it to her or his public persona. Combining fashion photography and portraiture, the star fashion shoot – where the fashion photographer's celebrity status is often equal to that of their subject – is a hybrid form, designed to enhance the star's public profile.

Just as the fashion photograph of a movie star must work to naturalize the constructed character of the star persona, photographs featuring professional models must also conceal the constructed character of the model's 'look'. This issue is brought into sharp focus by Stephanie Neda Sadre-Orafai, who examines how model development and casting use racial, national and regional classifications to classify models as specific racial and ethnic 'types'. A combination of visual aesthetics and linguistic classifications, the 'type' forms the grammar of the modelling industry. Like racial passing, typing involves the management of perception and the exploitation of seemingly rigid categories of race and nationality. In the modelling industry, however, language and naming also play a key role. Such classifications have powerful affective potential and act as framing devices to shape a model's image. Where Barthes studied the use of written text to limit and anchor the meaning of the fashion image on the magazine page, Sadre-Orafai shows how text is used in the casting process simultaneously to ground and exploit the visual ambiguity of the photographic image.

The following text also considers meanings that are not immediately legible in the image. Isabelle Loring Wallace focuses on features of Steven Meisel's 2000 Versace ad campaign that were overlooked by the art press and the viewing pubic. Beneath the campaign's frank display of 'extravagance' and 'LA-excess' lie aspects not covered in any straightforward sense by this rhetoric. Meisel's campaign takes shape around images of sameness and twinning; around androgynous and sexually indifferent subjects of malleable gender. In their compelling representation of bodies as neither mortal nor sexed, Meisel's images act out life in Baudrillard's 'era of the clone' – a time when immortality is secured by means of plastic surgery and in vitro fertilization rather than human biology. In Meisel's campaign, argues Wallace, we find an acknowledgement of cloning's appeal for a global fashion industry that promotes mass-produced garments, rather than individual bodies, as a means of marking out difference.

The separation of the lived body from its representation is also taken up by Karen de Perthuis, who reflects on the Barthesian notion of the 'absolute body' in the representation of fashion. Just as the fashion image represents garments free from practical considerations such as comfort and practicality, so the body of the model in the image is often purged of any corporeal references. No longer the property of a real individual, the body comes to stand for fashion itself. Extending Barthes's ideas, de Perthuis explores digital fashion photography's ability to free fashion completely from the limitations imposed by the corporeal body, creating imaginary forms where body and garment dissolve into one another. In this 'synthetic ideal', the photographed body is entirely purged of all references to the living, breathing body, existing instead as pure representation.

The final section of the book takes up the dialogue between representation and the real from the perspective of cultural politics and phenomenology. Taking as its subject the documentary style of fashion imagery made popular in early 1990s, 'Reassessing the Real' examines the fashion photograph's unstable status as a document and its problematic relationship with the 'real'. Here we find claims that the photograph is an empty signifier divorced from any real content. Posed alongside these, however, are questions about fashion as a situated process, and fashion imagery as a media form that is created, consumed and enacted by embodied agents.

From the 1960s onwards, the street has been acknowledged as a site where fashion is defined and constructed. In the 1980s, this idea was given visual form in *i-D* magazine through its use of the street-fashion photograph or 'straight-up'. As a fashion image, the straight-up presents the fashionable city dweller as a representative of the city and its inhabitants, and a kind of shorthand for the vitality and creativity of the street. As Agnès Rocamora and Alistair O'Neill remark, the popularity of the straight-up is due, in part, to its presentation of the 'real' and the 'everyday' in the context of modern urban fashion, and the street as a legitimate site for the creation of fashion. As they go on to point out, however, the reality of the street has become as constructed as the studio context it aims to challenge. Stripped of its complexity and diversity, the street, as it is represented in the contemporary fashion press, no longer functions as a real, situated place, but as an imaginary site that readers can fill with meaning.

The reality of the street is also mediated through the body of the found model. Writing about the use of 'ordinary' people as models in 1990s fashion photography, Kate Rhodes examines the way that the appearance of the everyday is used to redirect consumer desire. Like Rocamora and O'Neill, Rhodes sees the difference between the professional model and his or her carefully chosen amateur counterpart as more than a simple substitution of 'reality' for 'fantasy'. The imperfect body of the non-professional stands, on the one hand, for individuality and a challenge to preconceived notions of beauty. On the other, it is also a kind of aesthetic novelty, a form of seduction which turns difference into a commodifiable spectacle. Though they may have started out with documentary motivations, many of these images of the everyday, argues Rhodes, have come to be emptied of any real social content.

For fashion advertisers, the 'real' is a negotiable and highly marketable quantity. In other contexts, it stands in a different relationship to the illusory and the imaginary. My own chapter engages the notion of the real by examining our emotional and visceral – 'affective' – responses to the body in fashion photographs. This chapter reflects my own critical interest in the crossover between sight and touch, and the way that images act as sites of embodied exchange between image and viewer. Drawing on the field of cognitive neuroscience, I show how the fashion image is experienced in both visual and tactile registers. Here, perception involves more than conscious, rational looking: it also comprises emotional and physiological responses, many of them unconscious. Examining the combination of affective response and signification in Juergen Teller's collaborative work with model Kristen McMenamy, I explore the fashion image as a material form, produced and consumed by embodied agents.

*   *   *

The question of whether fashion imagery can provide a valid form of social critique is never far from the surface in the following essays. The difference between the artistic and the merely decorative or commercial is often understood to hinge on this possibility: for Abigail Solomon-Godeau, it is its explicitly critical intent – the sleazy and 'decidedly uneuphoric insistence on the visibility of class, its injuries, and its violence' (2004: 196) – that distinguishes art photography from other forms. Market success notwithstanding, fashion photography has often been swept to the margins of cultural criticism on the grounds that it is less free to be outspoken about the world that it represents. Indeed, many critics – as well as a significant number of fashion-industry creatives – don't believe that fashion photography is capable of saying anything of real political or social significance.

Fashion photography's dealings with the beautiful and the ephemeral don't do it any favours either. Aestheticizing social issues is an effective way of reinforcing audience passivity and dulling the seriousness of events; beauty, as Ingrid Sischy remarks, 'is a call to admiration, not action' (Sischy in Levi-Strauss 2003: 5). Despite the fact that fashion imagery has cheerfully engaged with aesthetically challenging and politically unsettling subject matter for decades, fashion images are often said to pander to traditional ideals of beauty, denying agency to those they represent and those who consume them.

The textual and rhetorical forms of the fashion image are played out and consumed by real, situated individuals. Fashion is made up of discursive, textual and lived bodies, it is created and consumed by embodied agents without whom it would not exist (Entwistle 2000: 236). In many ways, the criticisms levelled against fashion photography reflect the anxiety of early critics of postmodern art, who applauded artwork that acknowledged its complicity with forms of power and domination, but panned work which did not comprise 'any effective theory of agency that enables a move into political action' (Hutcheon 1988: 3). The following chapters question the assumption that fashion photography necessarily denies agency to its subject, or to those who consume it. Images of fashion shape the body by addressing it as a social agent. The fashion image is an interface between lived body and the visible, public body. Like the garments it depicts, it mediates between private experience and public address, and the essays that follow examine this mediating function from a number of different angles. Focusing on both the address and denial of the body, on the ways that the body is shaped by images, and on the ways that it exceeds capture in images, these essays show that the creation and consumption of fashion images is also a means of expressing and performing an embodied self.

George Steiner once described classical art as 'art by privation' – art that still managed to deliver a message even though it had recourse to rigorously limited means. It's time that this argument was extended to fashion photography. It is the tropes of fashion, argues Lipovetsky, that influence the form taken by advertising, not the other way round: 'With advertising, communication…is caught in the net of the fashion form. At the opposite extreme from totalitarian logic, it is immersed in superficiality, in fantasy and gimmickry…' (1994: 157).

Today's advertisements are no longer tied to simple demonstrations of use value; instead, they deal in superlatives, in 'preposterous and extravagant communications' (158), and their effectiveness is a function of this 'playful superficiality' (160). Here, seduction proceeds not by means of coercion or totalitarian logic, but through the celebration of artifice. Ephemeral yet underpinned by a shifting matrix of social and historical circumstance from which they draw, fashion images can, and do, comprise complex forms of ideological address. It seems only fair that we give them their due as powerful forms of social and political critique.

WORKS CITED

Barthes, Roland (1985) *The Fashion System*, trans. Matthew Ward and Richard Howard (London: Jonathan Cape)

Breward, Christopher (2003) *Fashion* (Oxford: Oxford University Press)

Burgoyne, Patrick (2002) 'Sex and Shopping', *Creative Review* 22 (3) March 2002: 33–37

Craik, Jennifer (1993) *The Face of Fashion: Cultural Studies in Fashion* (London and New York: Routledge)

Derrick, Robin (2002) 'The Golden Age of Fashion Photography is Now', *Creative Review* 22 (3) March 2002: 63–67

Entwistle, Joanne (2000) *The Fashioned Body: Fashion, Dress, and Modern Social Theory* (Cambridge: Polity Press)

Goldman, Robert (1992) *Reading Ads Socially* (London: Routledge)

Hutcheon, Linda (1988) *The Politics of Postmodernism* (London and New York: Routledge)

Knight, Nick (2006) 'Nick Knight on Advertising' (interview with Penny Martin), http://www.showstudio.com/advertising/Nick_Knight_on_advertising_REF.mov (accessed 2 August 2006)

Lipovetsky, Gilles (1994) *The Empire of Fashion: Dressing Modern Democracy*, trans. Catherine Porter (Princeton and Oxford: Princeton University Press)

Levi-Strauss, David (2003) *Between the Eyes: Essays on Photography and Politics* (New York: Aperture Books)

Saville, Peter (2006) interview with the author, London, 25 July 2006

Solomon-Godeau, Abigail (2004) 'Dressing Down', *Artforum* 42 (9) May 2004: 193–96

PART I

Critical Contexts

1   A Shop of Images and Signs

Caroline Evans

This chapter is an extended version of chapter 2 of Caroline Evans (2003) *Fashion at the Edge: Spectacle, Modernity and Deathliness* (London and New Haven: Yale University Press).

'Fashion doesn't have to be something people wear, fashion is also an image,' said the designers Viktor & Rolf in 1999 (Gan 1999). That year, their third couture collection, made entirely in black and white, was shown on the catwalk twice: first in black light that picked out the white elements of the clothes and concealed the black, so that the audience saw only a frill, a trailing ribbon, a disembodied white ruff, or a dancing skeleton with hips of white bows; and then in white light that revealed the collection to be a series of variations on the theme of the black tuxedo. At that point it became clear to the audience that the skeleton 'bones' it had seen earlier were stitched onto a black suit; and the plain white trouser suit turned out to be outlined by a huge black ruffle projecting from its side seams. At once macabre, whimsical and spectacular, the ghostly presentation evoked the double meaning of the term vision: it was quite literally a vision on the catwalk, and one which embodied the designers' vision. At the same time, it suggested the other meaning of the term: a ghost, shade or apparition. Viktor & Rolf's presentation was also spectral in terms of manufacturing and selling: the clothes were not intended to go into production but were made as a series of ideas. This black-and-white collection was an inventory of the shapes that Viktor & Rolf had been working on since the start of their career, and they intended it to be their last spectral collection before they launched themselves in the real world of embodied fashion and commerce, making clothes to go into production and be sold in the shops. As such, the collection, and its presentation, typified the spectacular nature of modern fashion and marketing. The word spectacle designates a sight, or show; the spectre a ghost, or a vision. Etymologically they have the same root, both coming from *specere*, the Latin verb 'to see'. The spectacle of fashion is the subject of this article, which is concerned with fashion as image rather than as photograph. It looks at the catwalk show as a key medium through which fashion images were created and then disseminated via new electronic and print media at the end of the twentieth century.

In the 1850s Baudelaire wrote that 'all the visible universe is nothing but a shop of images and signs' (Buck-Morss 1991: 177). A hundred and fifty years later, in the 1990s, new communications produced mutations in consumer culture that transmogrified the fashion object into image and sign. In the altered visual economy of fast-changing information technology and global markets, media images were, for most people, their first and only point of contact with top-end fashion. Fashion shows became characterized by dramatic showpieces – implausible garments made of feathers and shells, or resin and metal, that were galvanized by electricity or consumed by fire in a spectacular finale. Showpieces never went into production, and after the show disappeared into the designers' archives, only occasionally to reappear in the occasional museum exhibition. Their brief appearance on the catwalk would, however, be fixed in the amber of the press photograph, and would circulate in both digital and print media as an image and memory of a fleeting moment in an evanescent spectacle. More pragmatically, the showpiece would have done its job for the designer if it had attracted the requisite press coverage and, in the early stages of a designer's career, potential backers. As the catalogue for a British Council touring exhibition of cutting-edge design, *Lost and Found*, stated in 1999,

> Fashion designers work in a world whose currency is the magazine front cover; the editorial spread; the styled photo shoot… Successful designers are under extraordinary pressure from hundreds of magazines all over the world, wanting photographs or clothing samples to fill their editorial pages. As a result, a network of support teams has grown up to serve the

fashion industry, consisting of press and public relations people, publicity co-ordinators, editorial stylists and fashion photographers. For most people, the media provides the only contact with experimental or couture fashion. These garments are either too expensive or unsuitable for mainstream retail distribution, and we are left to consume fantasy images of magazine photo shoots. (1999: 97)

Thus the fantasy images of the elaborate and spectacular fashion shows of the late 1990s, in which the fashion object mutated into image, increasingly echoed Baudelaire's observation, from the heart of mid-nineteenth-century Paris with its specialist shops full of luxury goods, that the entire 'visible universe' consisted of no more than a vast emporium of signs and images. In 1967, in *The Society of the Spectacle,* Guy Debord (1994) anatomized that visible universe and its relation to capital; he saw it as a world colonized by false desires and illusions, epitomized by the ubiquity of the commodity form. In many respects the fashion show is the paradigm of Debord's notion of spectacle, which he described as narcissistic, self-absorbed and self-referential. So too is the catwalk fashion show, sealed into a hermetic world of its own with its attendant protocols and hierarchies. Like the spectacle, it spatializes time and destroys memory (Debord 1994: para. 19). It is 'the triumph of contemplation over action' (Jay 1993: 428) and the quintessential form of commercial seduction through theatrical novelty and innovation. Its spectacular displays are calculated to obscure its financial heart. Only the gilt chairs in the show, each with a journalist's name on it, and the banks of photographers, hint at the complex professional networks to which the spectacle is tied and through which its imagery is disseminated worldwide.

In their black-and-white collection, Viktor & Rolf's ghostly presentation recalled the nexus of image, spectacle and commerce described by Debord nearly forty years earlier. He too made the connection between ghostliness and money: 'the spectacle in general, as the concrete inversion of life, is the autonomous movement of the non-living', and in his commentary on Debord Martin Jay glossed Debord's definition of the spectacle as 'the deathgrip of desiccated images' (Jay 1993: 425; Debord 1994: para. 2). Taking his cue from Marx, Debord sought in this passage to describe the vampiric operations of capital, the ruthless energy and drive with which it sucked life from its victims (Carver 1998). In the 1990s, the British fashion journalist Sally Brampton (1998) used an equally bloodthirsty metaphor to describe the increased attendance at the Paris fashion shows as 'a media feeding frenzy as newspapers and television stations around the world give increasing prominence to fashion'. By the late twentieth century, in an ever more visualized global market dominated by new technologies of the image, it became all the more important for designers to produce strong, graphic runway images that could be transmitted round the world via print and electronic media. Brampton argued that the London-trained designer John Galliano was partly responsible for the 'media feeding frenzy' of mid-1990s fashion shows. In 1995 Galliano briefly became principal designer at Givenchy, before moving to Christian Dior in December 1996, where he remains today. At the time, Brampton described him as 'the greatest image-maker in the world' (Frankel 1999: 12). Particularly with the support of a major Paris couture house, Galliano was able to stage a range of fantastical and opulent mis-en-scènes on the catwalk: a suburban sports stadium transformed into a forest scene with forty-foot-high spruce trees; the Paris Opéra converted into an English garden where the fashion photographers were given straw hats on entry; and the Carousel du Louvre, the official venue for the Paris collections, made over as a snowy rooftop scene, complete with battered chimney stacks, designed, like most of his shows, by the set designer Jean-Luc Ardouin.

In every case, Galliano's transformation of the space involved effacing its real characteristics in the interests of imposing his own fantasy vision on the space, weaving instant mythologies and creating something out of nothing, very much like the nineteenth-century consumer displays identified by Rosalind Williams (1982) as 'dream worlds'. Williams describes how, in nineteenth-century Paris, consumers were seduced – even duped she suggests – by fantastical displays of goods in department stores and world fairs. The seduction lay precisely in the way the real, commercial nature of the transaction was veiled in seductive 'dream worlds' in which the shopper lost him- or herself in fantasy and reverie. Galliano's shows too create this kind of dream world, occluding the commercial reality behind the spectacle. His fabrications evoke the opening words of Debord's *The Society of the Spectacle*: 'in societies where modern conditions of production prevail all of life presents itself as an immense accumulation of spectacles. Everything that was directly lived has moved away into a representation' (1994: para. 1).

It is important to remember that in Debord's formulation the spectacle is not merely the image but society as a whole. The spectacle is not a collection of images, but 'a social relation among people, mediated by images' (Debord 1994: para. 4; Jay 1993: 429). In other words, we come to the spectacle via images, and those images both mediate and structure our social relations and our desires. Nevertheless, for Debord, the visible form of the spectacle is the commodity which occupies everyday life: the spectacle, according to Debord (1994: para. 1), is 'capital become an image'; the sight of the journalists and photographers at work in the fashion show reveals both sides of the way in which capital is constructed as image, first in the show itself and in its dissemination by the press. And while, as I will go on to argue, Debord's analysis is only of limited use in relation to new media, it does still have some currency with regard to the fashion show itself. In Antonio Berardi's Spring/ Summer 2000 collection capital became pure image in his crystal corset made in hand-blown Murano glass from Venice. Berardi's glass bustier was a fairy-tale object, as evocative as Cinderella's glass slipper, and, in real life, just as unwearable. In the realm of the symbolic it paraded the dreams and arcane craft skills of elite fashion production, as did Berardi's hand-made lace dress that took Sicilian lace-makers three months to complete. The glass corset was about the obvious display of wealth, a monument to conspicuous consumption. But it was also a reflective object, mirror-like: its fragile glass surfaces both deflected the gaze of the observer and reflected the world back onto itself. In the bustier, simultaneously both image and object, capital was magically invisible and yet made real. The transparency of glass was rendered opaque, just as the commodity both flaunts and disguises its commercial nature in spectacle. Here is capital turned into an image, at once fragile and precious, an emblem of Debord's idea of 'spectacle'.

In Alexander McQueen's Spring/Summer 2001 collection, 'Voss', the life of the catwalk image and object was extended beyond the catwalk, even though the pieces never actually went into production. One dress consisted of two thousand glass microscope slides, each one hand-drilled and hand-painted red, then hand-stitched onto an elongated bodice above a skirt constructed of tiered red ostrich feathers over a crinoline. It took six weeks to make, yet it appeared on the catwalk for less than two minutes, almost as excessive a monument to conspicuous labour as the Berardi glass corset was to con-spicuous consumption. As a rule, dresses such as this are archived after the show, so they exist only as a memory – for those who saw it – or as a photographic trace of an evanescent moment. It is in this sense too that the showpiece is ghostly, or spectral. Worn once for just a few seconds by the model on the catwalk, after its disappearance the memory of it can fade slowly like a retinal image after the real object has gone. Only the photographs of the showpiece remain, a marker of its recent presence, testifying to the indexical power of the photograph that records the object so briefly exhibited and so instantly lost in the recent past.

This particular dress was, however, briefly retrieved in the V&A museum's 'Radical Fashion' exhibition in London in 2001 and displayed on a mannequin in a glass box that re-created elements of the runway show. A version of the dress also made a second appearance as a worn garment when the singer and musician Björk wore it on stage in a concert where, as she danced, the tinkling of the glass plates against each other was amplified and incorporated into the music, turning the dress itself into a percussion instrument. Its history exemplifies the way in which so much contemporary fashion enters the realm of the commodity and circulates obliquely, not always as an embodied practice or worn garment but as an image, an idea, or a conceptual piece, as likely to resurface in a museum or a music venue as in a shop.[1] It is in this way that the image is no longer a representation of an original (like, say, a fashion advertisement with a photograph of a dress for sale) but has become the commodity itself, a new kind of commodity that we consume through various new, often digital, or digitally manipulated, media.

It is this change in commodity and image culture that makes Guy Debord's hitherto fruitful analysis of the 'spectacle' of only limited value. His analysis has proved a useful model for understanding a number of other periods, from the Paris of the Impressionists to the commodity culture of nineteenth-century London, and including the relationship of women, spectacle and modernity.[2] On the face of it, late-twentieth-century fashion appears to be a paradigm of the spectacle, the starriest of star commodities: 'when culture becomes nothing more than a commodity, it must also become the star commodity of the spectacular society,' wrote Debord (1994: para. 193). Yet the relevance of Debord's arguments from the 1960s to late-twentieth-century consumer culture is limited by subsequent shifts in the nature of commodity and image in the electronic age. Debord's descriptions were rooted in a Marxist critique of the commodity form as economic object; however, the overarching transformations of the 1990s (globalization, new technology and new communications) have radically altered its form. As electronic media and global markets have developed, and service industries have replaced older forms of industrial production, information has become a valuable commodity in its own right.[3] In the shifting constellations of the 'culture industries', fashion has begun to signify in a number of different registers, as demonstrated in the case of McQueen's red slide glass dress. Debord's sour denunciations of the image seem curiously redundant in a culture in which the fashioned garment circulates in a network of signs as both image and object: no longer represent-ation, the image is frequently the commodity itself, as I have argued, be it in a fashion show, magazine, website or even as an idea. Indeed, Thomas Richards (1991: 258) suggests that the days of spectacle are numbered, and that 'it may turn out that the semiotics of spectacle played a transitional role in capitalist mythology'.

The way in which object, image and commodity are meshed in many designers' work today suggests that perhaps we need a more nuanced account of the society of the spectacle than Debord's analysis from the 1960s can provide. Hussein Chalayan, for instance, has constantly worked on the cusp of the digital and the real, two and three dimensions, the virtual and the actual, even before the advent of accessible and cheap digital technology made this play between different realms so seductive. Both in his relatively early show 'Panoramic' (Autumn/Winter 1998/99) and the later 'Ventriloquy' (Spring/Summer 2001), the slippage between image and reality was incorporated as a structuring device of the show. 'Panoramic' was staged against a mirrored set, and as the show progressed the human elements of performance receded. The models wove mesmerizingly in and out of the set, appearing to disappear into walls and emerge from mirrors, until the difference between image and reality was effaced and their bodies became mere patterns in a moving picture. This visual play of models appearing and disappearing was mirrored by a slide show on a white wall to the side, in which a scene was gradually reduced to a set of abstract elements. The show played on the visual links between the 2-D images off-stage and the live action on the catwalk. In 'Ventriloquy', Chalayan made a comparable link between digital film and real action, opening the show with a computer-generated film of wire-frame models whose pixellated actions prefigured the real-time show in which the models played out a narrative that harked back to the film narrative. Chalayan thus created a relay of action between real time and virtual time, as when, for example, in the show's finale the models smashed each others' hard resin dresses to echo the way in which the figures in the film had shattered and destroyed each others' image.

Many fashion historians as well as consumers have tended to privilege image over object, a point invoked in Chalayan's oscillation between image and object in his shows. In Chalayan's innovative and sophisticated games with representation, the commodity form returned via the very structures that denied it, through the instability of the image in the modern period and its ambiguous role in the society of the spectacle. For all his modernist experimentation – his use of avant-garde musicians, his engagement with philosophy, and his 'white cube' sets more evocative of art installations and performance than of fashion – Chalayan's repetitive turn to the image, and to the seductions of new technology, also chimes with consumer culture and the society of the spectacle. These fashion shows invoked the duplicitous and sophisticated play of image and idea that began to underwrite capitalist production, consumption and, particularly, marketing, from the mid-nineteenth century when Baudelaire wrote that 'all the visible universe is nothing but a shop of images and signs' (Buck-Morss 1991: 177). Much as they looked forwards experimentally, Chalayan's mirrors and computer animations, because they existed in the context of late-capitalist fashion, also harked back to the duplicitous vitrines and mirrored windows of nineteenth-century Parisian department stores, whose dazzling displays reflected the image of the new consumer back to her- or himself while simultaneously multiplying and fracturing the image of the goods on display.[4] While 'Panoramic' referred to the high-art gravitas of the installation, the faithlessness of the mirror also testified to the slippery instability of the surface in modern consumer culture, with its constantly changing flow of signs, images and information. Its mirrored set was shimmering rather than reflective; instead of telling the truth it dazzled and confused, perpetrating an act of deception, like consumerist display. Although Chalayan is a very different type of designer from Antonio Berardi or Alexander McQueen, his illusionistic use of mirrors in 'Panoramic' is comparable to the visual trickery of both Berardi's glass corset and to McQueen's red microscope slide dress, which was shown in a two-way mirrored glass box.

In her book *On Photography*, Susan Sontag has argued that in the modern period our perception of reality is shaped by the type and frequency of images we receive. Sontag wrote that from the mid-nineteenth century 'the credence that could no longer be given to realities understood in the form of images was now being given to realities understood to be images, illusions'. She goes on to cite Feuerbach's observation of 1843, also cited by Debord at the beginning of *The Society of the Spectacle*: 'our era prefers the image to the thing, the copy to the original, the representation to the reality, appearance to being'[5] (Sontag 1972: 153). Yet the sophisticated play between image and object in Chalayan's work suggests that this is a false opposition and that we may, in fact, prefer 'both-and' to 'either-or', as Robert Venturi (1977: 16) defined the architectural choices of postmodernism. In 'Ventriloquy', Chalayan played on the contrast between computer model and fashion model, between virtual and actual body, between image and object. This technological play is a feature, Gilles Lipovetsky has argued, of 'a society structured by fashion, where rationality functions by way of evanescence and superficiality, where objectivity is instituted as a spectacle, where the dominion of technology is reconciled with play and the realm of politics is reconciled with seduction' (1994: 10). The conjunction returns the argument yet again to Debord. My final two examples are geared towards a consideration of this idea of reconciliation (or not) of politics and seduction in 'a society structured by fashion'.

When, in his Autumn/Winter 1997/98 show, Martin Margiela diverted his models from their planned route in the scheduled venue and sent them on an impromptu walk through the city streets dressed in deconstructed pattern pieces, or when, in his Spring/Summer 1999 show, he imported the street figure of the sandwich-board man to the catwalk to 'advertise' an image of a garment that was not actually being shown on the catwalk (the sandwich-board man being clad in Margiela's trademark white lab coat), such tactics could be argued to be a subversion of the spectacle. The former equates to the situationist stratagems of *dérive* (urban drift), the latter to *détournement* (turning something around or back on itself) – precisely the stratagems prescribed by Debord to counter the operations of the society of the spectacle. Unlike John Galliano's catwalk effects, such stratagems do not generate dramatic or seductive imagery for wider dissemination, and one could argue that this in itself is a tactic to avoid recuperation by society of the spectacle. If so, Margiela's undoubtedly innovative ways of showing could be said to amount to an anti-capitalist stratagem, were it not for the fact that he is, and was, a highly successful Paris-based designer working at the heart of the fashion industry. It is, therefore, more plausible to argue that, because they require a new kind of cultural recognition from a fashion elite, Margiela's shows, far from overturning the spectacle, simply expand its repertoire in novel and original ways.

The point, however, is not whether they amount to either-or (either subversion or recuperation), which is what Debord's analysis asks us to decide, so much as the degree to which they succeed in being both-and. There is no better exponent of the capacity to be both-and than Viktor & Rolf, who served as the opening example in this chapter. Their fifth collection, Spring/Summer 1996, 'l'Apparence du Vide', was shown in the Galerie Patricia Dorfmann in Paris. Made entirely from gold, a colour they associated with wrapping paper, they claimed that the collection was a criticism of the circus surrounding the industry. The following season, apparently in response to journalistic indifference to this installation, for Autumn/Winter 1996/97 they produced no collection at all and simply sent the fashion editors a poster which read 'Viktor & Rolf on strike', and fly-posted Paris with a similar range of images. Such tactics suggested that the designers were well aware that fashion is the ultimate example of a product that emphasizes consumption at the expense of production, making the latter invisible in classically Marxist fashion. Being 'on strike' as fashion designers and producing no clothes is to make a joke about production, arguably at the expense of the industry.

Yet Viktor & Rolf managed simultaneously to critique the spectacle and to be part of it in an ironic and knowing way in their Spring/Summer 1998 couture collection. In it a model wore a white silk evening dress that was accessorized with a porcelain boater and a huge necklace consisting of gigantic white porcelain beads. On the catwalk, she divested herself of both these items and hurled them to the floor, where they lay in shattered fragments. Like a bonfire of the vanities, the gesture could be construed as a violent repudiation of the fashion system. Yet it was so spectacular that it could not avoid recuperation as a capitalist spectacle even as it sought to destroy its emblems. Just as Antonio Berardi's precious treatment of the glass corset reified the spectacle of the catwalk, so too did Viktor & Rolf's violent destruction of their over-scaled china accessories. Similarly, their Spring/Summer 2001 show modelled by a troupe of Dutch tapdancers in Busby Berkeley line-ups, rather than the usual fashion models, undercut any notion of resistance to the spectacle by paying homage to Hollywood musicals. At the end, the two designers came on in white suits and pencil-thin moustaches to take their bow, only to be themselves willingly incorporated into a dance routine like twin Fred Astaires.

This show seemed to acknowledge that as cultural producers and consumers we can be simultaneously seduced and entranced by the spectacle even as we understand that we are being manipulated by it, caught up in a virtuoso display of tap-dancing capitalism.

NOTES ON CHAPTER 1

1   For a discussion of the way the fashion commodity mutated in the 1990s, see Evans 2000.
2   See Clark 1984, Richards 1991 and McPhearson 1999. Thank you to Carol Tulloch for bringing this invaluable article to my attention.
3   See Bell 1988 and Gershuny 2000.
4   Émile Zola's *The Ladies Paradise* opens with one such description.
5   For more empirically based studies of the impact of new visual technologies on sensibilities see Crary 1990 and McQuire 1998.

WORKS CITED

Bell, Daniel (1988) 'The Third Technological Revolution and its Possible Socio-Economic Consequences', University of Salford, Faculty of Social Sciences, annual lecture

Brampton, Sally (1998) '"Extravagant" Galliano Uses Simplicity to Combat Critics', *Guardian*, 14 October

British Council, Nick Barley (1999) *Lost and Found: Critical Voices in British Design* (Basel, Boston and Berlin: Birkauser)

Buck-Morss, Susan (1991) *The Dialectics of Seeing: Walter Benjamin and the Arcades Project* (Cambridge, MA and London: MIT Press)

Carver, Terrell (1998) *The Postmodern Marx* (Manchester: Manchester University Press)

Clark, T.J. (1984) *The Painting of Modern Life: Paris in the Art of Manet and His Followers* (Princeton, NJ: Princeton University Press and London: Thames & Hudson)

Crary, Jonathan (1990) *Techniques of the Observer: On Vision and Modernity in the Nineteenth Century* (Cambridge MA and London: MIT Press)

Debord, Guy (1994 [1967]) *The Society of the Spectacle*, trans. Donald Nicholson-Smith (London: Zone Books)

Evans, Caroline (2000), 'Yesterday's Emblems and Tomorrow's Commodities: The Return of the Repressed in Fashion Imagery Today', in Stella Bruzzi and Pamela Church Gibson (eds) *Fashion Cultures: Theories, Explorations and Analysis* (London and New York: Routledge): 96–97

Frankel, Susannah (1999) 'Galliano', *Independent* Magazine, 20 February

Gan, Stephen (1999) *Visionaire's Fashion 2001: Designers of the New Avant-garde*, ed. Alix Browne (London: Laurence King)

Gershuny, Jonathan I. (2000) *Changing Times: Work and Leisure in Postindustrial Society* (Oxford: Oxford University Press)

Jay, Martin (1993) *Downcast Eyes: The Denigration of Vision in Twentieth-century French Thought* (Berkeley and Los Angeles: University of California Press)

Lipovetsky, Gilles (1994 [1987]) *The Empire of Fashion: Dressing Modern Democracy*, trans. Catherine Porter (Princeton: Princeton University Press)

McPhearson, Heather (1999) 'Sarah Bernhardt: Portrait of the Actress as Spectacle', *Nineteenth-Century Contexts* 20 (4): 409–54

McQuire, Scott (1998) *Visions of Modernity: Representation, Memory, Time and Space in the Age of the Camera* (London: Sage Publications and New Delhi: Thousand Oaks)

Richards, Thomas (1991) *The Commodity Culture of Victorian England: Advertising and Spectacle, 1851–1914* (London and New York: Verso)

Sontag, Susan (1972) *On Photography* (Harmondsworth: Penguin)

Venturi, Robert (1977) *Complexity and Contradiction in Architecture* (London: Architectural Press)

Williams, Rosalind H. (1982) *Dream Worlds: Mass Consumption in Late Nineteenth-century France* (Berkeley, Los Angeles and Oxford: University of California Press)

Zola, Émile (1995) *The Ladies Paradise*, trans. with an introduction by Brian Nelson (Oxford University Press, Oxford and New York)

2 Fashioning Fiction in Photography Since 1990

Susan Kismaric and Eva Respini

The following essay is an edited excerpt from the catalogue essay for an exhibition entitled *Fashioning Fiction in Photography Since 1990*, held at New York's Museum of Modern Art in 2004. The full text of the essay can be found in *Fashioning Fiction in Photography Since 1990* (2004) (New York: Museum of Modern Art).

Fashion photography has followed the move of the fashion industry from the salon to the street. Like fashion, photography relies and thrives on change, not only through advances in technology but, more importantly, through the countless shifting cultural, social and economic forces that drive the effort to sell clothes. Both fashion photography and fashion have shifted from being primarily reflections of the aspirations of the haute bourgeoisie to a new status emblematic of a diverse, rapidly evolving and increasingly younger, visually sophisticated commercial environment in which the pace of change has taken on a new industry-driven rhythm.

This essay focuses on a key aspect of fashion photography during the 1990s, a decade during which the genre moved away from the paradigm of an idealized and classical beauty towards a new vernacular allied with lifestyle, pop and youth culture, and the demi-monde. Key factors in this shift are changes in fashion itself, its audience, and the way it is marketed. Of great importance, too, was the emergence, within art photography, of techniques borrowed from commercial fashion imagery. One of the most significant changes in fashion photography, in this fertile chaotic environment, has been that its subject – clothing – has become subordinate to the photographic description of lifestyle: transformed from a frozen object of beauty to a tantalizing aspect of a narrative. As a consequence, much fashion photography has ceased to capture a timeless moment, and instead attempts to represent a moment in time. Two of the dominant narrative modes in fashion photography of the last decade are the influence of the cinema and the snapshot. Both of these strategies create storylines and interrupted narratives, which imbue the images with dramatic complexity and an aura of personal intimacy and authenticity. All of the work in this essay is examined through one of these lenses, which are also central to contemporary art photography. By using these two inter-related narrative strategies, the fashion world has turned to current trends in art photography, and in some cases turned to the artists themselves.

Some of the photographers featured here can be defined principally as artists, others as commercial professionals. However, the fluidity (and some would argue futility) of these categories represents a particularly fruitful moment in the exchange between fine art and commercial photography. The dialogue between the two photographic fields has always been vital, and the character of this relationship has varied over time. To be sure, art has always influenced fashion, and there have been instances when earlier fashion photographs have been perceived as art, as seen in the work of Edward Steichen, Cecil Beaton, Baron Adolf de Meyer, Horst P. Horst, Irving Penn and Richard Avedon, among others. The cross-fertilization has always benefited both art and applied photography, and continues to do so today.

The 1990s, however, have been particularly ripe for the exchange between art and fashion photography. The use of commercial photographic techniques by art photographers and the influence of art photography on fashion photography reflect a somewhat fraught exchange of sensibilities between the contemporary art world and consumer culture. The feedback between art and fashion photography has provided an environment for fashion photography to evolve rapidly and in close relationship with art photography. This vibrant exchange has helped alter the look and subject of fashion photography over the period.

*   *   *

The memorable fashion photographs of the generation of photographers who began working in the late 1940s functioned primarily to describe clothes as they appeared on the model. As in a still life, the clothes and the women are artfully arranged with meticulous attention focused on the uniqueness, originality or stunning detail of the garment. Irving Penn and a select few other photographers of this generation saw their task in the strictest sense as the interpretation and description of clothes as the embodiment of perfection and elegance. It is a task that Penn himself performed brilliantly and with considerable wit. At the same time, Penn's photographs and those of other highly talented fashion photographers of that era reflect an intrinsic value system. Their work displays idealized members of an upper social class, whose chief characteristics are good breeding and refinement. In these pictures, the power of privilege is understood as absolute, as are the crisp and elegant standards of beauty that are integrated with it.

In the wake of the 1940s and during the ensuing Cold War, however, the notion of an idealized social hierarchy could never be the same. The place it had held in the pictorial firmament was challenged by its democratic opposite, the notion of a popular and populist anti-establishment, which took its values from mass culture. During this time, prêt-à-porter eclipsed haute couture as a trendsetter in fashion.

Among the formative developments of the anti-establishment's new vision was the work of William Klein. Klein, who had studied art with Fernand Léger, used a 35mm camera on the run, often surreptitiously. His negatives were often exposed in shadows or low light, or at a slow speed so that a print from the negative included highly visible grain and blur. Klein's aggressive photographic style broke through the theatrical plane of staged artificiality, even as it brought the notion of theatricality into the street. In the mid-1950s, Klein began working on assignment for *Vogue*, and has been involved with fashion photography ever since. In Klein's photographs, the model has become a woman whose visage is refreshing, tough and not altogether pleasing. The viewer was slowly, incrementally, being drawn down a path that was bringing the images of fashion closer to the 'realities' of life.

Klein and the new anti-establishment photographers were changing the relationship between consumers of fashion and the images themselves; in the same way they were changing the subject of fashion photography. Readers of fashion magazines or viewers of fashion pictures were no longer just observers, but implicit participants. As fashion photographers changed the models from objects into active humans in realistic situations, they began to make the viewer an extension of these situations. Everything – model, clothing, background, lighting, situations, image and viewer – participated in a narrative fantasy.

In their day, photographers like Klein (and later Guy Bourdin, Helmut Newton and Richard Avedon) were the fashion industry's avant-garde. By definition, they stood out from a less inventive pack; the majority of fashion photographs being made, then as now, were straightforward pictures of women with a clear view of the clothes. But over time, the field of fashion photography slowly absorbed the precedents set by these earlier leaders. By 1990, sporadic but adventurous, racy and highly individualistic bodies of work made for fifty years had coalesced into a trend that infiltrated the main body of the fashion-photography world. The expansion of the subject of fashion photography from clothing to lifestyle reflected a major change in the fashion industry. As it adapted to the interests and concerns of a contemporary audience, it radically broadened the range of possibilities for the photographer.

Fashion and fashion snobbery still exist, but in addition to top labels, design is now equally determined by the consumer or the 'street'. Young people are the largest targeted audience for consumer goods, and they wield the economic power effectively to project their ideas and preferences back to the top. The high-end designers, in turn, are inspired by their vitality and more than willing to accommodate their whims. Fashion photography logically followed increasingly idiosyncratic clothes, culture and markets. The mass marketing of street fashion, such as low-slung baggy jeans, paradoxically helped precipitate strong narrative elements and striking imagery in fashion photography. Once again, fashion photography drew its inspiration from the world of art photography, where the same problems – the multiplicity of imagery in everyday life, the resultant exhaustion of traditional dramatic gestures, postures and situations, and the constant jostling of diverse forms of expression – had long challenged the foundations of traditional artistic expression. In the post-Andy Warhol art world, photographers were also making use of explicit or implied narrative techniques to augment the vitality of their work.

Fashion photography was quick to join in. Ironically, just as the narrative techniques of art photography were beginning to insinuate themselves into fashion photography, fashion was receiving recognition as a budding aspect of art. The February 1982 special issue of *Artforum* magazine featured a cover photograph of a rattan bodice and nylon polyester skirt by avant-garde Japanese designer Issey Miyake. This was the first time fashion was showcased on the cover of a contemporary art magazine. Since 1982, fashion has become increasingly visible on the pages of *Artforum*, as brand-name advertisements and as the subjects of articles, artwork and exhibitions have featured in the journal. The influence of art in fashion magazines is just as vibrant, as seen in the increasing number of artists seeking the limelight in mass-consumer fashion magazines, either photographing for fashion editorials or appropriating commercial techniques of fashion photography in their own artwork.

In London, a former art director at British *Vogue*, Terry Jones, founded *i-D* in the summer of 1980. Inspired by London punk and street culture, *i-D* featured gritty, straightforward black-and-white photographs of street fashion, and layouts modelled after punk 'zines. Along with *The Face*, another influential magazine launched a few months earlier, *i-D* was to become a visual diary of a new generation. Both magazines were instrumental in encouraging photographers such as David Sims, Glen Luchford, Craig McDean, Juergen Teller and Corinne Day to express their ideas.

The American counterparts to *i-D* and *The Face* were magazines like *Interview* and *Punk*, though neither of these was specifically fashion oriented. In 1985, the New York newspaper the *Village Voice* launched the fashion insert *View* (after the first issue spelt *Vue*), which sought to showcase innovative photography, design and fashion, without being directed by trends. *Vue* did not employ established fashion photographers or feature professional models in its pages; instead, photojournalists and art photographers such as Nan Goldin, Laurie Simmons, Gilles Peress and Philip-Lorca diCorcia brought their own art practices into the stories they made. *Vue* was discontinued after six issues, but the strategies employed by Mary Peacock, fashion editor, and Yolanda Cuomo, art director, presaged the thinking behind many of the independent magazines in the 1990s.

The flood of independent magazines that began in the 1980s gave a new boost to the inclusion of art photographers in the fashion field. Founded in the 1990s, magazines like *Dutch*, *Purple*, *Tank*, *Self Service*, *Big*, *Surface* and *Sleek* bridged the worlds of art and fashion, showcasing young and unknown photographers and designers. Their circulation was small, and many were short-lived, yet these independent publications encouraged creativity and innovation, and fostered an artistic approach to fashion, often interspersing art within the pages of fashion editorials. Photographers, stylists and editors all expressed ideas, constructed narratives and made images that spoke to their own generation. Editorials were born not from trends seen on the runway, but rather from a conceptual beginning, either a literal, cinematic or psychological impetus that made for a compelling story. These magazines fostered an intersection for art, music, fashion, design and youth culture, and helped usher in a boom in fashion photography that focused even further on originality and personal expression.

*   *   *

The prevalence of narrative in fashion photography leads to another, enormously influential aspect of the medium: cinema. Ever since the pioneering work of Eadweard Muybridge and Étienne Marey at the turn of the nineteenth century, the link between the two art forms has been explicit. Film is perhaps the most popular language of the twentieth century, and it was inevitable that both art and fashion photography should also begin to appropriate the imagery and narrative constructions of their more powerful cousin. For fashion photography, in particular, the impulse to appropriate imagery and narratives from the movies was also grounded in the glamour that was explicitly created by the moving medium. Glamour and melodrama, the chief sources of cinema's mass appeal, became a kind of visual shorthand that fashion photography could easily appropriate to amplify the impact of its own narratives. Thus, characters from Hollywood films, especially those of the 1950s and 1960s by Alfred Hitchcock, Jean-Luc Godard and Michelangelo Antonioni are continually recycled in fashion photography. In the cinematic fashion photograph, the glamour of movies is joined with the glamour of fashion.

Ironically, this has brought back the importance of the studio system, but with a different twist. With the advent, in the 1970s, of narrative subjects created by art photographers in the studio, the photographer became a kind of film director. Sets were constructed as backgrounds for narratives, models and friends enlisted as subjects, and lighting specialists called in. These cinematic tactics can be seen in the work of Gregory Crewdson, whose photographic tableaux appear to be scenes from movies. In Crewdson's work what is left out of the frame of a photograph is as important to the viewer's experience as what is within it. To enter secretly a narrative over which we have no control, except for in the imagination we bring to it, further instigates the impulse to fantasize without repercussions, and the story happening outside the frame underscores our voyeuristic sense, because the voyeur is always at a tantalizing disadvantage.

The cinematic techniques adopted by contemporary fashion photographers range from the actual scripting of stories with fully drawn characters to the use of lighting and camera angles normally used by filmmakers. The magazine format offers the photographer the opportunity for an extended narrative over a number of pages; this means that a telling detail, a lingering camera shot of an object, or a person leaving a room, suggests a more detailed narrative to be completed by the viewer.

Perhaps the best-known contemporary exemplar of the fusion of self-conscious cinematic technique with photography is Philip-Lorca diCorcia. DiCorcia's personal style of picture-making emerged after he graduated from Yale University's two-year MFA programme. DiCorcia understood that to create works that were genuinely new, he needed to distil the culture that had most profoundly influenced him. This was primarily cinema, which he mixed with photographic history into a brew that applied cinematic narrative to the ever inspirational incidents of quotidian life.

DiCorcia's photographs are carefully planned images that combine the seductive powers of cinematic and commercial photography with a deeply felt perception of the possibilities of meaning in the prosaic: how the ordinary can become exceptional when framed with intelligence and imagination (Plate 1). DiCorcia is a member of a generation for whom the hyperbolic dramas of Douglas Sirk and camp classics such as *Valley of the Dolls* were shown alongside the post-war foreign films of Roberto Rossellini, Federico Fellini, Ingmar Bergman and Jean-Luc Godard. The intellectual, emotional and, most significantly, visual impact of these films replaced the literary influence of books and the history of art as formative elements in a new photographic vocabulary with which many contemporary photographers would subsequently work.

The fashion photographs of diCorcia are cryptic moments from a narrative that has no beginning or end. His *Cuba Libre* portfolio appeared in *W* magazine as a 30-page photographic essay in 2000. The story opens with a panoramic overview of Havana, such as one might see in a film. The protagonist is a woman alone, and a clandestine current of repression dominates the scene, although the explicit plot of the narrative is never revealed. Its essence is pure intrigue and melodrama, without apparent beginning, middle or end.

DiCorcia's voyeuristic views often describe people (most often alienated women) who live in existential despair. The surfaces of the pictures are seductive; their lights and darks, through the advantage of digital printing where colour is seen even in the blacks (another similarity to cinema), achieve an atmosphere of morbidity in which the characters are trapped.

What diCorcia does explicitly, other photographers have done more elliptically. Cedric Buchet's ethereal overhead photographs, shot by a camera on a high crane, resemble the landscape and mysterious encounters of Federico Fellini's 1963 film *8½*, in which a successful filmmaker is alternately accosted and soothed by a crowd of producers, friends, wives, family and mistresses as he struggles to make his next film. Several times in the film we see the central figure wandering aimlessly through a veritable fog from which living and dead characters mysteriously appear and disappear. Buchet's overhead views were printed as two-page spreads to accommodate the scope of the images. The photographs invite us to linger in spaces swathed in transcendent light, a world of shifting characters in beach scenes that embody both the real (conscious) and the dreamed (unconscious). Protagonists, faceless for the most part, cross paths dressed in Prada's newest designs, and when full-figured characters appear they project the energy of robotic puppets (Plate 2). With Buchet, the reference is not only to cinema but, as with Fellini, to the surreal.

David Lynch's 1986 film *Blue Velvet* describes the potential strangeness lurking beneath the surface of our lives. A mystery/suspense drama set in a small American town, the film contrasts an unnatural brilliance in daytime with scenes photographed at night, where details revealed in the shadows heighten our sense that something hidden and forebidding lurks beneath the surface. In his 1997 and 1998 campaigns for Prada, British photographer Glen Luchford translates the dark side of *Blue Velvet* into provocative stills from an extended cinematic narrative filled with tension and ambiguity.

Luchford started working in the early 1990s, at a time when British fashion photography embodied the adventurous and creative. Nick Knight was the editor of *i-D* magazine, and hired photographers Nigel Shafran and Craig McDean; art director Phil Bicker at *The Face* gave unknown photographers Corinne Day and David Sims their first jobs. Stylists such as Alexandra White and Melanie Ward also worked with the same group of photographers. Their images felt fresh and new – a change influenced in part by the predominant grunge and rave culture in Britain at the time, and an attitude towards dressing which ignored the dictates of commercial fashion brands. Personal expression became more important than actual clothes, and independent start-up magazines such as *Purple, Self Service* and *Dutch* all contributed to this shifting definition of fashion. Luchford's first images were made during this period; rife with tension, eroticism and theatricality, they challenged the delineation between fact and fiction, using fashion as a mere prop.

In most of Luchford's pictures for the Prada campaigns, only parts of bodies or figures are seen. The photographs are cinematically lit, and the ambient light, sets, props and careful framing create a claustrophobic environment imbued with the mystery of film noir (Plate 3). In one image a woman fearfully looks back over her shoulder as if someone is lurking in the shadows of the room. In another photograph made for the 1997 campaign, a woman's illuminated legs with the red ribbon of her shoes tied suggestively around her ankles lie lifeless on the damp and murky grass, leaving viewers to draw their own conclusions about her unfortunate end. Luchford's images propose a way to address concerns beyond the synthetic surface of fashion by utilizing cinematic strategies to heighten a complex psychological and emotional state.

*   *   *

The cinematic tendency in fashion photography represents what might be called the public aspect of modern photography – the aspect that is in play in our representation of others. But there is another tendency in photography that has come to exercise a dominant if paradoxical influence on both art and fashion photography: the private aspect. It derives from the vast realm of images that were not taken with the objective of public display in mind. Their birthplace is the snapshot and the family album.

'Of all photographic images, [the snapshot] comes closest to the truth,' declared the photographer Lisette Model. The candid family snapshot is understood as casual, innocent and unorchestrated, capturing life and people as they really are, devoid of the pretension and constructions of art or studio photography. It is oblivious to the rules of serious photography; its subject matter is more crucial than original composition, accurate colour and print quality. With its apparent emotional immediacy, the snapshot fills family albums, visual diaries and scrapbooks, depicting domestic interactions and treasured moments. The family photographs that we cherish today arise from two distinct photographic traditions: the formally posed nineteenth-century studio portrait and the spontaneous images derived from the Kodak Brownie and the 35mm tradition. Both kinds of photographs are beloved keepsakes that privately track our personal histories and memories.

While family photographs allege honesty, they do not necessarily memorialize an event truthfully, and the stiff frontal posing of the studio portrait still dominates many family photographs today. As if on instinct, even the most recalcitrant 12-year-old will smile for a split second when the camera clicks, before slumping back in boredom. This presentation for the camera is a cultural ritual in which families participate year after year, and points to the complexity of the layers of meaning in the autobiographical picture.

The snapshot's emotional authenticity and the degree of empathy it inspires between the viewer and the subject have made it attractive to art and fashion photographers alike. Amid the clamour of commercial imagery, the possible ties that bind the viewer to a memory – real or false – of the subject are powerful and intriguing tools of perception. In a generation of photographers who grew up surrounded by such photographs, the possibilities were not going to be ignored. By 1990, the snapshot and family album aesthetic came to inspire fashion photography almost as much as the cult of cinema did. The inspiration came in two forms: posed and candid. When posed, the snapshot recalls ritualistic moments and perfected scenarios of family interaction, while the candid snapshot introduces a sense of reality or authenticity to the magazine page.

The line between casual amateur and skilled commercial photographer is often intentionally blurred in 1990s fashion imagery. Photographers emulating the snapshot deliberately avoid the studio aesthetic, and instead opt to make photographs that are, or appear to be, autobiographical and uncontrived. Some contemporary photographers started using point-and-shoot cameras to capture friends, family and real-life situations, unobtrusively – fashion as it is lived. The spontaneity that characterizes their work harks back to photographers whose work blended reportage and fashion, among them Martin Munkacsi, William Klein and Jeanloup Sieff.

In the 1990s, photographers such as Corinne Day, Juergen Teller, Mario Sorrenti, and Terry Richardson regularly photographed their friends and lovers in 'real-life' situations for fashion magazines. As a consequence of Corinne Day's controversial photographs of the unknown skinny teenager Kate Moss in British *Vogue* in 1993, the unfortunate terms 'waif' and 'heroin chic' became household expressions. Conservative critics alleged that these images offered thinly veiled references to drug use and glamorized unhealthy lifestyles. But the real point was different and paradoxical: fashion photography was presenting itself as bypassing fashion photography.

As part of this turn of events, models began to be cast from real life and from the street, and the credit line 'clothes model's own' became commonplace on the magazine page. Not only were the models and narratives atypical, but the photographs themselves often appeared to be snapshots. The images were read as subversive and authentic challenges to the conventions of the fashion image, and as introducing 'realism' into a glamorous genre. They acknowledge not only Nan Goldin's *Ballad of Sexual Dependency* (first shown in 1979) but also Larry Clark's *Tulsa* (1970), an autobiographical study of the author's drug-addicted friends and their lifestyle. Yet the new 'spontaneous' photographs were as fabricated as any other fashion images, and inevitably became as mannered and self-conscious as the studio portraits they were replacing.

The appropriation of the snapshot aesthetic in the 1990s was paralleled by a rise in deconstructed clothes and the resurgence of vintage fashion, which champion a more individualized expression of style. In opposition to the label-conscious 1980s, mixing and matching high-end labels with department-store brands became commonplace, even in the most commercial magazines that emphasized the selection of clothes as an important symbol of personal style. Simultaneously, street style and music influenced the vocabulary of haute couture more than ever.

In 1985 a precedent was set for this new direction in fashion photography that would become commonplace by the mid-1990s. Nan Goldin's shockingly unglamorous and straightforward photographs of four women in lingerie, taken in the Russian Baths on New York's Lower East Side, presages the snapshot aesthetic of many 1990s fashion images (Plate 4). Goldin's editorial, *Masculine/Feminine* (the title of Jean-Luc Godard's 1966 film), was published in 1985 in the 'High/Low' themed premier issue of *View*. The women modelled simple cotton briefs and tank tops (masculine) as well as flirty lacy lingerie (feminine) while lounging around the deteriorating stone benches and tiled pools of the bathhouse, seemingly indifferent to the camera. The lighting is amateur, the framing is loose, and the models rarely pose and smile for the camera.

Deborah Turbeville's 1975 soft-focus bathhouse photographs for *Vogue* became somewhat of a benchmark in fashion photography when they were accused of creating a 'great scandal' by taking the model out of the glossy studio and inserting her in a moody scenario with intimate undertones of sexuality. While the narrative is similar to *Masculine/Feminine*, Turbeville's carefully posed and artfully constructed shots of professional models contrast with Goldin's more straightforward pictures, which resemble casual snapshots. Reportage, art and fashion are blurred in Goldin's images, which have more in common with personal mementos than stylized fashion images.

Goldin's pictures are decidedly unpretentious, and the decrepit locale and low-quality printing add to their grittiness. The models are Goldin's friends, and the relationships among the women, rather than any idealized notion of beauty, are the central focus of the photographs. In effect, the clothes are held hostage to the pictures – a fresh way to define and sell fashion. This approach was possible in a publication like *View*, which did not need to pander to high-end clothing advertisers and well-to-do purveyors of style, but was aimed at young readers who followed the art and music scene of New York's East Village.

Unlike traditional fashion photography in women's magazines, where one image usually fills an entire glossy page, the *View* layout featured Goldin's photographs in varying sizes, often overlapping, and allowing only two images in the editorial to bleed to the full page. The layout is similar to that of a scrapbook or personal album. One of the largest photographs is of a very pregnant blonde woman in a gold bra and panty set, and this untraditional underwear model turns the lure of a lingerie shoot on its head. Instead of posing seductively for the camera, she looks down as she fiddles with her bra, her panties almost hidden under her swollen belly, a surprising picture of womanly sensuality. The lingerie is not sexed up but matter of fact, suggesting that a fashion photograph can simply be defined by the credits that identify the brand of clothing worn by the model. In Goldin's images, a fashion photograph is just somebody wearing clothes, with no need for professional models or elaborate sets, and the resulting picture is just as persuasive, if not more so, to potential consumers.

Another photographer inspired by the autobiographical picture is Mario Sorrenti, who became known at a young age for his Calvin Klein *Obsession* ad campaign in 1992, which featured a nude young Kate Moss in an idyllic beach setting, photographed in luscious black-and-white. Because Sorrenti was involved with Moss at the time, the photographs also function as intimate snapshots of a relationship and a particular moment in his life. Although Sorrenti has subsequently photographed in many differing styles, documenting his life and friends remains at the core of his practice. In his editorials and diaries, fashion is an appendage to a certain lifestyle rather than the subject of the photographs.

At the beginning of his career, Sorrenti carried a 35mm camera with him at all times. Because he couldn't afford to print the frames he took, he cut up contact sheets and stuck them in his diary, a constant source of inspiration that has subsequently influenced the design and content of a number of fashion features. The subjects in his essay *One*, published in *Another Magazine* in 2001, are not beautiful women but, instead, a wheelchair-bound boy smoking a bong in a graffiti-plastered room, and a band practising in a dark and cluttered apartment (Plate 5). Sorrenti is actually featured in several of the photographs, adding to the illusion that they offer an authentic moment or experience, rather than merely selling a product.

Juergen Teller is another photographer who uses our belief in the authenticity of the snapshot to create narrative tension in his fashion work. Teller meshes spontaneous moments captured on film with carefully constructed scenarios that appear to be casual. For an editorial titled 'The Clients', in the March 1999 issue of *W* magazine, Teller photographed some of haute couture's biggest clients, such as Princess Marie-Chantal of Greece and Vicomtesse Jacqueline de Ribes (Fig. 1). These wealthy women are not the idealized beauties we regularly see modelling garments on the pages of magazines, and Teller's pictures of the clients are straightforward and uncontrived. He used a 35mm auto-focus point-and-shoot camera to photograph each woman quickly in markedly mundane environments. The results are startlingly honest and blunt, not always portraying the women in the most flattering light. The pictures communicate a frankness that reveals Teller's sharp sensibility for composition and humour. As viewers, we feel as though we might be in the room with these women, that perhaps we ourselves could have taken this picture, and that just maybe

1. Juergen Teller,
The Clients,
Haute Couture:
'Marie-Chantal of
Greece, Paris',
from *The Clients,*
W, March 1999.

this fantasy of beautiful clothes is not so far removed from our own experience of life.

The conventions of the family photo album also play a strong role in fashion images and stories made during the 1990s. Well-known art photographers Larry Sultan and Tina Barney used the format of the magazine to create narratives reminiscent of images in family albums. Sultan's photographs for the Kate Spade 2002 Fall/Winter campaign embody frozen moments of idealized domestic interactions. They take advantage of the artifice of fashion to create exaggerated narratives that address domestic conventions of family harmony or the promise of suburbia, while Barney incorporates the tradition of the family photograph to explore contemporary versions of domesticity.

Sultan's photographs for the Kate Spade campaign, *Visiting Tennessee*, are about an American upper-middle-class family's trip to New York to visit their young adult daughter Tennessee. The layout mimics the format of a photo album of a family's adventures on their annual trip to the Big Apple. We follow the Lawrences, a culturally sophisticated and stylish family, as they check into New York's Carlyle Hotel, trek through Chelsea art galleries, shop in Chinatown, and finally enjoy a nightcap back in their well-appointed hotel room. The Lawrences are portrayed as the model American nuclear family, and the images are reminiscent of 1940s Kodak advertisements, which similarly featured highly stylized domestic scenarios. In the images, the characters are perfectly pulled together in the way they could be only if attended to by makeup artists and stylists.

Larry Sultan is best known for his project *Pictures from Home* (1983–92), which follows the life of his parents through photographs taken over many years. A member of the post-war baby-boom generation, Sultan documented his parents in an attempt to come to terms with a childhood defined by media representations of the American Dream. *Pictures from Home* includes photographs of his parents performing their daily rituals, details of their personal belongings, as well as family snapshots and stills appropriated from 8mm home movies made between 1943 and 1972. Inspired by *Pictures from Home*, Kate Spade's creative directors asked Sultan to make similar photographs of their fictional family. The campaign's punchy colour and graphic framing are reminiscent of Sultan's earlier art project, and similarly addresses the schism between memories as informed by family photographs and lived reality.

The narrative and look of Sultan's photographs suggest nostalgia for a happier and less complicated era. The images are iconic, and present a family that is familiar yet unattainable. Their over-saturated colours veer towards kitsch, and the pictured moments are clichéd, creating scenarios that are no longer real, but exaggerated constructions of authentic encounters. Sultan's images affirm and recognize their own commerciality, and point to the constructed nature and essential falsity of such representations and longings for the 'good life'.

Tina Barney uses the family-photograph motif to create stories rife with complexity and tension. Her pictures provide intimate insider views of the privileged circle of wealthy East Coast families in which she grew up. Her family scenarios are autobiographical and feature her parents, siblings and friends in typical domestic events such as Sunday brunch. The photographs are partly contrived, but are born from everyday exchanges between family members. Her prints are often up to five feet in length, and the large-format four-by-five camera she uses reveals each detail in the utmost clarity, so that every nuance in gesture, pose, decor and dress informs the viewer's reading of the relationships among the people in the photographs.

In her fashion work, Barney composes similar family narratives and scenarios. For her 1999 magazine editorial 'New York Stories', Barney photographed some of the city's well-known cultured residents, such as the writer Joan Didion, and the families of painter Brice Marden and gallery owner Angela Westwater. Like her artwork, these photographs provide a glimpse into a world few ordinary people see. But unlike Barney's large photographic prints, the small scale of the magazine editorial creates a sense of intimacy embodied in family albums. In the photographs, fashion is an accessory, just like the sofas, art and lamps that decorate the environments. The families are posed, so that what once might have been a spontaneous moment of a mother holding out her hand to her young child (as in the photograph of actor Julianne Moore's family) becomes frozen. Every photograph is carefully arranged to communicate a narrative, but a flick of the head or a statement caught in mid-sentence belies the constructed story and works within the conventions of the impromptu family snapshot. The viewer becomes entrenched in the dramas and the complex relationships among family members and does not focus on the clothes.

*　　　*　　　*

Fashion photography in the 1990s is marked by a desire to communicate narratives outside the world of fashion. Adopting the aesthetics of cinema and of snapshots and cherished family photographs represents an attempt by practising photographers and editors to enrich their images with a resonance and meaning that address the concerns, desires and realities of youth culture. More than ever, fashion photographs no longer function solely to dictate hemlines and silhouettes, but also to acknowledge their position as vehicles for an expression of cultural attitudes. Whether candid or staged, the snapshot and family album motif and the cinematic picture demonstrate that these fashionable fictions are no longer confined to the commercial codes of the magazine but, rather, have social, psychological and cultural implications beyond the hermetic world of fashion.

3 The Celebration of the Fashion Image: Photograph as Market Commodity and Research Tool

Philippe Garner

This chapter is based on a presentation made at the National Portrait Gallery.

Fashion is an elusive medium. An area of creativity in constant flux, change is its very essence. Yet great fashion photographs – images that succeed not just in capturing the specifics of garments and styles, but in immortalizing evocative nuances of gesture, mood and context – provide a tangible legacy of this fluid form of expression. They become the seminal and iconic reference points for historians and collectors eager to grasp something lasting from the organic, fluid branch of performance art that we call high fashion. These images can permanently fix the defining moments from an endlessly evolving, ever inventive spectacle. In May 2004, against the background of their Cecil Beaton exhibition, London's National Portrait Gallery, in collaboration with the University of Westminster, hosted a study day on the subject of fashion photography. I was asked to be one of the speakers.

I have been an auction specialist for thirty-three years. Thirty-one of those were spent at Sotheby's and, after a two-year spell working on New York sales for Phillips, I have now joined Christie's, working internationally, but still based in London. My fields are photographs and twentieth-century decorative art and design. While I have a wide-ranging curiosity and have developed a broad knowledge across the full history of photography, I have a particular fascination with fashion photography. This passion well predates my professional involvement with the medium. I can, in fact, be more specific – I started saving fashion and related photographs as tear sheets from magazines in the very early sixties, aged 13. My curiosity embraced beauty and celebrity as well as pure fashion – the full sweep of professional photographic images of sophisticated, styled and – to use a current term not then in common currency – 'constructed' female icons. This field of photography today occupies a position of enormous influence in our culture, a mirror of our ideals, vanities, ambitions, desires and insecurities. It is hardly surprising that exemplary images should have acquired such a potent aura and been allowed, even encouraged, to assume a considerable fetishistic authority.

It is as a professional involved in the marketing of fine and rare photographic prints that I was invited to discuss how images from this particular branch of commercial photography can become transformed into commodities worthy of being collected, studied and of course traded. I was to speak as an experienced market specialist, and not without qualification, since over the years I had personally brought down my gavel on a very wide range of fine vintage fashion prints by some of the masters of the medium – from Beaton to Penn, Horst to Newton, Parkinson to Bourdin, de Meyer to von Wangenheim. Among all these lots were memorable treasures, distinguished by the combination of the power of the image and the inherent magic of the print as object. I have always been acutely conscious of the evident implication that through my professional activity I was endorsing the value and importance of these rare prints as keys to the subject of fashion photography. The auction and gallery market seems to suggest that the most desirable form in which to collect and preserve the story of fashion photography is through the original prints made by or for the photographers. In certain cases these were made as working tools in which case stamps and annotations on the reverse may well testify to their primary function. Many others – and probably the majority of the prints that are the stuff of the art market – were made specifically for collectors in high-quality editions, as in the case of Irving Penn's wonderful platinum prints.

But I was also speaking at the NPG as a consumer of fashion images, a passionate and perhaps unusually well-informed consumer. For me, the first point of contact with fashion photographs was always through the perusal of a magazine, purchased from a newsstand, or enjoyed as a supplement to a newspaper. The more I thought about this question, the more I felt that fashion photography was perhaps being done a disservice by the art market's emphasis. I felt obliged to suggest an alternative approach – one that could sound like a professional heresy. While fully acknowledging the power and relevance of beautiful individual prints, my suggestion was that the true medium through which to study and appreciate fashion photographs is the magazine – for this was the original point of interface between the photographers and their intended audience.

Fashion photography has in common with photojournalism the underlying principle of making images by photographic means that will be translated by photomechanical processes into ink on paper destined to reach as wide an audience as possible. Clearly a front-page picture on a big national daily newspaper will reach more people than a fashion story in the finely printed pages of a luxurious fashion magazine such as French *Vogue*. But the principle is the same – photography as a medium with a swift and wide reach, an open means of communication in an image-hungry and photo-literate world (Plate 6).

Implicit in the notion of the magazine as the true conduit for fashion imagery are certain central truths regarding this field. First, magazines remind us that fashion photographs are not created in a vacuum. They have a specific commercial purpose and they are the product of a complex collaborative process. The challenge for ambitious fashion photographers is to define and express their individual point of view within a team project that involves editor, fashion editor, art director and, of course, the fashion designer whose work they are illustrating. To this list must be added the hair and makeup artists, the stylists and the models, who all become players in the mix. The photographer is a ringmaster whose role is to bring together all these talents and to create persuasive images that are undeniably artificial constructions yet which have the ability to seduce and inspire. The pictures must have a quality of credibility that persuades the viewer to suspend disbelief. Which brings us to another key characteristic of fashion imagery that becomes evident in magazines, namely that the pictures are usually conceived in series. The objective is to draw the viewer not just into one single image, but into a narrative sequence, a picture story that exerts an extended hold (Fig. 2). The choice of theme and the sequencing become crucial. Certainly, exceptional individual images can burn themselves into one's memory. Isolated from their context, such images are used in books and exhibitions as landmarks in charting the history of fashion photography. They are arguably more telling, however, in their original contexts than isolated as solitary icons.

To explain my thesis I presented a slide show of magazine spreads. My aim was to show certain very famous images as published in the original magazine features. Pictures by Steichen, Penn, Avedon, Newton, Weber and others were situated in the lively cocktail of the magazine spreads, each image working as part of an overall concept with other photographs as well as with typographical and illustrative elements (Figs 3, 4 and 5). The starting point

2. Bob Richardson, *Une nuit blanche*, fashion shoot for French *Vogue*, 1967. Richardson brought a new dimension to fashion photography in the 1960s. He used fashion as the pretext to explore mood and expressive gesture in picture stories that convey an authentic sense of emotional engagement between his models.

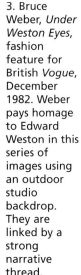

3. Bruce Weber, *Under Weston Eyes*, fashion feature for British *Vogue*, December 1982. Weber pays homage to Edward Weston in this series of images using an outdoor studio backdrop. They are linked by a strong narrative thread.

4. [opposite, upper] Franco Rubartelli, *Jungle Look: Une grande aventure au Coeur de l'Afrique*, fashion feature for French *Vogue*, July–August 1968. Aristocratic German model Veruschka and Italian photographer Rubartelli teamed up in the late sixties and used the sponsorship of international fashion and other magazines to create exciting, inventive, celebratory images that situate fashion in the realms of pure fantasy and transform the conventions of modelling into a branch of performance art.

5. [opposite, lower] Deborah Turbeville, 'Isabella Weingarten and Ella in a Wood', Montova, Italy, published in the photographer's book *Wallflower*, 1978. An experienced fashion photographer understands the dynamics of the context in which their images will be published. Here, a landscape-format image has been constructed taking full account of the double-page spread in which it will appear, and proves highly effective in its form and its content – steeped in melancholy and with a strong graphic impact.

JUNGLE LOOK:
UNE GRANDE AVENTURE **AU COEUR DE L'AFRIQUE**

24 PAGES DE
RETOUR À L'ÉTAT DE "NATURE"
DANS LA MODE
ET LES MAQUILLAGES

"Partis du Bourget à 6 h du matin, Franco Rubartelli et moi étions à 5 h
du soir à Bangui, au cœur même de la République centrafricaine,
grâce à U.T.A. L'on me donna un arc, et, vêtue de cuir blanc,
Paco Rabanne!, je me plongeai à
mi-mollet dans ce marigot
plein d'hippopotames."

Veruschka

was a feature from the April 1911 issue of *Art et Décoration* in which a fashion picture story by Edward Steichen was elegantly laid out with relevant text and with charming illustrations by Georges Lepape (Fig. 6). This was perhaps the first great art-directed photographic magazine fashion story. I then showed a cavalcade of glorious fashion pages from mainstream fashion magazines, notably *Vogue* and *Harper's Bazaar*, and chose to broaden the presentation by drawing attention to the more ephemeral, and sometimes more adventurous, aspects of fashion publishing, to the work that appears in newspapers and newspaper supplements, destined to have a life-span of only one day, or in lower-budget, smaller-circulation, so-called 'style' magazines such as *i-D* and *Dazed & Confused* (Plates 7, 8 and 9). It is thrilling to see new talent and new directions emerging in the pages of such publications, to identify the contemporary equivalents of the pictures and picture sequences that have come to define aspects of social and photographic history (Plates 10 and 11).

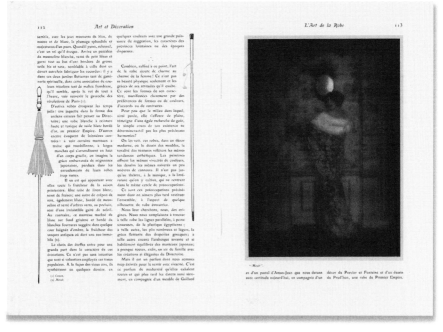

6. Edward Steichen, *L'Art de la Robe*, fashion feature for *Art et Décoration*, Paris, April 1911. This feature on the creation of couturier Paul Poiret combined photographs in the secessionist manner by Steichen with illustrations by George Lepape. The resulting spreads are of a consummate refinement and constitute a historic first in the sophisticated, photographic presentation of fashion.

These magazines, from the most established titles to the provocative upstarts, present fashion photography in its most immediate and authentic form. If they include fashion features that engage or inspire you, then you are face-to-face with a vital expression of our visual culture. This – ink on paper, pictures in a context, images integrated with words – is the precious data that will define the history of fashion photography.

WORKS CITED

Turbeville, Deborah (1978) *Wallflower*, edited and designed by Marvin Israel and Kate Morgan (London: Quartet Books)

4 The Fashion Photograph: an 'Ecology'[1]

Margaret Maynard

Three intriguing black-and-white fashion photographs, taken by significant photographers working for the Australian fashion press in the 1960s, are the subject of this essay. The first is a streetscape by Laurence Le Guay,[2] known as 'Untitled (Fashion Queue with Masked Child)', a double spread concluding a six-page shoot *How to Stand Out in the City* (*Flair*, August 1960: 34–39) (Plate 12). The second, also by Le Guay, is one of a double-page set of textually linked, generically complicated images of billboards, 'Forsaken Mermaids Need No Longer Despair…' (*Flair*, October 1961: 28–29). The third is by Helmut Newton,[3] entitled 'Beautiful Beast Looks' (*Vogue* [Australia], Early Winter 1961: 91), the last of seven photos of caged models, wearing leather and fur outfits: 'les belles sauvages'.

My intention is to apply the metaphor of an 'ecology' to elucidate from these images more than appreciation of glossy attractiveness, straightforward socio/cultural shifts or issues of gender politics. Without wishing to diminish the role of aesthetics in evaluating these images, nor to deny the usefulness of an auteurial approach of analysis per se, I suggest there are better ways to understand the orchestration of Australia's photographic industry at the time. By examining the appearances of these images, plus complex inconsistencies constituted by unstable sets of external variables surrounding production, publication and circulation, the internal factors of the 'look' can be 'reframed' by those elements which lie beyond. We need to ask what relevance a wider understanding of what we call the 'genre' of fashion photography can have. A broadened approach may allow us to deduce cultural information from these examples beyond stand-alone stylistic analysis, chronological detailing, feminist studies of the female body, sexuality and desire, or indeed the semiological readings of texts.

We speak categorically of the 'genre' of fashion photography as having its own coherent histories, practices and expectations (Ramamurthy 2000: 185). But it is better understood by recognizing that its generic status is not essentialist; rather, it is a rhetorical practice, informed by provisional, external engagements and framing procedures that play with relational contrasts. In other words, considering fashion photography as a genre is to understand it as constituted by sets of regularities, sufficient to mark out particularities, but at the same time without consistent rules or ingredients (Freadman and Macdonald 1992: 25–26, 43). The latter writers argue that all texts are defined by competing taxonomies, therefore no text is generically pure (45). In earlier writing Freadman explains that rather than the discovery of an essence, what positions something as generic is more aptly 'the tracing of boundaries' that arise from the positioning of certain differences or sets of contrasts (1988: 79).

Various 'ceremonial' frames which, for fashion photography, may be layout or captioning, technical procedures etc., enact these differences, and 'it is the system of their relations' that creates a place for meaning to occur (1988: 90–91). As Freadman says, 'framing is not usefully restricted to that which is outside the text, but strategically includes those things which the text does to situate itself in relation to its social, formal and material surroundings' (1988: 92). Considering fashion images located in such a dynamic matrix, we step back from a tendency to see emphatic coherences and similarities, finding instead what is most interesting emerging from differences within placements, series of contrasts or even 'non' descriptors. Thus in reviewing presumptions about 'genre' we can extract further meaning from the images under consideration.

In accepting the notion of a matrix, the term 'ecology' is used to explicate both the circumstances and the milieu of the chosen photographs. This means acknowledging the fragile sites of these photographs and their re-siting as they become embedded or re-embedded in presentation and publication frameworks. The fashion image, like any photograph, is a 'site of intersection of various orders of theoretical understanding relating to its production, publication and consumption or reading' (Wells 2000: 34). Such frameworks speak as well to the viewer.

Explicitly dealing with the ephemeral, fashion photographs are paradoxically the most pictorially stylized of images. Frosh, in an essay about stock photography, suggests we regard such imagery as sharing structured conventions, assumptions, expectations and classifications, all of which bind viewers, images and producers in 'a common framework of meaning', freeing them from isolated significance (2001: 638). Their meaning is produced by viewer expectations from resemblance to 'other images'. Fashion representations are, of course, not necessarily 'stock', despite frequently close ties in subject matter, poses and standardized body shapes that constitute a degree of agreed protocols.

But these photos also extend boundaries and can be alive to personal creative practices; they can be constituted by the conventionalized, but also the radical and the artistic. Being fleeting and glamorous arrangements, they are naturally highly responsive to motile social and historical factors – the period and possibilities in which they were made. Subject matter (fashionable clothes, hairstyles, body postures, notions of beauty) change, although not necessarily at the same time.[4] According to Craik, fashion images constantly play with definitions of sexuality, their conventions neither fixed nor purposeful. Rather they are a nexus between fashion and selfhood; the desire generated for consumers is constantly being reconfirmed as natural (Craik 1994: 114).

To summarize, we should accept that rather than demonstrating repetitive formal features in the established sense of 'genre', images often have a provisional stability of related techniques and protocols which can be read as purposeful, and of singular interest beyond the superficial look of 'the convention'. But while conventions can be stereotypical, images are not templates. They can be meaningfully irregular, not least in external framing. To speak of a stereotypical beach or cityscape fashion shot, or an exotic one, may be to accept the image as 'stock', but this can dismiss possible challenges to generic boundaries, or depth and complexity within the image's external contextual matrix. Identifying external factors, together with elements germane to the internal organization of the image, we find fashion photography is not just about surface idealism, desire and triviality, or the chemical magic of illusion (Marsh 2003: 265). Nor is it necessarily a reflection of society's anxious preoccupations. Rather it is far more variously, even densely, anchored.

The photographs discussed here show the instability of genre, constituted as they are by a slipperiness of subject. In each case singular rhetorical framing – publication conventions, lighting, page layout, technical know-how or protocols, titles, descriptions and production practices – show the visual text situating itself variously in relation to its surrounds. The creative acumen and reputations of Le Guay and Newton remain undoubted. But we should see this in relation to other manifold and mutable registers and articulations. Only a few can be explored here: the input of style coordinators, the acquired or trained body techniques of fashion models, use of colour or black-and-white film, descriptive textual accompaniments, magazine layout and conventions, tone, production practices and circulation. Other registers include lighting expertise, available types of film, photographic apparatus, input from designers and fashion companies, editorial policies, shifts and weighting of content, technical back-up, aesthetic preferences, commercial directives and factors of distribution.

Thinking in terms of the 'ecology' of fashion photography, or those 'differences', indeed boundary framings of Freadman's revisionist notion of genre, is one way to be actively aware of the myriad influences at play, not least the shoot itself. In fact lack of attention to factors of production has led to significant overemphasis of the role of the fashion photographer during the 1960s. Practitioners (David Bailey is a good UK example) certainly orchestrated photo sessions, wielding considerable influence (Craik 1994: 106), but this wasn't fully the case in Australia. During this period magazine photo shoots, as today, could be joint projects, balancing acts between stakeholders, with the photographer but one element. The mystique of the all-dominating, sexy male photographer is something of a construct, certainly encouraged by the photographers.[5] Nor did the shoot necessarily follow rigid details set out by an independent art director (Ewen 1988: 87). At most some commercial ideas were roughed out by an artist, but it was relatively common for shoots to be informal, managed by a fashion coordinator, demonstrating framing factors to be differentially enacted. In 1958 the Sydney *Draper* explained that as well as the creativity of the photographer, planning by a good coordinator was essential. Almost always a woman, she selected good fabrics, new lines and impeccable accessories – 'she usually has to have ideas of her own on this' (7).

Another complicating factor was the active input of models, the best of whom, like talented actresses, had natural ability and the personality to make clothes come alive. With little formal training, they worked hard.[6] *Flair* magazine noted that models had just as much responsibility in producing a good photograph as photographers (1956 Olympic Issue: 55). The actual moment of image-taking (acknowledged by photographer Henry Talbot), could be driven by the model, with all the attendant differences this might entail. For Talbot it was an almost passive situation, a matter of patiently waiting for her to assume the 'right' pose: 'I would always set up a mirror beside me and the lady would move, watching herself. When the moment hit, I would take the shot. It would always depend on the model, that moment, and I had to be ready for it.'[7]

The three images here appeared in two magazines, the Australian version of *Vogue* first released as independent from the mother UK magazine in Midsummer 1959,[8] and the smaller, more daring but less affluent *Flair*. The latter commenced in 1956, edited by Dorothy Dale Ryman and from 1962 by Mary Wilkinson.[9] Although we have no precise figures, neither seems to have had extensive circulation. Aside from these, there were only two other major style-related magazines published in the early 1960s in Australia, the mass-produced *Women's Weekly* (1933–) and *Woman's Day* (1953–80), neither dedicated to fashion. Early in the decade *Flair* and *Vogue* Australia were consolidating their reputations as premier-quality fashion publications, although journalistic layout and image links between *Vogue* and its parent remained strong. Clearly different in tone, size and format, *Flair* had fewer pages but was more lively, its youthful content aimed at 16–25-year-olds. *Vogue* Australia (edited by Rosemary Cooper in the early 1960s) was larger but fundamentally genteel and conservative,[10] its target consumers slightly older.

The 1960s was an increasingly confident and cosmopolitan period for Australian fashion, and local photographers like Henry Talbot, Le Guay and Geoffrey Lee spread their wings to practice in Europe and the US, occasionally sending their work home. Dispelling notions of an inward-looking fashion photographic industry, some gained recognition working for overseas publications and designers.[11] The present examples appeared at a moment when fashion photography, the fashion press and modelling in Australia were self-consciously trying to create a new sense of professional acumen. Yet the polish of the published page could disguise the 'make-do' elements behind the scenes, such as multiple tasking at *Flair*, an indicator of financial strictures and limited circulation.

The three photographs offer generic complexities. Our principal concern is the 1960 street scene 'Fashion Queue' by Le Guay. Le Guay was one of Australia's most inventive photographers, and by all accounts 'touched by an endearing larrikinism' ('The Age', *Good Weekend* magazine, 17 March 1990: 19). He worked regularly for *Vogue* Australia and *Flair* (allegedly the latter's most favoured photographer) and was responsible for launching many of Australia's finest models, like Margot McKendry. This sleek image is one of his best-known, even iconic works (acknowledged by the magazine a month after it was taken as still causing a stir, surely for its unusual content). Collected and exhibited as 'art', as far as we know it has always been reproduced or shown without its captions, thus significantly diminishing its meaning and context.[12] It is formally powerful, well-lit, and with a vivid, even picaresque narrative.

It was shot at Wynyard Park, Sydney early on a Sunday morning when the traffic was not a problem (*Flair*, September 1960: 90). Le Guay is known to have been less a technician than a dark-room operator, an admirer of Man Ray, fascinated with the possibilities of photomontage. But this is not a print made up from several different negatives, rather it was chosen by *Flair*'s editorial department from a set of contact prints. It is one of a number of dramatic images he made of central Sydney's post-war commercial expansion and 'go ahead' urban life. Fascination with the bustle of the city, its seamy side as well as its spectacular construction boom, had featured in much of his fashion work for some years. Internationally this was not unusual. We see this linking of the ebb and flow of city life and fashion in images by David Bailey, and much earlier with Erwin Blumenfeld. In terms of Le Guay's carefully calculated tone though, the work seems closer to Norman Parkinson, Richard Avedon and to an extent William Klein.

It is interesting to note the differences between the drama of 'Fashion Queue' and an unusually bland series made in Melbourne by Helmut Newton at the same time, entitled 'The Young Idea – Pretty City' (*Vogue* Australia, Summer 1960: 58–59). These illuminate the problems of too readily describing images as 'generic'. The largest of the set (in portrait format) extends over much of two pages. Lacking Le Guay's firmly staged and dense narrative, this charming image is set against a misty urban view. It archly pictures two sprightly young typists with hats and gloves holding hands with a suited man, gaily skipping (albeit decorously) along a riverside ledge. There is no direct connection between the images, but in terms of our reconstituted understanding of the generic, the visual text and setting situates itself palpably in relation to publication differences. These include the captions focused entirely on the 'fresh', 'free as air' clothes and the genteel tone of *Vogue* Australia.

By contrast, Le Guay's image balances fashion and everyday documentary: a mix of different ages, sexes and economic conditions, suspended in time, yet it gives the appearance of a reporter's snapshot. Natural settings and documentary features linked to fashion were by then no novelty. But Le Guay was interested in the commonplace, not in social reform, despite editing *Contemporary Photography* (1946–50) which initially had social concerns (Willis 1988: 193). Nor does he casually interject models into everyday street scenes, as did Jerry Schattzberg for *Vogue* in the late fifties. 'Fashion Queue' is more contrived, with ironic, even humorous, details, perhaps a macabre quality with the masked child. Craik contends that sexuality was the central and explicit motif of post-war photography, even though it also utilized social commentary and contrived spontaneity (1994: 104–5). My reading of this work is that any sexual imperative has been over-ridden by its wit and irony, thereby reframing our understanding of it as generic.

Many years ago Nancy Hall-Duncan tried to define what constituted a fashion photograph, as opposed to a fashionable portrait. She called it 'its fashion intent' because of its commercialism (1979: 9). But perhaps there is more to the notion of 'intent' than she suggests. Is it not the context of the magazine, the advertising of product and accompanying text, or even some inbuilt coding or presupposition that bodily conventions and expression are read as fashionable images? Yet hers is an interesting remark, for the Le Guay, and the Newton 'Beautiful Beast Looks' discussed shortly, obviously have 'fashion intent'. Yet both vacillate between being fashion photographs and something beyond. For it is the 'beyond', the street characters and the Newton paparazzi-like photographer/observer which challenge their status as generically pure.

A fashion photograph is not a portrait, but it may incorporate aspects of portraiture. Le Guay's 'Fashion Queue', for instance, includes recently identified, well-known fashion models and photo-shoot 'actors' in various down-market street clothes. This duality makes the image complicated. Only the roles played by each of the players are described in the captions (Fig. 7). Of the three fashion models, on the extreme left is Dawn Diedrickson, next right is Anne Felton (the following year a top model in New York), and the 'teenager' is Del Hancock, *Flair*'s model of the year in 1960.[13] They are captioned as 'traffic stoppers', those who stand out in the city, having caught the interest of the father in the middle. What *Flair* termed 'our beatnik' (the figure on the extreme right) was Mary Wilkinson, then Assistant Editor, someone who undertook a variety of roles for the magazine, including appearing in images.[14] She was responsible, among other things, for calling on advertisers and selecting suitable items from the ranges of leading designers, organizing shoots and often choosing locations. In this instance she preferred to remain anonymous, what *Flair* termed 'a staff member in disguise' (September 1960: 90). Captioned 'How to Stand Out in the City in a sadly un-*Flair*-like fashion', Wilkinson acts as one who signals those contradictory differences between fashion and the reportage of everyday dress.

How does a reconsidered notion of genre expand our understanding of this photograph? There are plenty of shots of fashionable dressing in cityscapes in Australian magazines. Norman Parkinson and others drew on the documentary tradition for fashion images years before, but the present work takes its own approach, although we know nothing of its commissioning. With a landscape format that echoes its subject matter, the image is a combination of

7. Laurence Le Guay, *How to Stand Out in the City*, *Flair*, August 1960.

visual wit, narrative captions, symbolic suggestions of beauty and the beast, and a representative range of ages and class. Its very strangeness sparks desire for its products.

In terms of Freadman's concepts of 'framing', the captions, with their sexist overtones, tell us much about gender relations. 'Number 1 in the Queue' (extreme left) is smartly dressed. Absorbed in the *Financial Review,* he is described as 'a good catch', not advertising fashion, as no retail details are given, but clearly fashionable compared to the other men. Le Guay did not use professional male fashion models then, and all three are probably friends, the seated woman one of their wives. So is 'Number 1' fashionable by default? Stand-alone male fashion photography was then in its infancy in Australian women's magazines, so possibly male fashion photography is imperceptibly being introduced into a representational category primarily focused on women. Here is evidence of a destabilizing of fashion photography as a female 'genre'.

The second example is the right-hand page of Le Guay's double spread of fashion billboards (Fig. 8). Billboards are normally associated with large-scale city advertising, but the motif is occasionally used in magazine adverts.[15] Entitled 'Forsaken Mermaids Need No Longer Despair...' the images complicate our understanding both of cityscape images and beach scenes, fitting with neither. Although nothing specific is known of their making,[16] the shots follow on a series 'Men at Work', dealing with particular fashion designers, yet these concern retail products only. More relevant is an uneasy association between fashion, physical activity, sexual attraction, ironic playfulness, confusions of physical size and more.

Le Guay had a fascination with the sea and was no stranger to beach photography. He was the first Australian photographer to grace the cover of *Vogue's Supplement for Australia* (Spring–Summer 1956), with his, by then, quite dated Munkacsi-like image of Margot McKendry in beach gear, running towards the viewer on Tamarama Beach. In the mermaid shots the poses are equally lively, but set on billboards not a beach. *Flair* has broken with convention to publish images over two full pages, the images' size responsive to the subject. Visual anomalies of location are accompanied by the slightest details of product acknowledgement. With a backdrop of clouds, the billboards appear set on gravel or, perhaps ambiguously, at the bottom of the sea. The image responds to captions telling us the models can rest content as deep-sea 'Prince Charming' frogmen (a hint of fairytale here), dressed in siren

8. Laurence Le Guay, 'Forsaken Mermaids Need No Longer Despair...', *Flair*, October 1961.

suits, can retrieve them from any depth.[17] The right-hand image contains toy-sized frogmen. Are they setting up the billboard, destroying it or scaling it? Further confusion is provided by a small diver curiously situated on the billboard, thus linking him to the fashion intent. Generic complications arise in that the models can 'gambol in deep waters' but also on land, while the divers geared for underwater work are positioned on land as well as the billboard itself.

The final example is Newton's photograph 'Beautiful Beast Looks' (Fig. 9), published in 1961, the year he left Australia for good (Featherstone 2005: 116). His choice of a model with 'knowing looks'[18] and subject matter stands out vividly for its trademark inventiveness, yet links to a fascinating, recurring magazine motif of the late 1950s and 1960s, 'the fashion photographer at work'. These differ markedly from candid photographs taken of fashion photographers at work. Despite format variations, these images resituate the genre of fashion photography in specific relation to the photographer with apparatus, and/or lighting expert as audience; the image captured from outside the scene includes the photographer taking the photograph. This image type, used by Le Guay, Gerard Herbst, Henry Talbot and others,[19] constitutes a framing device that bears further analysis. Perhaps this was self-promotion, as photographers sought greater visibility and status for their profession, matching that of the celebrity model. Alternatively it accentuated the model's femininity by dramatizing the masculine role of observer/photographer. Earlier images give negligible account of the fashion photographic process and practitioners, so perhaps here is a modernist desire for spectator participation as specific witness to the photographer, his technical apparatus and working methods.

9. Helmut Newton, 'Beautiful Beast Looks', 1961.

Newton's representation is self-reflexive: the photographer stands back from being present, yet explicates his role. The suited photographer (a self-portrait or stand-in?) is accompanied by a male spectator, and both 'look' into the cage of fashion, being themselves looked at. Fashion model plus zoo visitor and photographer are co-subjects, a genre (the fashion photograph) within a genre (the making of a fashion photograph). The haughty model, dressed in a Myers store leopard-skin jacket and pillbox hat, is caged but not cowed. The caption notes 'a leopard worth stalking', while stereotypical terms like rare birds, sleek beasts and crazy cats describe other images in the set. The brooding sexuality could not be more different from the Le Guay. Newton boldly challenges the respectability and genteel upper-class tone of *Vogue* Australia, heading the dramatic shot with the words 'Keep away – dangerous'. He says in his biography, he 'slipped' this kind of racy image into *Vogue* wherever he could (Newton 2003: 171). Although we are familiar with his more erotic, voyeuristic and shockingly explicit images of the seventies (Craik 1994: 109), his liking for strange artificiality and mysterious non-narrative is also at work here.

Where commissions allowed, Newton was fascinated with the dramatic. He believed, like fellow photographers, that models needed acting ability to be truly successful. He admitted to Australia's *Fashion Trade News* (July 1949) that fashion photographs should be approached in 'a spirit of adventure' (14–15). An unusual background, for instance, often creates special interest and makes the picture eye-catching, although it may not represent the precise circumstance under which a frock would normally be worn, surely the case here. But there is more than sensation at work, for Newton emphasizes the falsity of fashion photography itself (Brookes 1992: 23). Entrapped zoo-like in a cage, the model is caught in the dual looks of photographer and another voyeur. The generic aspect and intention of the work is complicated, as the artifice of fashion photography is as much the subject as Newton's model. Fashion is shown worthy of being photographed, but the image is framed by that which is most relevant: the observers of the wearing.

Fashion photographs are commonly regarded as visual ephemera – the 'transitory image par excellence' (Brookes 1992: 17). They are inevitably prejudiced by the commercial interests of retailers and, like fashion itself, incontrovertibly superficial in their preoccupations. Fashion photography is about creating desire. The image's success (sales value) is dependent on the extent to which model and photographer combine to put forward convincing and attractive products or concepts. Newton said in 1949 that if you can catch the eye of the prospective buyer with spirited layout, background and imaginative, even adventurous, content then you will give them something to think about and talk about and encourage spending (*Fashion Trade News*, July 1949: 15). But we now know fashion photographs are 'incomplete' visual statements – rather they respond to the continuous interplay between themselves and external framing factors, model input and comportment, production layout, captions, conditions, and oftentimes circulation afterlife to produce full meaningfulness.

While we use the term 'genre' in a conventional sense to describe these images, a broader reading yields more subtle understandings. They are in effect generically 'unstable'. This instability lies partly in their visual content, although the visual text is but one constituent of a creative and production 'ecology'. The notion of an 'ecology' shows how mutations in visual and other conventions, partly the result of external factors including circumstances of publication, can extend the capacity of photographs for wider understanding. Sekula's view that a photograph is an 'incomplete utterance' requiring appreciation of delicate and continuous interplay between external factors and conditions, and indeed its circulation afterlife, for full readability is manifest (1982: 85). Meaning lies not just in what photos appear to be (their surface glamour of attractive bodies and formal design), but in how they respond to the external conditions of their making. Their surface artifice is only one aspect of a constantly shifting matrix of relationships between production techniques, editorial decisions, mass circulation and readership, commercial interests, creativity, national and international proclivities, style and the feminine body. A reconsideration of preconceptions, and a wider understanding of 'genre', is one way we may review Le Guay's representation, known today as 'Untitled', to show its meaning indeed reflects something quite the reverse.

NOTES ON CHAPTER 4

1   Funded by an Australian Research Grant (2005–7). Research by Kerry and Miranda Heckenberg, and information from Anne-Marie van de Ven, Powerhouse Museum, Sydney, Candice Le Guay, David Mist, Mary Wilkinson (Mrs Paget-Cook) and Margaret McGurgan gratefully acknowledged.

2   Le Guay established his first commercial studio in Sydney in 1938. From 1947 until 1961 the firm was known as Le Guay and Nisbett Pty Ltd.

3   Newton opened his advertising studio in Flinders Lane, Melbourne after World War II. He worked with Henry Talbot from 1956 as Helmut Newton and Associates.

4   Lois Banner (1984) claims that the conventions of beauty change more slowly than fashionable dress.

5   Women were also fashion photographers. Fashion model/photographer Janice Wakely was a notable example.

6   There were few model agencies in Sydney at this time, more like charm schools, according to Mist (2005: 61).

7   George, Sheryn (1998) 'Visions Splendid', *The Australian Magazine*, 25–26 April: 57.

8   *Vogue Supplement for Australia* was first published in 1955.

9   *Flair* was published by Fashion Publications Pty Ltd, Sydney.

10   In 1960 *Vogue* Australia had 124 pages, with 52 pages of advertising at the start. In 1961 *Flair* had 84 pages including covers. Both had coloured covers and some coloured interior images.

11   Talbot worked for Pierre Cardin and *Jardin des Modes*.

12   See *Architects of Glamour and Masters of Style: Excerpts from a Century of Fashion Photography* (2003), Queensland University of Technology Art Museum.

13   Information obtained from a personal interview with Mrs Paget-Cook, formerly Mary Wilkinson, editor of *Flair*, 1962–73.

14   Mary Wilkinson wrote under various *noms de plumes*, did shoot coordination, fashion sketches and even fashion photography under her own name, and from 1960 as Marie Boam.

15   See the billboard advert for E. Lukas and Co., Melbourne, *Vogue* (Australia), Summer 1961: 45.

16   The model in the striped bathing suit was Dawn Diedrickson, and the model jumping with a net beach coat probably Colleen Fitzpatrick.

17   Le Guay did another image of fashion and divers, 'Girl in White Swimsuit with Underwater Divers', c. 1960, National Library of Australia, Pic-an 25120806.

18   Maggie Tabberer, a model at this time, notes in her autobiography *Maggie* (50), that he liked big tall girls with knowing looks, as compared with Le Guay, who liked healthy girls who caught buses.

19   An example is Henry Talbot, 'Studio of Leonard, Paris', National Gallery of Australia, Canberra, 89.1470.

WORKS CITED

Banner, Lois (1984) *American Beauty* (Chicago: Chicago University Press)

Brookes, Rosetta (1992) 'Fashion Photography: The Double-page Spread: Helmut Newton, Guy Bourdin and Deborah Turbeville', in Juliet Ash and Elizabeth Wilson (eds) *Chic Thrills: A Fashion Reader* (London: Pandora Press)

Craik, Jennifer (1994) *The Face of Fashion: Cultural Studies in Fashion* (London: Routledge)

Ewen, Stuart (1988) *All Consuming Images: The Politics of Style in Contemporary Culture* (New York: Basic Books)

Featherstone, Guy (2005) 'Helmut Newton's Australian Years', *La Trobe Journal* 76, Spring: 105–23

Freadman, Anne (1988) 'Untitled: (on genre)', *Cultural Studies* 2 (1): 67–99

Freadman, Anne and Amanda Macdonald (1992) *What is This Thing Called 'Genre'? Four Essays in the Semiotics of Genre* (Mt Nebo, Queensland: Boombana Publications)

Frosh, Paul (2001) 'Inside the Image Factor: Stock Photography and Cultural Production', *Media Culture and Society* 23 (5): 625–46

Hall-Duncan, Nancy (1979) *The History of Fashion Photography* (New York: Alpine Book Co.)

Marsh, Anne (2003) *The Dark Room: Photography and the Theatre of Desire* (South Yarra, Victoria: Macmillan)

Mist, David (2005) *Exposed: A Life Behind the Camera* (Leichhardt, New South Wales: A&A Book Publishing)

Newton, Helmut (2003) *Autobiography* (New York: Doubleday)

Ramamurthy, Anandi (2000) 'Constructions of Illusion: Photography and Commodity Culture', in Liz Wells (ed.) *Photography: A Critical Introduction* (London: Routledge)

Sekula, Allan (1982) 'On the Invention of Photographic Meaning', in Victor Burgin (ed.) *Thinking Photography* (Houndmills: Macmillan Education)

Tabberer, Maggie (1998) *Maggie* (Sydney: Allen and Unwin)

Wells, Liz (2000) 'Thinking about Photography: Debates, Historically and Now', in Liz Wells (ed.) *Photography: A Critical Introduction* (London: Routledge)

Willis, Anne-Marie (1988) *Picturing Australia: A History of Photography* (North Ryde: Angus and Robertson)

5 Lee Miller's Simultaneity: Photographer and Model in the Pages of Inter-war *Vogue*

Becky E. Conekin

The October 1930 issue of French *Vogue* announced the surrealist Jean Cocteau's first film, entitled *Blood of a Poet*. The two-page article informed readers that 'Miss Lee Miller' was playing the lead female role as a statue (French *Vogue*, October 1930: 90–91). Tied up, draped and covered in butter and flour, Miller appeared in the first scene of the film as an armless classical sculpture. In later scenes her arms were set free and she was allowed to play cards and to be chased by a bull (Penrose 2002: 35–36). In *Blood of a Poet* Miller was, as she so often was in the late 1920s and early 1930s, simultaneously active and passive, subject and object. By the Autumn of 1930, this twenty-three-and-a-half-year-old from Poughkeepsie, with her ideal inter-war look, had already been on the cover of US *Vogue*, perfected the Sabbatier photographic effect – often referred to as 'solarization' – with her lover and teacher, Man Ray, and was regularly appearing in the pages of *Vogue* magazine as both model and photographer.

Her work and her story problematize dominant narratives of fashion photography. To say that Miller's singular experience radically undermines the dichotomy between model and photographer would perhaps be going too far. She was a rare individual. But her experiences and their subsequent writing (and re-writing) make us keenly aware of the way in which these stories have been told. In turn, they encourage us to call those now-commonplace narratives into question.

Although there is no large-scale, scholarly historical study of photo-graphic fashion modelling, the story has generally been told – or, perhaps more accurately, implied – in a range of texts in terms of talented – even genius – photographers and beautiful models.[1] Underlying such accounts are issues of agency and gender, in which photographers are assumed to be active, male subjects (with a few female exceptions) and models are portrayed as passive, female objects. Photographers are artistic auteurs and models are, at best, their muses. However, in the early days of professional photographic modelling, if not always, when the cameras were so slow and the studio lights so hot, successful models were certainly collaborators in the construction of their images. In addition, Lee Miller was unique in that she both modelled in and photographed fashion images for *Vogue* in the inter-war period. Working on both sides of the camera provided her with insights that other models could only intuit.

Born Elizabeth Miller in 1907, her father was an amateur inventor and photographer, and by about 1910 works manager of the De Laval Separator Company in Poughkeepsie. According to her son and biographer, Tony Penrose, Lee Miller inherited her father's 'wilfulness, an insatiable curiosity about all things mechanical and scientific, and a completely unabashed manner of asking questions' (Penrose 2002: 8). Less positive is Jane Livingston's account of Miller's relationship with her father. Livingston asserts in her book, *Lee Miller: Photographer* (1989):

> It is clear from all that is known about Lee Miller in her formative years that her father, Theodore, exerted a powerful and lifelong influence on her…Lee must have internalized from her earliest consciousness Theodore Miller's fascination with inventive technique; certainly she inherited his facility. And the two of them remained close throughout their lives. But she may also have had a troubled relationship with him – while he was a direct source of strength and a powerful mentor, he became for a time a somewhat obsessed photographer of her, and she a compliant model. The closeness between them, especially when Lee was in her early twenties, may have bordered on an unhealthy intimacy. In any event, Lee Miller would always have difficulty in establishing long-term relationships with other men. (27)

Livingston is here alluding to the fact that Lee Miller's father photographed her over and over again from birth. According to her son, his grandfather's 'carefully annotated albums are crammed with...feats of modern engineering [but they] came a poor second to the studies of Lee which fill the books' (Penrose 2002: 11). Penrose writes that by the time she was 21, Theodore Miller had dragged Lee back from Paris to Poughkeepsie and bought a stereoscopic camera: 'his secret passion was nudes. Lee posed for him count-less times, indoors and out; cool, poised and at times a little solemn. Her self-consciousness only creeps into the shots where she is posing together with nude girlfriends' (Penrose 2002: 13–16). And two and a half years later, when Lee Miller was again living in Paris, this time with Man Ray, whom Theodore liked very much, her father arranged a business trip to Stockholm, collecting her first. Father and daughter spent Christmas 1930 together at the Grand Hotel in Stockholm, 'where Theodore took the opportunity of making several stereoscopic nude studies of his daughter' (Penrose 2002: 37). The disquiet such information creates in the contemporary reader is not acknowledged by Penrose. But this obsessive – most probably intrusive – camera wielded by her father was not the only violation Lee Miller had endured as a child. We can never know the truth of what happened to her at the age of seven, but she was sexually assaulted and contracted venereal disease, which necessitated (in the days before penicillin) an excruciating medical treatment, administered by her mother, who had been a nurse. Miller's parents enlisted the help of a psychiatrist, who advised that she be told that sex and love were not related and that sex was merely a physical act, in the hope that she would not suffer from guilt, as well as the physical pain precipitated by this dreadful event (Penrose 2002: 12). Whether this can explain why Miller was especially sexually liberated, yet prone to bouts of depression and, as some claim, unable to be truly close to people she loved, we can never know, of course. But it does seem that the combination of being continually photographed, often nude, by her father and early, if horrific, sexual experience and resulting counselling may have contributed to Lee Miller's extraordinary abilities as a photographic model. She seems never to have been self-conscious; she had that required, yet rare, ability to look beautiful and feminine, and in her aloofness not quite human – the ability that has been key to the display of serious fashion on the printed page across the twentieth century.

Once she started modelling professionally in 1927, she quickly became one of Edward Steichen's favourite models. Steichen was Condé Nast's chief photographer and the wealthiest artist in America by the time he began photographing her. One of Miller's biographers speculates that she was one of Steichen's favourites 'because she paid attention to their work together' (Burke 2005: 60). Another famous fashion photographer for *Vogue* Paris, George Hoyningen-Huene, had a reputation for being fierce, looking at the nervous models waiting to pose for him and asking disdainfully, 'Is this what you expect me to photograph?' (as quoted in Keenan 1977: 136) Yet Miller was his favourite model when she worked in Paris; he greatly enjoyed the conversations they had about photography (Penrose 2002: 28–29).

LEE MILLER BECOMES A *VOGUE* MODEL

In 1927 Miller had been living weekdays in Manhattan, in a small brownstone apartment on East 49th Street, paid for by her father, and studying theatrical design and lighting at the Arts Students League (Penrose 2002: 15). But her life became more exciting and truly cosmopolitan thanks to an 'accidental' meeting with Condé Nast. The publisher saved her from being run over, and he was so impressed with her looks, her European clothes and her babbling in French that he offered Miller modelling work at New York *Vogue*. She appeared as the cover girl for the March 1927 issue, designed by George Lapape, featuring the glittering, night-time Manhattan skyline behind her elegant, cloche-hatted head. From then on, Steichen and Arnold Genthe frequently photographed her, and she established a close friendship with *Vanity Fair*'s Frank Crowninshield (Livingston 1989: 28). Although she was a success in New York, Miller 'was now twenty-two, and obsessed with the idea of returning' to Paris, where she had been a few years before as a student at the l'Ecole Medgyes pour la Technique du Theatre[2] (Penrose 2002: 20, 13–15).

So, in 1929, with a letter of introduction to Man Ray from Steichen and another from Condé Nast to Hoyningen-Huene, Miller returned to Paris with her best friend from art college, Tanja Ramm. Also thanks to Condé Nast, Miller had a small job for an American fashion designer. That job led to Miller's first serious foray into photography. She was hired to sketch clothing details in Renaissance paintings in Florence to be used in contemporary fashion designs. Miller found the work so tedious that she decided to attempt to photograph the paintings instead, using a folding Kodak and a spindly tripod. The results seem to have satisfied her American employer and galvanized in

Miller the idea of becoming a photographer. She went to Paris to meet Man Ray (Penrose 2002: 22). She later recounted this meeting in a café near his apartment:

> He kind of rose up through the floor at the top of a circular staircase. He looked like a bull, with an extraordinary torso and very dark eyebrows and dark hair. I told him boldly that I was his new student. He said he didn't take students, and anyway, he was leaving Paris for his holiday. I said, I know, I'm going with you – and I did. We lived together for three years. I was known as Madame Man Ray, because that's how they do things in France. (Miller, as quoted in Keenan 1977: 136)

THE HISTORICALLY SPECIFIC CONTEXT OF MILLER'S WORK

Lee Miller was among the first generation of professional models, as the fashion magazines moved away from their earlier reliance on portraits of society women (Chadwick 2003: 211–12). In New York City, the first modelling agency was established in 1921 by John Robert Powers (Gross 1995: 31). But even in the mid-1930s *Vogue* photographer Horst P. Horst recalled that in Paris 'in those days we had no hairdressers, makeup people or modelling agencies. Girls just turned up or somebody knew somebody' (Horst, as quoted in Gross 1995: 51).[3] But, unlike other models, Miller found work in photography as well (Kerr and Ware 1994: 219).

She was young, female, cosmopolitan, fashionable, sexually liberated, and involved in surrealism. Surrealism differed from the formalist, modernist movements – post-impressionism and cubism – that preceded it; it was very interested and involved in the world of fashion. In his book *Fashion and Surrealism*, Richard Martin argues that 'Fashion became Surrealism's most compelling friction between the ordinary and extraordinary' (1988: 9). Martin explains that by the 1930s Surrealists had 'entered the realms of fashion, fashion advertising, and window display' and that the Surrealist style was 'pervasive' 'among the major fashion publications, most especially *Vogue* and *Harper's Bazaar*' (1988: 217). Jean Cocteau, Leonor Fini, George Hoyningen-Huene and Man Ray, among others, 'were recruited as the unlikely missionaries for the stylistic revolution' (217).

MODELLING AS COLLABORATION, AND MODELLING AND PHOTOGRAPHING SIMULTANEOUSLY: 1930–32

Lee Miller positioned herself at this important intersection of art and fashion in the summer of 1930 at the white-themed 'Bal Blanc'. Man Ray's photograph of a group dressed in white as classical statues accompanied the French text in *Vogue* (*Vogue* [France], August 1930: 50–51). He explained in his autobiography (1963) that the Count and Countess Pecci-Blunt had installed a white dance floor in their garden, with the orchestra hidden behind the bushes, and that he had been 'asked to think up some added attraction'. Man Ray had taken with him 'as assistant a pupil who studied photography' at the time, and they both dressed in tennis whites, hers 'very smart' and 'especially designed' by the Paris designer, Madame Vionnet. This 'assistant' was Lee Miller: 'A slim figure with blond hair and lovely legs, she was continually being taken away to dance, leaving me to concentrate alone on my photography. I was pleased with her success, but annoyed at the same time, not because of the added work, but out of jealousy; I was in love with her' (Man Ray 1963: 168; Penrose 2002: 24–25)

Miller said decades later that Man Ray had 'taught her everything in her first year [with him]: "...fashion pictures...portraits...the whole technique of what he did"' (Miller, as quoted by Amaya 1975: 55). And, in turn, she studied studio lighting with Hoyningen-Huene, as he photographed her for *Vogue*. Hoyningen-Huene was a baron, born in Leningrad seven years before Miller, and is considered by Gross to be one of 'the four pioneers of fashion photography' (Gross 1995: 39). Tony Penrose explains that 'these modelling sessions with Hoyningen-Huene were rather like a privileged tutorial, allowing Lee to experience the work on both sides of the camera at the same time' (Penrose 2002: 29). She was an excellent student, and by the winter of 1930 she had her own apartment and studio in Montparnasse and was regularly landing assignments as a photographer for leading Paris couturiers, including Patou, Schiaparelli and Chanel (Penrose 2002: 32–37). Also in 1930, as Man Ray's student, Miller made many surrealistic photographs for non-commercial purposes, including one of a breast she had recovered from a radical mastectomy, which she arranged on a dinner plate, with a knife on fork on each side and salt and pepper shakers positioned nearby, and a now famous one, 'Exploding Hand', of a woman's hand reaching for a door handle, as the glass door appears to shatter (Penrose 2002: 30).

A further emblematic example of Miller's extreme versatility in this period comes from her work in the winter of 1931. In addition to working as a camerawoman in England on a Paramount film, *Stamboul*, she collaborated with Man Ray in Paris on a limited-edition brochure celebrating electric power commissioned by the utility Compagnie Parisienne de Distribution d'Electricité. Intended for their best customers and accompanied by a poem by Pierre Bost, Man Ray was hired to produce any photographs he wished, as long as they somehow illustrated the wonders of electricity. Man Ray asked Miller to serve as his model, muse and photographic collaborator on the project, ultimately entitled simply *Electricité*. He photographed Miller as a 'dangerous Goddess' with rays undulating on her torso for one illustration and in another, 'Salle de Bain', she is at her toilette, a white line connected to a cylinder on her headless torso (Burke 2005: 117). Miller later recalled that 'curious things happened in the collaboration' (Miller, as quoted in Amaya 1975: 56–57). Working simultaneously in this period as an artist's model and muse, filmmaker and art photographer, as well as fashion photographer and fashion model surely provided Lee Miller with a deep sense of her own aesthetic presence across all of these realms. And this aesthetic awareness must have contributed to her ability to produce both fine commercial fashion photographs and astute portraits of her private clients.

Much of her photographic work for *Vogue* Paris focused on objects rather than people. Yet her surrealist eye for shadows is apparent even when she was only shooting backgammon boards, as was the case in April 1931 (61). But two *Vogue* fashion layouts provide extraordinary examples of Miller's unique capacity to move with ease from one side of the camera to the other. In these pages of *Vogue* from 1930 and 1931, in each case, she appears on the same page as the model in the upper image and the photographer in the lower (*Vogue*, 15 September, 1930 and 10 June 1931; Figs 10 and 11 respectively). What must this have been like, and what might these images offer to a re-writing of the history of fashion photography, especially in this period when the equipment was still so bulky and demanding and the shots so slow? For one thing, these fashion spreads further problematize the active/passive/ male/female/photographer/model dichotomies that underlie most narratives of fashion photography. Here we see Miller performing both roles simul- taneously. Actually, according to current practice at London *Vogue*, since Miller is the only credited photographer on the page, today we would assume

10. Lee Miller, 'Soft Outlines in New Types of Felt and Velvet', *Vogue* (US), 15 September 1930. On this page, Miller is the photographer and the model.

11. Again, here Lee Miller is the photographer and the model. *Vogue* (UK), 10 June 1931.

that she was the photographer for both pictures and credit her as such (Button 2005).[4]

Another important insight provided by these pages of *Vogue* is that Miller clearly helped to create her look and her image, once again undermining the notion of the passive model. The photographs of Miller on those pages may well be self-portraits. Furthering this contention, there are two series of self-portraits that she took in 1932, after she had set up her own studio in Manhattan with her brother Erik as her assistant.[5] They specialized in high-end advertising photographs and portraits of society figures and for playbills. As the Depression in the US worsened, portraits became the mainstay of their business (Penrose 2002: 245). Lee Miller clearly used self-portraits to experiment with innovative angles and lighting. Acknowledging the roles she played as both model *and* photographer in creating these images – this in addition to continuing to work as a fashion model for others in this period – suggests her centrality to the process by which she was constructed as a symbol of modern femininity. She understood in what light and at what angle she appeared most captivating. Armed with such knowledge, Miller brought agency to her modelling work. She was not simply created as an icon of modern beauty by the men who photographed her; she worked diligently on her crafts behind and in front of the camera. Thus, her story and her experiences once again call into question the assumptions of active male photographer and passive female model.

And, in fact, in the inter-war period some designers and photographers acknowledged the active role of their models. The couturier, Poiret, for example, wrote in his autobiography, published in English in 1931, that with at least one of his models, or 'mannequins', Paulette, he felt 'The way in which she gave life to everything I put on her could really be called a collaboration…' (Poiret, as quoted in Chadwick 2002: 212). Interestingly, Jane Livingston has much more recently written that many of Man Ray's photographs of Miller 'seem created through a process in which the model and photographer have collaborated fully as artists' (Livingston 1989: 35). Miller herself said of the photograph 'Primat de la Matière sur la Pensée', taken by her and Man Ray when they lived together in Paris, 'I don't know if I did it but that doesn't matter. We were almost the same person when we were working' (Miller, as quoted in *Atelier Man Ray* 1982: 56 and Burke 2005: 94). Surely this symbiosis extended to all of their collaborations, whether she was in front of or behind the camera.

LEE MILLER, PHOTOGRAPHER: 1932–53

Lee Miller also further developed her identity as an artist once she moved back to New York. In February and March 1932, Julien Levy, one of the few collectors and gallery owners to take surrealist photography seriously at the time, featured Miller's work in a Manhattan show of 20 artists entitled 'Modern European Photographers', which included Man Ray, Peter Hans and László Moholy-Nagy. A *New York Times* critic who did not generally appreciate the photographs in this exhibition praised Miller's photograph of a woman's manicured hand on the back of her curly-haired head (Burke 2005: 123).[6] Early in 1933, Levy gave Miller the only solo show of her life (Penrose 2002: 45). And in May of 1934, *Vanity Fair* listed her with Cecil Beaton as among 'the most distinguished living photographers' (51). Just as she was achieving such success in New York, however, in July 1934 Miller married Aziz Eloui Bey, a wealthy Egyptian with whom she had been involved in Paris, and moved to Cairo. In the desert near Cairo she shot some of her most arresting photographs. 'Portrait of Space', taken in 1937, is generally considered one of her best 'surrealist photographs' and it is said to have inspired Magritte's painting *Le Baiser* (Penrose 2002: 45–96).[7] But unfortunately Miller's marriage to Eloui Bey ended the impressive Manhattan phase of her photographic career.

Although she went on in the 1940s to serve as a staff photographer for British *Vogue* and then from 1944 to 1945 as *Vogue*'s official war correspondent in Europe, we have no evidence that Miller ever used herself as a model again. One can only speculate that donning fatigues, going 'for weeks without a bath or clean clothes', showering in portable showers and using the latrine with US servicemen changed her forever (Miller, as quoted by Gold and Fizdale 1974: 162). In her first article as a war correspondent, published in both British and US *Vogue*'s September 1944 issues, we can see that Lee Miller still watched herself, even if not with her camera. The British version opened,

> As we flew into sight of France I swallowed hard on what were trying to be tears and remembered a movie actress kissing a handful of earth. My self-conscious analysis was forgotten in greedily studying the soft, grey-skied panorama of nearly a thousand square miles of France … of freed France.
>   The sea and sky joined in a careless watercolour wash … below, two convoys speckled the fragile smooth surface of the Channel. Cherbourg

was a misty bend far to the right, and ahead three 'planes were returning from dropping bombs which made towering columns of smoke. This was the Front. (35)

Here Miller saw herself, as she approached the front from the air, as like a Hollywood actress, but also as an artist noting 'watercolour washes'. It is worth commenting on the way Miller's prose exemplifies John Berger's contention that women see themselves seeing – that, is that unlike men, women are taught to think of themselves as always being on view. Or in his words, 'Women watch themselves being looked at (Berger 1972: 45, 47). As a woman so photographed, and also as a woman who was a photographer, Miller must have been extremely cognizant of the way women carry around this acute awareness of being continuously subjected to the gaze. In fact, in an article for the *Poughkeepsie Evening Star* in November of 1932, Miller had told her interviewer that it was easier to take women's portraits than men's because 'women are used to being looked at' (Miller, as quoted by Blanshard 1932).

But, was it merely the act of becoming a World War II war correspondent or the specific, horrifying realities of that war that meant that Miller no longer moved from one side of the camera to the other? She was one of the first people to enter the Dachau concentration camp, photographing it on 30 April 1945. She also photographed Buchenwald, reporting on both for *Vogue*. Some of the gestures in her pieces on the end of the war in Europe indicate that she questioned how life could ever return to normal for her, or anyone, after the knowledge of the Nazi atrocities. Not long after the war in Europe ended, though, British *Vogue* wished to return to normality as far as possible under post-war conditions.[8] But it is clear that Lee Miller found such attempts far from easy, if not impossible.

We can never know the answer to why she stopped using herself as a model and eventually, by the mid-1950s, ceased photographing or even responding to requests for her photographs and negatives. Her answer to enquiries was along the lines of: 'Oh, I did take a few pictures – but that was a long time ago'. And she was so persuasive that 'everyone was convinced that she had done little or no work of significance,' in her son's words (Penrose 2002: 209). Thus her extraordinary photography, along with the insights her work on both sides of the camera can offer a re-writing of the history of fashion photography were almost lost forever. Luckily, her son and his first wife, Suzanna, 'uncovered many boxes and trunks full of negatives, original prints and manuscripts' after her death from cancer in 1977, and the Lee Miller Archive was created (Penrose 2002: 6). No one else worked simultaneously as model and photographer in the pivotal, vibrant world of inter-war fashion magazines. And the very beautiful and somewhat androgynous 'Lee' Miller moved seemingly effortlessly between those roles – roles generally perceived in gendered terms, as well as in overly simplistic understandings of activity and passivity. Unlike the ways she has most often been represented between the wars, Miller should be remembered for her unique ability to be subject *and* object on the fashion page.[9]

ACKNOWLEDGEMENTS

Many thanks to Tony Penrose, Arabella Hayes and Carole Callow of the Lee Miller Archive, and to Janine Button, former librarian, and Brett Croft, current librarian, at Vogue House, London. A special thanks to Harriet Wilson of Condé Nast, London, and Nicky Budden, her assistant, for all their generosity, help and support. I happily acknowledge the support of the London College of Fashion (LCF) in the form of a senior research fellowship. Also, Dr Rob Lutton and Lance Tabraham at LCF offered assistance in securing images and copyrights. Many friends and colleagues have commented on parts of this work, but in particular I would like to thank: Marilyn Booth, Stephen Brooke, Amy de la Haye, Janine Furness, Bettina McNulty, Christopher Reed, Eugénie Shinkle and Adam Tooze.

NOTES ON CHAPTER 5

1   The best work is Gross (1995). Currently, Joanne Entwistle is editing a volume on commercial modelling.
2   By the spring of 1925 there were no more schools for Miller to attend, having been multiply expelled. A former French teacher took her to Paris to study classical arts and culture. But Miller soon escaped and announced that she was going to be an artist.
3   Although Miller's relationship with Man Ray is always noted, it is rarely acknowledged that Horst, who Hoyningen-Huene employed as assistant and apprentice at *Vogue*, was also housed in the servant's room above his apartment and became his lover (Gross 1995: 50).

4   This seems particularly likely in the 1931 spread, since the spherical shape
        of the 'red and white medicine ball' in the bottom photograph is echoed by
        the shape of the Art Deco lamp behind Miller on top (see Fig. 11).

5   The only photograph reproduced from either series appears in Penrose
        2002: 55 and Calvocoressi 2002: 24–25.

6   See the photograph, Penrose 2002: 46.

7   Magritte saw Miller's photograph in London in 1938 (Livingston 1989: 48).

8   Numerous goods and services were still rationed in post-war Britain
        (Clarke 1996: 243). Carolyn Steedman, born in 1948, writes, 'The war was
        so palpable a presence in the first five years of my life that I still find it hard
        to believe that I did not live through it' (1987: 27).

9   Penrose states, 'In spite of all Lee's work as a photographer, it was as a
        model that she created the most vivid impressions, then as now' (Penrose
        2002: 32). See Lyford 1994: 232. Miller actually said in October 1932, as
        she disembarked from the ship from Paris, 'I'd rather take a picture than be
        one' (Miller, as quoted by Burke 2005: 128).

WORKS CITED

Primary Sources

Anonymous (1930) 'Bal Blanc', *Vogue* (France), August: 50–51

Anonymous (1930) 'La vie d'un poete...premier film de Jean Cocteau', *Vogue*
        (France), October: 90–91

Blanshard, Julia (1932) 'Other Faces are Her Fortune', *Poughkeepsie Evening Star*,
        1 November

Button, Janine, Librarian, Vogue House, London, interview with the author, 22
        August 2005

Gold, Arthur and Robert Fizdale, 'How Famous People Cook: Lady Penrose, the
        Most Unusual Recipes You Have Ever Seen', *Vogue* (US), April 1974:
        160–61, 186–7

Miller, L., photographs and contact sheets, the Lee Miller Archive, Farley Farm
        House, Chiddingly, East Sussex, England

— (1944) 'Unarmed Warriors', *Vogue* (UK), September: 35, passim and as 'USA
        Tent Hospital', *Vogue* (US), 15 September 1944: 139, passim

— (1945) '"Believe It": Lee Miller Cables from Germany', *Vogue* (US), June:
        104–8

— (1945) 'Germans are Like This', *Vogue* (US), June: 101–3, 192, 193

— (1945) 'Germany – the war that is won', *Vogue* (UK), June: 40–42, 84, 86, 89

— (1945) 'Hitleriania', *Vogue* (UK), July: 36–37, 74

— (1945) 'Loire Bridges/How the Germans Surrender', *Vogue* (UK), November: 50–51, 82, 90

Secondary Sources

Amaya, M. (1975) 'My Man Ray', *Art in America*, May–June: 55

Atelier Man Ray (1982) Paris: Centre Georges Pompidou/Phillippe Sers

Berger, J. (1972, 1990) *Ways of Seeing* (London: Penguin)

Burke, C. (2001) 'Framing a life: Lee Miller', in Roland Penrose, *Lee Miller* (Edinburgh: Scottish National Gallery of Modern Art)

— (2005) *Lee Miller* (London: Bloomsbury)

Calvocoressi, R. (2002) *Lee Miller: Portraits from a Life* (London: Thames and Hudson)

Chadwick, W. (2002) 'Claude Cahun and Lee Miller', in T. Lester (ed.) *Gender, Nonconformity, Race and Sexuality* (Madison: University of Wisconsin Press): 141–59

— (2003) 'Lee Miller's Two Bodies', in Whitney Chadwick and Tirza True Latimer (eds) *The Modern Woman Revisited: Paris Between the Wars* (New Brunswick, NJ and London: Rutgers University Press): 199–221

Clarke, P. (1996) *Hope and Glory* (London: Penguin)

Conekin, B. (2005) 'Lee Miller and the Limits of Post-war British Modernity', in C. Breward and C. Evans (eds) *Fashion and Modernity* (Oxford: Berg)

— (2006) 'Lee Miller: Model, Photographer and War Correspondent in *Vogue*, 1927–1953', *Fashion Theory* 10 (1 and 2): 97–126

Gross, Michael (1995) *Model: The Ugly Business of Beautiful Women* (New York: William Morrow)

Keenan, B. (1977) *The Women We Wanted to Look Like* (London: Macmillan)

Kerr, J. and K. Ware (1994) 'Women Photographers in Europe 1919–1939', *History of Photography* 18 (3), Autumn: 219

Livingston, J. (1989) *Lee Miller: Photographer* (London: Thames and Hudson)

Lyford, A. (1994) 'Lee Miller's Photographic Impersonations, 1930–1945', *History of Photography* 18 (3), Autumn: 230–41

Man Ray (1963) *Self Portrait* (Boston: Little Brown/Atlantic Monthly Press)

Martin, R. (1988) *Fashion and Surrealism* (London: Thames and Hudson)

Penrose, A. (1985, 2002) *The Lives of Lee Miller* (London: Thames and Hudson)

— (ed.) (1992) *Lee Miller's War* (Boston: Bullfinch Press)

Steedman, C.K. (1987) *Landscape for a Good Woman: A Story of Two Lives* (New Brunswick, NJ: Rutgers University Press)

PART II

Processes and Politics

6 Interview with Rankin

Eugénie Shinkle

We spoke with Rankin (Waddell) on two occasions. The first time was at a public event held at the University of Westminster's Old Cinema in Regent Street in May 2004, where he was interviewed by Roger Hargreaves. Eugénie Shinkle also spoke with him in October 2006 at his studio in Old Street, London. The following text contains material from both interviews.

ES: Can you talk a bit about how you got started?

RW: I was from a lower-middle-class family who really had no formal education in art or culture. My grandfather had died when my father was quite young, and he'd had to go to work very early. Because of that, my parents kind of guided me towards very straightforward subjects like maths and physics, so I ended up doing an accountancy diploma at Brighton Polytechnic, and I just happened to be in residence with all of these art students. In the eight or nine months that I spent with these art students, I ended up having everything reassessed very very quickly, and realizing that although I quite liked the idea of commerce and business, I hadn't really explored this other area of self-development. So I went back home and said, 'I can't do this,' which didn't go down very well with my parents. I didn't really know what to do. I'd had this friend of mine at school who took photographs, and I really loved film, and my dad was really into film, and I thought, 'If I do photography, then maybe it'll get me into film.' I just thought I'd be good at it. So I started taking photographs, and I started to enjoy it immediately.

ES: Did you have any formal training?

RW: Not at that point. Photography was quite expensive, so I started getting part-time jobs to pay for this hobby that was becoming more and more important to me, which I think gave my parents a certain amount of confidence that I was quite serious about it. I worked as a cleaner and a hospital porter, at anything, really, then I applied to do a BTEC[1] national diploma. I'd spent a lot of time reading Susan Sontag, and Roland Barthes, and Umberto Eco, and all of these commentators on photography, and ended up having an opinion about photography, and then I went to do the BTEC, which was a very technical course. I rebelled against the technicism of it, but at the same time, because I'd done physics and maths, I was kind of into it as well. I didn't finish accountancy, and I didn't finish the national diploma. I applied everywhere to do a BA: Nottingham, and PCL [Polytechnic of Central London],[2] and LCP [London College of Printing], and I got into LCP. I went there and totally objected to their approach to tuition, and their theories. I really loved photography, and I was interested in the cultural study of photography, but they were just about theory. I remember asking one of my tutors, 'Do you ever take photographs?', and she looked at me like I was mad. There's a thing about photography that is quite magical, and it was almost like it had been demystified by this intense study. So I was a bit freaked out really. All of the kids in my year were really into taking photographs, everyone was taking photographs, with so much energy and passion. We were in a lesson one day, and the tutor was talking about a shot in the *Sunday Times* which had a camel and a pyramid and a guy sat on it, like a tourist photograph. She said, 'Can you deconstruct this photograph?', and I remember everyone in class going 'It's just a guy on a camel in front of a pyramid! You really need to get over this deconstructing of every single image. It doesn't have to have a meaning.'

That was an interesting period for me, because I rejected everything that I'd been taught, in principle. At LCP, that approach, everything was so coded, there's no emotion, you're not capturing anything. I stayed five years, and I did two sabbaticals as a student union rep., and I really enjoyed being part of the college, but I didn't finish my degree properly.

In the end, I got so obsessed by doing magazines, and creating exhibitions and getting work out there, that I kind of lost sight of the cultural theory side of it. I started taking photos and portraits, and thinking, 'I'm getting something out of these people that they're not, and that other people aren't.' I suddenly realized that actually there is an emotional aspect to it, and there is an emotional thread that runs through everything we do in our life. I look at art and I have an emotional response to it, I don't have a semiotic, encoded/decoded response to it. LCP's approach was very postmodern, but I didn't really believe in it.

ES: You were also sowing the seeds for *Dazed & Confused* around this time.

RW: One of the reasons I set up *Dazed & Confused* was because I loved photography, and I wanted to promote other photographers. We were quite naive in that with *Dazed & Confused* the idea was that it was a democratic magazine, and you could send your work in. Our approach was that everybody should be looked at, and given time to consider their work and be honest about it, and it shouldn't be elitist in any way. Some of those things that I'd learned at college were seeping into my work. Plus, I'd learned about conceptual art, and a lot of that had really seeped into my ideas about how we should do a magazine. It was a strange mix. And LCP was great, because it was so bad. It was so hard to get stuff done there, and to get people to accept it, that it was almost like the real world. You were really put through the mill to get a result. So coming out and being in the real world was just the same as college: people say no, and they don't like your work. So my attitude was 'Fuck 'em, I'm just going to do what I want,' and ended up growing up in public, which was quite strange.

ES: *Dazed* was started by yourself, Jefferson Hack and Katie Grand…

RW: …and there was a guy called Ian Taylor, who was designing it. We all went to LCP, apart from Katie, who went to St Martin's.

ES: But it was the three of you created most of the content.

RW: Yeah. We very much led it. We were kind of competing against each other. If you've got Katie, Jefferson and me in a room, we're very competitive, and Phil Poynter as well, who was my assistant and ended up going on to become photo editor and then quite an amazing photographer. It was kind of like, 'Who's got the best idea? What can we do now? What hasn't been done?' It was very exciting, and then we all started to make a bit of money, and it all fell apart really. Katie started to drift away and wanted to do other stuff, and Phil left, and then it just became Jefferson and myself. We got a load of new people in who all worked for us, as opposed to working with us; it was a different dynamic.

ES: What was your relationship with advertisers early on?

RW: We went bust three times. We were terrible about paying people. For us, the end product was the most important thing, and however we got there, by hook or by crook, was fine. I became very good at negotiating with people. You'd do a deal with people, and then you'd write them a letter and say, 'Sorry, we can't pay you, can we pay you in nine months?' – all this stuff that you learn from being a kid in the late eighties. Jefferson for a long time at the beginning did the advertising himself. We went out and we did presentations, and learned how to do proposals, and get sponsorship. We kind of invented advertorials in *Dazed*. We realized that a lot of magazines took for granted their advertisers, they didn't work with them, they didn't develop their relationships or do productions with them. Content-led marketing was something that wasn't even discussed. That's where you take a brand and actually use it, and show the product in a way that might be useful to the customer. We did something with Sony Minidisc, and we'd say, 'We'll go and use your Minidisc to interview people, and record them, and we'll put it into this package.' We'd do advertorials all the time, we would try and create marketing imagery that would compete, and be more in touch with the consumer than their advertisers. At that point advertising was done by people in their forties in ad agencies, and they didn't really know what was going on, and we did. We were going to clubs, and taking e's, and we knew what these kids were about.

We had a ready-made market for ourselves, who had high disposable incomes, and we had a way of talking to them and reaching them that nobody else had. It was a market that was ripe for exploitation, but only because everybody was becoming more media savvy, and everyone was becoming a little bored of being told what was cool. It was similar to the punk revolution, but it was a drug revolution, an ecstasy revolution, so there wasn't that aggression. We were just dropping out, and saying, 'You're so far away from what we're doing at the weekend that you can't talk to us.' The advertisers couldn't communicate, whereas we could, and we did. *i-D* had become a fashion magazine, and was too elitist, and *The Face* had completely lost its readership, because it was changing constantly and it didn't really understand what was going on. It had this 'We'll tell you what's cool' attitude, whereas we were never like that. We were always trying not to mediate to our reader. We'd do Q&As; don't tell them what's cool, ask them what's cool. We had a policy of never being negative about people. We were very influenced by Andy Warhol's *Interview* magazine, and their approach to editorial and interviews. It was about making the celebrity seem approachable, but at the same time about making anybody a celebrity. If we decided somebody was great, we would promote them. We would take risks on people – we did Beth Orton as a front cover five years before she did anything, on the basis of one album. It was a new way of doing it – it wasn't a very sophisticated way of doing it, but I think that appealled to people.

With *Dazed*, if you look at the early ones, it's a bit of a joke, but it was an interesting period politically. We'd been brought up in this strangely entrepreneurial era. There was a massive black economy around the late-eighties and early-nineties drug culture. Eighty-nine to ninety-one was totally drug-oriented. Everybody in England that was between 18 and 30 was suddenly doing ecstasy. People were making cash in hand doing nightclubs, doing anything really, to make a buck. We were very much part of that; you were entrepreneurial because you had to be entrepreneurial. The recession brought out a lot of creativity, people thinking for themselves and doing things because they had to survive. There was nothing to lose, there wasn't a great economy, I know I'm not going to go straight into a job, and I'm not going to have everything that society says I'm supposed to have. So we never thought we'd ever carry on, we thought, 'Well, we'll just get this one out, and then the next one out...'

It was great when we first started, but then two or three years in, we started to be seen, and when people started looking at it I think we probably overstretched ourselves. That's what I mean about growing up in public. There was a point in my career where I might have become more of an art photographer, and done more conceptual stuff, but I ended up being more and more commercial in order to keep *Dazed & Confused* going, thinking that was the right thing to do. Actually, it was probably the wrong thing to do creatively at that point in my career. After about four years of being creative and doing great work, I was then doing pretty average, pretty boring work. I think there's a massive dip in my work about '95, '96, just when *Dazed* was starting to really do well. My portraiture work was steady, but all the fashion work or the art ideas that I was doing, they really nose-dived. I started doing a lot of work for ad agencies, and I didn't really know why I was doing it. I couldn't really understand why they were hiring me or what my job was within the whole process of advertising. There's a period where I look back on my work and I think, 'God, I did some really fucking diabolical work in that period.' I'm embarrassed by it.

Also, we'd become minorly famous, and I think some sort of success is really bad for you creatively. I became successful, got married, and had a kid in the space of a year and a half. It was getting to the point where people knew who I was, and I was thinking I was the dog's bollocks. I was being stretched in a lot of different directions, I was partying a lot. I was doing all the wrong things, really, all the things you'd expect when anybody does well and suddenly you've got more money, and I was stretched by my home life and my work, and going out, and I could never balance it. I could never focus on the work, and I didn't really understand my relationship with ad agencies until about '99, when I suddenly went, 'Oh, you're paying me to tell you what I think, as opposed to doing what you want me to do.'

ES: Was that how you'd approached it at first?

RW: Yeah. I was always quite craft-driven, so I always wanted to do a good job and give them what they wanted. At that point I didn't try and question it, and didn't try to push the ideas, which is what they pay you for. The only thing that came out of that period was that I kept doing portraits. I was doing it all the time, it was like a band rehearsing and rehearsing, and suddenly it was like, 'I can do this.' Somebody would stand in front of me, and I'd just know how to communicate with them. You don't have to have David LaChapelle kinds of sets to challenge someone, you just need to talk to them, to have some communication with them. So that was probably the only good work that I was doing, and I was really happy with it. I was doing it for magazines, but that didn't really matter – doing portraits for magazines is not like working for advertising agencies or clients, because you do what you want, really. If I do a portrait for a magazine, it's actually become very concept-led over the last few years.

So you can say, 'Look, I'd like to do something like this,' and they go, 'Okay,' and the art director will come to the shoot and say, 'That's great.' It's really simple.

I also went to America around 1998–99, and did some magazine work there. I'd started to get a bit stronger about my own work, and my agent opened an office in America, so I thought it wouldn't be too hard to work there. It was really, really hard work. Everybody was really worried about their jobs, or about what the editor was going to say, or if you were going to get the shot. It's actually become a lot like that in the UK market. They're buying into your success, or your talent, or whatever, but then they're not 100 percent confident in their own opinions. In America, it's a proper business: you've got to have the credits, you've got to do this, you've got to do that. The way you do ads is to do proposals, and treatments, and you do a lot of development work, and there's a freedom in doing that, that you can allow yourself, or that the client can allow you, or the art director, or the editor. But there wasn't much of that, and I couldn't get used to it. I loved America, but I found the work so dry and so frustrating that I gave up on it, really, in about 2000.

ES: What was it about the work that frustrated you?

RW: I just felt that there was a kind of pressure, someone over your shoulder worrying and worrying. Everybody was 100 percent tense when they came onto a photo set, no matter what they were doing. I don't work in that kind of environment, I like to have a really happy set, a confident, positive set, and not have that kind of creation of tension which a lot of photographers love. They love to create tension on a set because it creates tension in the images, but I'm very much of the opposite opinion. Tension doesn't paralyze me, but it bursts my bubble and demotivates me, and I always find I end up doing really average work.

ES: A lot of fashion photographers work under similar constraints these days.

RW: Yeah. Everybody wants to know what they're going to get, you've got to do a certain number of shots, it has to be this and that. But I don't think that's coming from the magazines, predominately, it's coming from the advertisers, not the editors. It's a business, it's a big business. Everything, all the way down, is controlled. You get great editors and managing directors, and there are shit ones, and if you get a shit one, they don't allow you to express yourself, and it becomes formulaic. You need a strong editor who can balance it but not put too much pressure on you creatively. To tell them what you're going to do is difficult. Some of the best stuff that happens is not an accident, but it starts with an accident, and becomes something else. It's not prescriptive. I use a lot of tear sheets in my work as mood boards, and you take that, and you go in a different direction with it. The best situation is to take that and show it to them and say, 'Well, this is kind of what I'm going to do, but it's going to look completely different.' If they say, 'Well, I want that version of it,' then that fundamentally is a problem. It's prescriptive, and it's a problem being in a position where they want you to do exactly what they want you to do, and they want you to show them exactly how you're going to do it. It makes things look the same.

ES: And magazines are increasingly bound to pleasing the advertisers, even in editorial work.

RW: That's because most of them don't think about the art side of it. I guess that's what we tried to do with *Dazed & Confused*. And Juergen Teller is doing great things with Marc Jacobs. Designers like Marc Jacobs, they are artists, and they see themselves as artists, but they recognize that there is a commercial aspect to it. Juergen does those types of images that aren't really advertising, they're almost social commentary.

ES: It's also a matter of working with the right advertisers.

RW: Yeah. He's probably not even paid a great deal by Marc Jacobs to do it. But then there are people who do it terribly: Terry Richardson doesn't challenge me at all. Some of his work I like, he's got a great sense of humour, but *Kibosh* is shocking. It shocked me. It's like home porn – we've all done those photos. He's working with models that I know, and he's having sex with some of his models. It's quite misogynistic, actually, but in a very free-love kind of way. It's fantasy as well, but a different kind of fantasy. To be on that precipice of porn and to be able to piss into it is cool. But to fall in, it was like he was abusing his integrity. I think someone like Juergen does it with such class and humour and respect for the subject, and Terry Richardson just goes, 'Ah, fuck, 'em.' That sort of stuff is great for kids, kids love it, and that's why *Vice* magazine is so successful.

ES: They're both working in that snapshot aesthetic, but producing completely different work.

RW: The thing about Juergen is that he's a proper photographer, if you look at his work. I can remember when he was doing shoots for *The Face* or *Arena* or *Vogue*, and they were sophisticated, beautifully shot, beautifully executed imagery. They were well lit and everything was perfect, and he obviously rejected it all. I'm a big fan of his work.

ES: How would you describe yourself as a photographer?

RW: I just call myself a photographer. In interviews I've always said I'm not a fashion photographer, I'm a portrait photographer who does fashion. Really, I just like photography. I did cars last year and I really liked that. I love the process of photography.

RH: Had you wanted to go into fashion?

RW: No. I hated and loved fashion with a kind of equal passion. I've got to the point where I kind of feel like I'm influencing fashion now, where you feel like you can do something with it. It took me a long time to realize that fashion is an escape, a fantasy. If you treat it as a fantasy and an escape, that's fine, but if you are influenced by it as an individual to the point where you feel bad about yourself, it's not very good.

RH: But there are other photographers who are enamoured by that fashion industry, by the labels, the style books…

RW: What's interesting about fashion is that the people that really love it love it more than anything in the world. Take Mert and Marcus, for example. They're a fashion team that used to work as assistants at *Dazed & Confused*, and then Katie Grand helped to mould them, and they became the most important fashion photographers in the world. The desire and the love and the embrace of the whole medium is scary. I can't take it seriously. The tiniest difference in a model will make the most massive difference to a photograph, and I don't work like that at all. I try and choose models and subjects for their individuality, I try and look beyond what's fashionable.

RH: Many of your stories are very knowingly working against fashion.

RW: The idea is taking the fashion medium and twisting it a little bit each time. *Big Girl's Blouse* used bigger models, and that became quite a culturally significant thing. We were doing all of these types of stories, they were concepts, but they weren't serious concepts, they were kind of funny at the same time as being things that we thought were important or interesting, and then it went through to the mainstream. We did a shoot called

Hungry, where the models were eating. At that time, it was so pertinent. Today, people are a lot more sussed about what a model is and what a model does, but then it was seen as okay to treat them as a production line and see them as cattle. I did a shoot called *Livestock* where all the models were animals. It was always taking that little jab at the fashion industry, and then of course what happens is that that becomes fashionable, and gets absorbed and regurgitated. That's what the fashion industry does, season after season.

I think that if you take photographs, you're documenting culture, whether or not you're actually working as a documentary photographer. My thing is always to push that, to ask, 'Why is this inappropriate?', 'Why are you disgusted by these photos?' *Hungry* seems tame now, but at that time they were quite serious photographs, people were shocked that we could do that. But then a season later, people were using them as reference points.

ES: How do you approach fashion work these days? Do you do much fashion work at the moment?

RW: Probably one or two shoots a month. Not a great deal. It's never been a comfortable bedfellow for me. I've never felt completely comfortable doing fashion. But the more I work with that discomfort, the more interesting my ideas have been. I've gone through periods where I've been doing a lot of erotic fashion. I really enjoy working with women and photographing women, and being honest about it. It's not sexual, but there's a sexual side to it. I think that has placed me, more recently, in a position where my approach has been, 'Well, let's not do fashion any more, let's do an idea.' I still do beauty stuff, I really enjoy beauty. I get a lot out of creating, and really enjoying faces and eyes, and makeup, and stuff like that: it's become quite weird. But I'm also quite business-minded, and I always categorize my work into personal work, concept work, fashion work, whatever. With my fashion, my approach has been non-committal. I haven't really committed myself to any one particular style, or look, or idea. Enjoying the process of doing it and enjoying the images you're creating is part of how you challenge yourself intellectually and creatively. You can sometimes just take beautiful photographs.

My fashion work has changed a lot. It's shifted into this new style which is a lot more cinematic. I've thought about lighting a lot more, and about performance. A fashion story is not obviously a story – you're trying to create a mood and an atmosphere, so this work is more about that. And it's also about being less of a cynic about it – I was so cynical about fashion for a long time, so I was trying to embrace it a little bit more, and see the good in it, and not hate myself for being part of that world. It's just a photo of a bird in a frock, but you're trying to enhance some mood or some emotion. I just try to have a sense of humour about it all the time.

Recently I've been thinking about things that are more unusual. I want to do shoots with bodybuilders, or dwarves. I want to get back to when I first started in fashion where I would do things like portraying older women, or children, within a fashion context. I want to have a bit more intellectual fun with it, taking a photograph that people find difficult to look at. I'm really fascinated by male erotica, and I'd like to do more idea-based fashion. There's a commercial side to fashion, and doing it well technically and making money, but there's a part of me that definitely wants to challenge myself and my perceptions of people. If I look at something that interests me, and at my preconceptions, when I start to do the work, I start to think about it. I use the camera and the project to bring out my feelings and thoughts. It's a good way of processing your ideas, asking, 'Why do I have a problem with male nudity? Why can't I look at it?'

ES: I often encourage my students to pay attention to work that they don't like, or that makes them feel uncomfortable.

RW: Self-portraiture is a really good example of feeling uncomfortable, so I explore that through photos, and generally you get to a place where you feel more at ease. When you see something that you don't like, it doesn't mean it's not good, it means you've had a visceral response to it. Ten years ago I'd have just said, 'It's shit,' but these days I've got to argue with myself, and that's projected into everything I do, being a business person, being a manager, being a boss. Being a bit more considered about everything is something that comes from photography – having a tremendous amount of self-belief, but at the same time thinking I can't always be right.

ES: This takes me back to something that we were talking about right at the very beginning. A lot of critical writing on fashion photography takes semiotics as a sort of default critical approach. I've always found this angle a bit frustrating because I think that fashion images that really work strike you in a very visceral way – at least that's the case with most of the work I like.

RW: I do believe in the visceral element of photography, because it does touch you in a really strange way. I think with any work, whether you hate it or love it, as long as you're passionate, that's important. I'm very passionate about liking or not liking stuff, I can be very opinionated. But obviously it's also about fantasy. That's what I've tried to do with the Dove stuff – it's not about saying this or that is the ideal, but that this is fantasy, and if you accept it as fantasy, that's fine.

ES: The Dove *Real Beauty* campaign has become a sort of showpiece in your work.

RW: It has, and I'm really proud of it, and it's really difficult to contextualize for me, because anything where you take commerce and combine it with social questioning or social critique is very complicated. The bottom line is that it's about selling soap. That kind of marketing with a kind of small-'p' political perspective can be interpreted in different ways. I've worked with people who take the Campaign for Real Beauty[3] very seriously, they are committed to the idea of it. It's impressive, the way they take the party line on it. But then you've got people in other countries who interpret it in a different way, and a much scarier way, really: it's about selling, it's about aesthetics, whether it's that of the 'real woman' or that of the model. They're all completely different. I've worked on some that have become very beauty-oriented. You're doing beauty, but you're doing it for 'real women'. It's really hard to say that the Campaign for Real Beauty is a stand-alone asset without the knowledge that it's also selling beauty products. Yes, it does help people, but to give it credibility as social commentary is difficult.

NOTES ON CHAPTER 6

1   The Business and Technology Education Council (BTEC) was a sub-degree-conferring council in the United Kingdom, set up in 1984 and offering further and higher educational awards in vocational subjects.

2   The Polytechnic of Central London (PCL) was established in 1970 and was one of the first colleges in the UK to offer a BA photography course. In 1992, PCL became the University of Westminster.

3   The Campaign for Real Beauty was launched by Dove in 2005, as a platform for challenging narrow views of female beauty. It funds research and outreach programmes to help improve self-esteem among women and girls, hosts public forums, and is the driving force behind Dove 'real women' advertising.

7 In the Business of Selling Dreams: Working in Fashion Photography

Sascha Behrendt

MODELLING

I started modelling in 1983 at the age of 18. I saw it as a fast way to gain independence in the world (Fig. 12).

12. Sascha Behrendt, 1983.

From a young age, I had loved dressing up, and had always been fascinated by fashion history and the radical shifts in style over the decades. I can remember at 14 watching a documentary on Yves St Laurent, showing Jerry Hall, Marie Helvin and many other models on the catwalk in Paris. The fashion world appeared very glamorous and exciting.

My father's girlfriend was an art director on a women's weekly magazine, and suggested that before approaching any model agency, photographs that were vaguely professional would be helpful. She arranged for a roll of 'test' pictures of me to be shot at the tail end of a studio knitwear shoot. It was all backcombed, super-curly hair and burgundy blusher, very scary. The set was surprising to me because I had not expected such an intimidating, artificial construction. Behind me was a backdrop colorama in a strangely flat colour; there was a huge square flash overhead, and the camera was trained on a stool in the centre where I was to sit. The makeup artist, hairdresser and crew stood around watching. I felt like I was under a giant microscope, and was shaking with fear.

Having survived the experience, and armed with the roll of film, I did the rounds of the five recommended model agencies in London. I was happy to join a small old-fashioned one on Bond Street, run by a plump motherly figure with whom I felt safe. My first serious money work came about during the time that I was building up my portfolio with further 'test' shots. I was sent on a 'go-see' to a client, Adel Rootstein on the King's Road. Ushered into a dark space resembling a car showroom, I could see in the gloom carefully arranged static figures, spotlit as if on stage. It was all a bit strange, but I didn't question it – I went on so many appointments each day. Later, having been assessed by Adel herself, my agency were told I had the job. This would involve sittings over three months to create an exact clay copy which would be used as the template for 'Sascha' mannequins. Adel was very proud to be the only manufacturer modelling shop window dummies on real individuals; she had done mannequins of Twiggy and Marie Helvin, among others. They did three different versions of me. It was funny to discover them in their different incarnations in my later travels. Some would have afro hair and chocolate skin, or blonde hair and neon pink legwarmers. Now I wonder where all these frozen replicas are: probably languishing in department store basements.

Over time I realized my agency was not a big player and Paris was suggested as a good market for me. In the early eighties in England, my quirky looks, narrow face and six-foot height didn't fit in so easily. Most successful models were very pretty or classical looking. Even trendy magazines such as *The Face* or *i-D* preferred a more square-jawed, sexy look. However, I was lucky to find a new London agency called Premier who had girls who were more off-beat, and who tended to work with more innovative photographers. Just seeing the style of the composite cards of the girls lined up on the wall reassured me I was in the right place.

Most model agencies build relationships with their counterparts in Paris, Milan or New York, and will swap or trade girls between them. In the UK it is often young new models that have not 'made' it yet who are of interest to the other markets. Clients in the UK at that time tended to want only to book successful models from Paris or New York, and would prefer not to risk using a new girl from London. This meant that up-and-coming models would have to go to Paris at some point to be taken seriously on an international level. In my case, I was lucky to be taken on by one of the leading Paris agencies, City Models. They were edgy and unafraid to represent girls who were unconventional or not just 'pretty'. Cecilia Chancellor, also from England, was with them; she was very tall and pale, with childlike features, and dressed only in men's clothes.

In Paris, the Japanese designers Yohji Yamamoto and Comme des Garçons had arrived on the scene as an exciting breath of fresh air, challenging ideas of what was considered beautiful within fashion. Yohji, together with art director Marc Ascoli, created beautiful fashion catalogues, with the clothes, casting and photography showing a new refined aesthetic. The catalogues themselves became beautiful objects to treasure, the concept, photography and graphic design seamlessly sophisticated. For me, working with these designers and other more traditional ones like Yves St Laurent, Sonia Rykiel and Claude Montana was a heady mix. Catwalk shows were fun, intense and magically ephemeral. Girls would run from show to show in heavy makeup and stiff sprayed hair, on the metro when the traffic was too bad, looking like strange exotic birds.

I remember being sent on a casting to Yves St Laurent with a view to being used for his catwalk show. The classical Parisian building in Avenue Marceau was grand and impressive, but I was surprised to be sent via the trade entrance to a small dingy room. Hurriedly I was asked to strip, put on six-inch black heels, red lipstick and a curious white wrap reminding me of a nurse's uniform. In the glittering, mirrored salon I then had to walk on a slippery Persian carpet, trying not to catch my own eye until, with a brisk nod, I was approved. At the subsequent fitting with the designer himself, again wearing the St Laurent 'uniform', I was told in hushed tones by the other models that I would have to show Yves myself nude, in private. He apparently would not accept any model until he had seen their body completely. It seemed he wished to work with a model as a whole person, not just as a coat hanger with a pretty face.

I felt privileged in being hired for his shows and getting to experience the fading, rarefied working environment in the process. His take on women was old-fashioned, but he was interested in a model's uniqueness as a person. He had always been unafraid to use a mix of models from different nationalities, and seemed to celebrate their differences. The Japanese shows were more impersonal. One rarely met the designers, but saw them backstage from a distance, and it felt a little like on a production line of a factory. Their strength lay in recognizing the power of image and translating their vision by working with important photographers – like Nick Knight, Peter Lindbergh, Max Vadukal and Paolo Roversi, all of whom had a strong signature style – for their press and catalogues. The photography, paired with beautiful graphic design, created a new edgy and sophisticated visual language. These designers were not afraid of pictures with dark suggestive shadows, or of concept over-riding product detail in the interests of dynamic and powerful communication. Preceding the supermodel era and mass branding, in the late eighties it seems retrospectively radical and visionary.

The fashion glossies in Paris in the mid- to late eighties commissioned quite a wide spectrum of photography: Peter Lindbergh's raw grainy black-and-white, Paolo Roversi's nineteenth-century studio style, to the soft glowing flash of Dominique Isserman. At the time I didn't realize that the Paris shows were where the big photographers and magazine editors went not just to check the clothes they may be shooting later but also the new girls in town. If you had been chosen for the shows by important designers, you were considered ready for the prestigious magazines.

Although I loved doing catwalk, I was actually very shy, and found being pinned down in a photograph quite difficult. I personally felt more comfortable working with women photographers, as they were happy to shoot me more as an individual and less as a performing sexual stereotype. I shot a lot with Sacha, for German *Vogue* and *Marie Claire*, and Dominique Isserman for *Elle* and American and French *Vogue*. Shooting the collections for both US and French *Vogue* was very exciting. Clothes had to be photographed through the night, having been whisked away from the designers immediately after the catwalk show. Security was tight: no one was to know which pieces were being covered.

When I worked with big-name photographers of that period, like Arthur Elgort and Patrick Demarchelier, I could see why they were so successful. They very quickly adapted their approach according to what would suit you. They didn't plonk you in the middle of a set and just hope that it would all work. They thought about what they were doing, and were incredibly sensitive to light and to what the girl looked like through the lens. Other individuals that I worked with were Peter Lindbergh, Paolo Roversi, Steve Hiett, Oliviero Toscani and Gian Paolo Barbieri. Each photographer had his unique approach to achieving his signature style, from the lighting and film, to how he would interact with you. Some, like Arthur Elgort, shot very fast, almost like reportage, keeping it light and humorous. Others, like Sacha, would insist on a pose being frozen on location, sometimes for up to an hour. It was a miracle if there was any expression of life left!

Truly great models are like chameleons, in that they know they look good in almost any lighting condition or setup and enjoy projecting different moods to camera. Girls who are naturally more off-beat need extra thought directed towards the styling, hair etc., in order to pull off a convincing coherent image. This is the biggest obstacle to those attempting to create their first fashion images. There is such precision required from every element, from casting to concept to clothing, until the delicate balance is achieved that leads to the successful shot.

I modelled for five years, which was quite enough. I made good money in a relatively short amount of time, and travelled all over the world to exotic places. There are not many professions where one can be in different situations and with new people throughout a week. I can remember being aware of the shift in mood in the mid-eighties when a new breed of model started to do the fashion shows. More American, athletic and classic…the beginning of the supermodel era. Time to move on.

PHOTOGRAPHY

Having felt rather powerless as a model within fashion photo shoots I was curious as to what I could achieve on the other side of the lens. I was less interested in the technical aspects of photography, and more in how to arrive at a satisfactory result through being sensitive to the subject. I was fascinated at how individuals react and relate differently to light and the camera. Portrait photography was in this respect perfect for me. I could apply and experiment with some of the ideas I had formed as a result of being a subject myself, without being bogged down by large crews for hair, makeup, styling etc.

My partner and I decided to work together as a team, 'Wilde and Behrendt'. We kept it low-tech, using an SLR Nikon and one single tungsten spot, sometimes mixed with daylight. Putting a few test shots together, we went to visit some contemporary magazines. *Blitz* was one that commissioned portraits from us on a fairly regular basis. However, I was not treating photography as a career move; it was, at the time, important and cathartic for me to be allowed simply to enjoy it. The politics of which magazines to work for, the hustle in order to meet the right people, promoting oneself, and the investment in a studio and lighting equipment did not interest me. I was aware, however, that for it to be a serious profession that would be required.

We flirted briefly with fashion photography, but a fashion story involves a minimum of six images that are consistent in style and content. Although location work would have been cheaper than a studio setup, English weather is unreliable, and often grey for the entire period one needs to shoot for a magazine deadline. Summer wear, for example, needs to be shot during November, so one is forced to consider a studio or pay for some serious long-haul travel.

Shooting in a studio is similar to a film set in that it requires the construction of an artificial universe through equipment, lighting and sometimes props. The technical choices of camera and film, and then the model, determine subtly the look of the image. Formats such as ten-by-eight force a photographer to work more slowly, as the cumbersome hardware and its shallow depth of field limit movement. The results are often very stylized and contrived. The advertising industry loves large and medium format, as they can be blown up to a large scale without degradation of quality. The models need to look convincing in this environment, so you need specialists in hair, makeup and clothes to achieve a 'natural' look. Good models manage to summon up vitality for the camera in spite of being prodded, poked and made up. If there is a consistency in content and photographic style over about six images, you have the beginnings of a potential fashion 'story'.

FASHION-PHOTOGRAPHY AGENT

In 1995, I was invited to set up a fashion-photography agency with a business partner and some backing. Both of us had worked long enough to know we wanted to represent photographers who had some kind of artistic integrity. For fashion photographers, however, the journey to getting commissioned work – whether quality editorial or advertising – is a long one. As an agent you are responsible for promoting their work, negotiating fees, and managing long-term career strategy. Sometimes for a fee an agent will do the hands-on shoot production, booking of crew, ordering of equipment, and location or studio finding.

Fashion magazines act as an important forum to display a photographer's abilities. Published stories, consistently well done in quality magazines (in the nineties, these were *The Face*, *i-D*, *Dazed & Confused*, *Purple*, *Self Service*, *W* , and *Vogue* Italia US, UK, France), were an important way to showcase a photographer's work within the industry and put the photographer in the running for commercial jobs. Most high-fashion advertising work is commissioned from Paris, New York or Milan, but the photographers are picked internationally once they have proved their worth editorially. England has produced many successful photographers: David Sims, Glen Luchford, Nick Knight and Craig McDean have all provided important work worldwide.

Getting a foot in the door to the most influential magazines is notoriously tricky. It is often dependent on a good introduction with editors, stylists or art directors attached to the publication. It is often necessary to be patient and turn down more mainstream editorial, as there is an unspoken snobbery within the industry. If you were to put a lot of work with a lower-market magazine into your portfolio and do the rounds you may not be considered for future work. Agents often have to support photographers financially and emotionally while they navigate this period. They have to be careful that commercial jobs do not undermine the possibility of quality editorial. It is also necessary to follow the published work of other photographers, stylists, hairdressers, makeup artists and models in order to be aware of what is going on. So much of people's time, reputations and money are at stake when a fashion shoot takes place.

On a shoot for a good job there is an understanding between the whole team that there is a delicate alchemical process at work. Photographers have to find certain patterns, either technically or in the way they shoot their subject, that become their personal formulas. These formulas can consist of a particular combination of camera format and lighting setup, alongside their choice of hair, makeup and model. All these elements contribute to the final image of this fragile chemistry. Most successful work is often a result of working again and again with the same crew and slightly varied setups until some unexpected magic starts within this constructed framework. This emerges eventually as a kind of style or 'voice' that clients or designers seek when commissioning work.

It takes practice and nerves of steel to maintain a steady vision throughout a shoot. With so many people and possibilities involved, it is important to be focused. This becomes essential on an advertising job where there is pressure to reliably shoot great pictures in sometimes difficult circumstances. Over time as an agent it was an understanding of the above that I looked for in a photographer. Talent in taking pictures was not enough. Fashion is a business, and it requires political savvy as well as creativity.

ART BUYER IN THE ADVERTISING INDUSTRY

I decided I wanted a change from being a photographer's agent, and began working as a freelance art buyer in London with corporate advertising agencies Grey's, St Luke's and M&C Saatchi among others. As an art buyer I worked within advertising agencies as a facilitator to source and commission the appropriate illustrators or photographers to realize a print campaign. Having been a supplier to an ad agency as a photography agent I found it fascinating to be on the client side, and to witness the chain of events that lead up to the final choice of talent. My experience as a photography agent was enormously useful, as I had a good grasp of the production issues when commissioning a shoot as well as cost estimates proposed by photographers. The shoot or illustration itself is often only ten percent of what is required to bring an advertising campaign to fruition. Before the commissioned work can take place there is usually much negotiation over budget and creative concept between the agency and client. Big agencies have account handlers who manage the client on behalf of the agency, but in the midst of negotiations they can sometimes seem to be working for the client! Art buyers are often caught in the middle, trying to justify a favoured photographer's production and fee estimate to the account handler while getting the art directors the talent they feel will best visualize their concept.

Freelance art buying usually involves a short contract, from a week to a month, covering permanent staff who may be off sick or away. At M&C Saatchi I was brought in as a specialist to work under the creative director Tiger Savage, updating her with contemporary photography and fashion as well as the usual art buying. We worked together for nine months on two big campaigns for Beck's beer and Pink shirtmakers among others, working with still-life/fashion photographer Richard Burbridge, based in New York. Tiger was interested in using photographers that normally shoot fashion for product advertising and vice versa, to bring an extra dimension to the imagery.

In the UK, unlike Paris or New York, it is unusual to find big fashion brands giving their business to conventional ad agencies. Generally it will be done in-house, through a graphic design company, or an independent freelance art director. The big London advertising agencies get excited at the prospect of proving themselves on a fashion campaign: they are rare and add glamour to the otherwise boring roster of washing powders, cars, electrical goods and insurance companies. They also get a chance to work with fashion image-makers, as conventional advertising is usually serviced by still-life or straight commercial photography.

A variety of skilled individuals are needed to bring about a print campaign in conventional advertising. Planners work out a long-term strategy and identity for clients, find new business, and work on market research, forecasts and mood boards to secure the success of a campaign. Account handlers are responsible for handling clients, the gross budget for an account, negotiation, reassurance and delivery. The creative team is the backbone of any agency. It is made up of a copywriter and art director, although sometimes both people may be comfortable with either role. They are briefed by planning and account handling and told whether a campaign is destined for TV, radio, viral (internet films) or print. They devise scripts, which are then drawn up into storyboards for TV (or scripts for radio) and/or draw up layouts with headlines and copy for print campaigns. Creative teams have to have their work approved by a creative director. Art buyers source the appropriate talent for a job, negotiate respective fees and budgets, and oversee production of shoots or delivery of illustrations. Graphic designers are generally used as artworkers in advertising, helping an art director who might be lacking in craft skills to refine the typography and layout of a print campaign. They are very rarely instrumental in the initial creative process. Project managers are part of the creative department. They track and produce workflow, draw up timing plans and media schedules that determine which finished images will go in what magazine or poster site, and when. They liaise between everyone to ensure timings are met. Finance staff take care of finance workflow and administration. Repro takes care of the printing side, tracking proofs (that will need signing off by creatives and the client before going off to print), and ensuring all final delivery deadlines. Whether working within a large organization or a small one, an advertising campaign still requires all of the above, more or less.

I was very lucky to be asked to be an art buyer with a small outfit called Milk Communications. They had been asked to pitch for UK high-street clothing store Oasis. The creative director had a great track record with edgy, interesting brands, but knew he needed specialist help with fashion. We co-wrote the pitch, illustrating current social shifts in women's career and leisure activities as well as the closing of the perceived gap in fashion in the 15–40 age range. Accompanying the writing was a mood board we put together of fashion images we felt were contemporary and appropriate. When we won the account I suggested photographer Marcelo Krasilcic to shoot the campaign, as he had produced many fresh and innovative fashion stories for *Dazed & Confused* and *Purple*. Too many of the other high-street competitors seemed to roll out the same safe imagery, and yet the audience they were selling to were highly sophisticated. To me there was no reason why the fashion photography should not be as up-to-date and current as the clothing had to be. Although we took a big risk in working with one of the more edgy photographers for such a mainstream client, I felt it was a success and hoped they would have the imagination to continue along that path.

From the experience of working so closely with the art director in pitching, winning the account and then helping to follow through on the shoot itself, I felt I had come full circle and was hungry to do more. I was now able to use the big-agency knowledge in a more personal setup with a big brand.

FASHION ART DIRECTION

Advertising art directors work on the visual side of advertising, usually in partnership with a copywriter who provides words. They may be involved in working with many different media: TV, print (posters and press), radio and the internet. Art directors working on a supplement or a magazine will decide on the visual material to be used. They will be responsible for the image content of that publication. An art director working for a *fashion* magazine, on the other hand, will be resolving the content rather than directing it. Fashion editors as a rule bring the fashion spreads they have commissioned to the art director to lay out. Alternatively, the big fashion houses may use an in-house art director whose job is to translate the individual designer's vision into images.

I officially started as an art director specializing in fashion when well-known graphic designer/art director Peter Saville invited me to come and work with him on the Stella McCartney campaign. Stella McCartney is based in London, and one of a roster of designers within the Gucci Group. As Stella retains creative control over her company, she is the person with final say over her advertising. It is both refreshing and exciting to be able to work closely with her as client on concept and choice of talent. Too often large fashion brands will have decisions made by committee, the marketing or business heads at odds with the more visionary approach of the designer.

Peter had already collaborated with Stella on one print campaign, and wanted help on the next. He operated as an independent art director, quite different to those I encountered while working as an art buyer within the big agencies. He did not have the support backup of account handlers, art buyers, finance teams and secretaries, yet the usual procedure to roll out an advertising campaign still had to be followed. Working with him, my past experience became useful as I found myself needing to take on all the above roles as and when they came up. At some points, especially when negotiating the budget while working creatively on the brief, I would find a conflict of interest would emerge. As an art director the priority is to deliver the best creative solution possible, and it can be painful to see that principle potentially undermined by economics, yet diplomacy, as always, is key. I found my previous experience in some situations a hindrance, as I could sympathize with differing points of view, forgetting that not all were in our best interests. Being pigheaded and blocking out other people's problems is sometimes necessary to push important work through. It was important to let go of feeling responsible for every factor going into a shoot; I had to learn that my job was primarily as a creative and not a supplier.

For a fashion campaign, we would get the brief from the client and then draw up a concept appropriate for that season. Further responsibility would then rest on us to commission talent to realize the approved concept, lay out and design the final chosen images, and then follow through to the repro stage until files are given to magazines to print. Each campaign can take between three and four months from idea stage to final delivery. Usually not until after the catwalk show are choices made on shoot dates or models, as the tug-of-war begins between big-name designers to see who gets the hottest girl of the season.

Advertising is a business selling dreams, but high-end fashion does not always follow the same methods as conventional advertising communication. Most product print ads use copywriting, wit and humour to add value. With fashion, the image and name are considered enough. Imbued with mystique and power, these two are supposed to evoke immediate desirability – the intrinsic value inherent in the brand. Fashion advertising rarely relies on tag-lines or jokes, because it operates on a more unconscious level. Presented with a beautiful woman, it offers the fantasy of what it feels like to be her, and even suggests that we *could* be her. Instead of witty one-liners as part of the advertising idea, fashion uses the choice of makeup, model, clothing and style of photography to influence the consumer. Fashion advertising demands precision in putting these elements together to be convincing, something experienced fashion photographers respect and understand.

Stella had a good grasp of these issues, but did not want to be overly influenced by contemporary fashion culture when we started on a campaign, preferring to look at vintage prints or modern art as sources of inspiration (Plate 13). I would look for the talent to realize the mood and feeling of our idea. Most fashion houses contract a photographer so they are guaranteed a certain 'look' or style they can call their own. Stella's campaigns were challenging, in that she wanted to start afresh each season, so sourcing new photographers took a lot of work but was braver than sticking with the same talent each time. I enjoyed working with a range of photographers and their teams where possible, these being David Vasiljevic, Camille Vivier, Mary McCartney and Cedric Buchet, all diverse in style. Working with these individuals gave me a chance to art direct in different ways. Some required close guidance and a second pair of eyes, others to be left alone, only wanting input when requested. It has always been important to be aware and not afraid to step in if the shoot goes too far away from the original agreed concept.

After deciding to go freelance, continuing to work with Stella, I was approached by a large ad agency to help on one of their biggest hair and beauty brands. Although this area is more specifically product-oriented than high fashion, similar principles still apply. From being responsible for so much on a job, going back to being a small part of the chain was a bit of a shock. No matter how passionately aware I was of potential pitfalls in this area of work, trying to raise the quality of work was hard within a large organization. Neither the vast numbers of people working within the agency nor the client, were educated in the culture of contemporary beauty and photography. The agency and client handled selling their product as if it was another washing powder or pet food. Entering the corporate world again was an interesting reminder that unless a company is organized to operate responsively around the fashion and beauty business it cannot hope to communicate impressively with its audience.

For me the most satisfying image-making has come out of small, close working relationships. Many factors can derail a fashion campaign, from lack of financial resources to too many parties having a say on final outcome. For me, the more the client has directly supported efforts to nurture the campaign through its sometimes tricky stages, the more chance it has of being a success.

8 Interview with Penny Martin

Eugénie Shinkle

SHOWstudio is a London-based online fashion broadcasting company dedicated to showcasing the creative process and examining fashion image-making from within the industry. I spoke with editor-in-chief Penny Martin in April 2006.

ES: Can you talk a bit about the history and development of SHOWstudio?
PM: SHOWstudio was officially launched November 2000, though it had been in development for maybe a year prior to that. It came out of a discussion that [photographer] Nick Knight and [art director] Peter Saville had on holiday. Peter had been approached by a German TV channel to create a programme about culture. He had been talking to Nick about whether he might like to be involved in it, and with the characteristic evangelical zeal that engenders Nick's way of thinking about things, he said, 'Okay, I'm interested, but why don't we make our own television programme? Why don't we make our own channel?' It was around 1999, with all the euphoria about dotcom, and the word on the street was that it was really cheap and quick to make websites. In the publishing culture that Peter and Nick were involved in, things took ages: you'd create something and it would be three months before you saw it. With the web, there was this idea of immediacy and spontaneity. So they set about, with designer Paul Hetherington, to start developing a website. That took ages,

because there was a real tussle between the way Nick wanted to work, which was fast and full-on, and Peter, who muses and takes a long time. Eventually, with Paul and a couple of other members of staff – a guy called Derek Michael, who was interactive designer, and our now chief designer, Paul Bruty, and a film editor, Adam Mufti – they launched the site, the container for SHOWstudio, in November 2000. At that point, it was kind of like a collection of editorial multimedia projects, centred to some extent around fashion, naturally, because they were commissioning a lot of their fashion peers. Before I came on board, they were creating four to six projects every four months or so. There were about thirty projects or so in the first year, and they were launched as and when they were made; there was no sense of impetus, or calendar.

ES: So it didn't have an editorial structure at that time?

PM: It had an editorial view, inasmuch as it was through the filter of what Nick and Peter wanted. By the time I started, Peter was no longer on the scene. He was a contributor, and he was very present, quite literally, because we shared a studio with him. But he was already diverted by the rebranding of Givenchy, so he wasn't involved in running it, and importantly, he wasn't funding it; it was Nick's money that was funding it. So by the time I came on board, I was working to Nick. In terms of editorial, there was definitely a taste implemented, and a kind of selection mechanism, because it was through their contacts that people were being commissioned. But it wasn't like a magazine that has a certain impetus to get things out once a month and follow a certain format. Alice Rawsthorn had been commissioning texts to explore some of the projects, but by the time I joined she had gone to the Design Museum to become the director. I was the first 'editor' as such, in terms of trying to create some structure. I started in September 2001.

When we started, it was very difficult to get people in the industry involved, even to find someone with an email account; they didn't use computers at all. All the other communities around design and architecture and music were logged on, but fashion wasn't at all interested. If you commissioned something, people would say, 'Look, computers aren't really my thing.' We enjoyed the luxury of having Nick and Peter's names attached to the project, so people wanted to do things with them, but very few of them saw the potential of multimedia and new media in fashion.

It's even difficult to get a lot of the very established brands interested now. We spent a long time trying to lead people by the hand at the start. When we first commissioned people, when we said, 'We want you to do a bit of multimedia because we're interested in your photography,' people didn't really know what we meant, and we would not really understand why they didn't come back to us with a finished project. Then we realized that actually they needed to collaborate with us, we had to support what they wanted to do. We really had to nurse people through, but that was great, because it meant that we really grew up.

ES: Nick says on the website that 'SHOWstudio is based on the belief that showing the entire creative process – from conception to completion – is beneficial for the artist, the audience and the art itself.' What other motives did Nick and Peter have for starting up the site?

PM: Nick's motives for starting SHOWstudio were very much underpinned by the fact that he's at a stage in his career, after twenty-five years in image-making, where what he's doing is generally well-received but he never hears anything about it, aside from a few viewer's letters, and what's written in magazines. He doesn't do a lot of the social things in the industry, so there's no way into a discussion about what he's doing, he just puts it out into a vacuum, really. He just felt that the atmosphere around dotcom was right, although it really wasn't targeted at fashion at all.

ES: It was also about creating a space where they didn't have the constraints of working for advertisers, wasn't it?

PM: Magazines are about selling advertising. They may have pretended not to be, but it's the way the whole system is structured. In magazines, the key fashion advertising issues, where the collections are profiled, are in March, April, September and October, when the shows are on. Inside you'd expect to find a variety of different kinds of editorial shoots, maybe a special or a trend piece. The collections issue is basically the way a magazine fulfils all its advertising credits. There's a full page devoted to each of its main advertisers, and it's shot by an important photographer. Your advertisers will count up how many shots they got per season. Tacitly, there's a sort of sliding scale of how well you showed their garments – shooting a full look counts for more than a shoulder strap. There are some brands that are known to count up how explicitly you've shown their garments, and will be talking to your head of advertising about whether you were in line or not. I think it's a mistake for people to think that photographers were ever able to do exactly what they wanted. Somehow advertising is a dirty word, and editorial was imagined to be clean of any commercial responsibilities. It's always been tacit advertising, it's just that the advertisers have really got the thumbscrews on designers and magazines now. PRs have also got an enormous amount of control now. Sometimes they won't lend out sample garments to a magazine if they're not quite right.

ES: Your look book project with Ebru Ercon (April 2004) also commented on the hold that advertisers now have, didn't it?

PM: They've changed fashion, look books; I'm fascinated by what they're for and what they've done. Fashion assistants and stylists no longer illustrate directly from the catalogue, they use look books instead. It's a way of seeing the collections afterwards, seeing the garments well depicted instead of flashing by you on the catwalk. The look book is a kind of catalogue for calling in garments to shoot; these days, websites like style.com or catwalking.com are used like look books. They were introduced as *aides-memoire*, but actually, look books have become a didactic agent in making sure fashion clothing is depicted in the way that the advertiser would like, and they can be quite aggressive. The advertiser – the commercial part of the company – is not so distant from the designer: they'll work together on creating a campaign and saying how the clothing should be represented.

ES: You've mentioned that companies will actually insist on a magazine shooting an entire look.

PM: The look book drives home the styling statement that the company wants to make. It's a much stronger statement when your garment doesn't get shown with a top by a competitor. If a magazine shoots a full look by Balenciaga, say, it's a really strong endorsement of their collection. As a magazine, ideally what you'd want to do is to be able to mix it up, so you could include lots of different advertisers and please them all. But if you just put in a top, or something like that, it's not going to cut it from the advertiser's perspective. People have become quite constrained in what they're allowed to do. Very recently, a reputable and important French fashion brand issued a dictum that you're not allowed to borrow in an item of its clothing to shoot if you don't shoot the whole look and the accessories with it. It happens with couture, but in editorial this was unheard

Plate 1. Philip-Lorca diCorcia, 'Untitled', from *Cuba Libre*, *W*, March 2000. Stylist: Joe Zee.

Plate 2. Cedric Buchet, 'Untitled', from Prada advertising campaign, Spring/Summer 2001. Stylist: Alastair Mackui; Art Director: David James.

Plate 3. Glen Luchford, 'Untitled', from Prada advertising campaign, Fall/Winter 1997. Stylist: Alexandra White; Art Director: David James.

Plate 4. Nan Goldin, 'Untitled, Russian Baths, New York City', from *Masculine/Feminine*, *View*, 1985. Fashion Editor: Mary Peacock.

Plate 5. Mario Sorrenti, 'Untitled', from One, *Another Magazine* 1, Autumn/Winter 2001. Stylist: Camilla Nickerson.

Plate 6. Philippe Garner, 'New York Newsstand', October 2002. Images vie for attention on the city street, stylized female beauty their most ubiquitous currency.

Plate 7. Jane McLeish, *Bombshell by the Sea*, fashion feature for *ES* magazine, 24 May 2002. McLeish appears to pose her model effortlessly to achieve a relaxed, seemingly spontaneous set of pictures in a soft, diffused light. The images are subtly infused with an engaging, understated sensuality that reveal a woman's take on the erotic. The story took its inspiration from a 1960s photograph by Dennis Hopper of Jane Fonda in a bikini shooting a bow and arrow in the artist's Los Angeles garden.

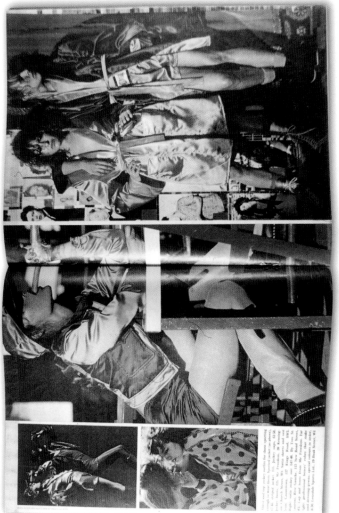

Plate 8. Hans Feurer, *Pick Yourself a Winner*, fashion feature for *Sunday Times* Magazine, 11 July 1971. These images anticipate the sharp, sexy, colour-saturated look that was to characterize so much fashion photography of the 1970s. The models play directly to the male gaze.

Plate 9. [left] Richard Burbridge. Stella Tennant models for the cover of *i-D*, London, April 2001. [right] Bruce Weber, *United States Olympic Special*, cover of Andy Warhol's *Interview*, New York, January–February 1984. Image and typography must work in harmony to make an effective magazine cover, exploiting the combined skills of photographer, art director and editor.

Plate 10. [left] Toni Frissell, 'United we stand', cover of American *Vogue*, July 1942. [right] Zanna, *England Rules OK*, feature on stylist Katy England for *ES* magazine, London, 28 September 1997. Fashion photography has been regularly exploited to develop concepts and themes beyond its overt purpose of presenting new styles in dress. Here, in different ways, it takes on a political dimension, in one instance consolidating a sense of shared destiny and purpose, in the other presenting a neo-punk posture of subversion.

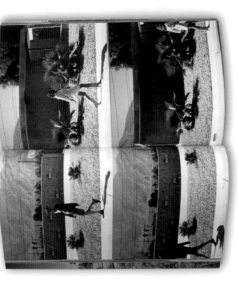

Plate 11. Terry Richardson, *Nancy, What's for Dinner?*, catalogue for Sisley, 2002. Following in the footsteps of his father Bob, Terry Richardson has brought his own twist to fashion photography. He is an iconoclast and a *provocateur* who has injected a healthy dose of spoof, vulgarity and near-pornographic eroticism into the often overly precious world of fashion.

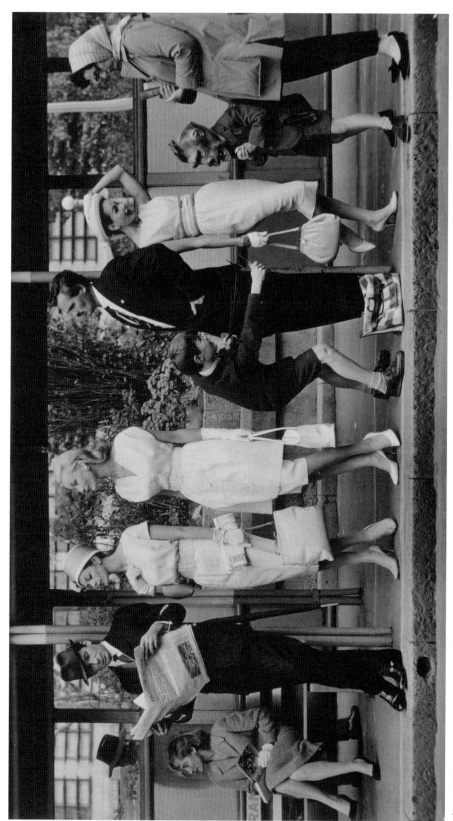

Plate 12. Laurence Le Guay, 'Untitled (Fashion Queue with Masked Child)', 1960.

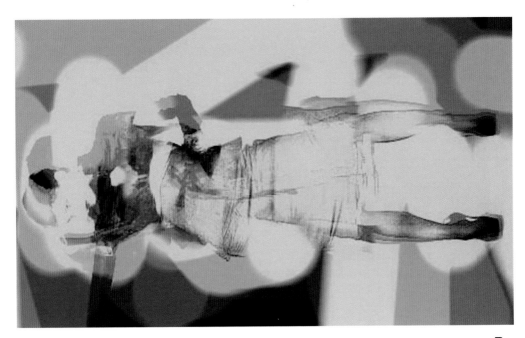

Plate 13. [left] Mary
McCartney, Stella
McCartney,
Spring/Summer
2004.

Plate 14. [right]
*Dress Me Up, Dress
Me Down,*
SHOWstudio
interactive featuring
Liberty Ross, 2005.

Plate 15. Nick Knight, 'It's a Jungle Out There', Alexander McQueen show invitation, 1997.

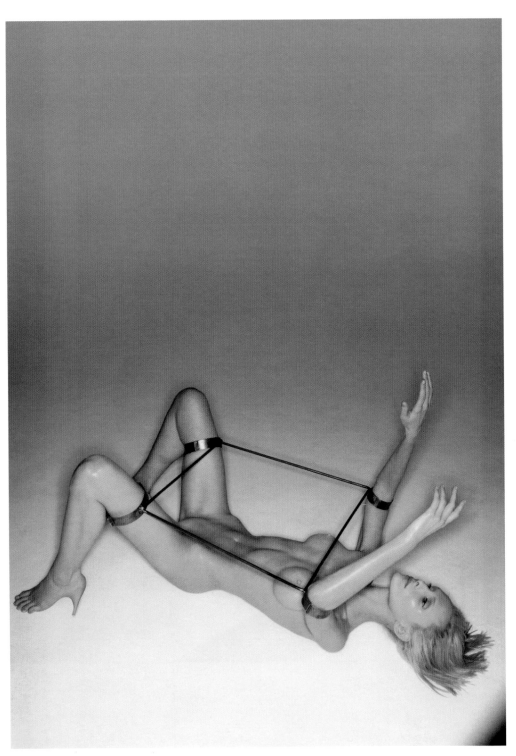

Plate 16. Nick Knight, 'Laura de Palma', *Visionaire*, 1997.

Plate 17. [left] Cover, *Street* 165, May 2005.

Plate 18. [below] Martin Parr, 'Junk Space', *Fashion Magazine* 1, Summer 2005.

Plate 19. Juergen Teller, 'Kristen Lifting Skirt', London, 2005.

of. If companies say you've got to shoot a full look, it prevents their outfit from being dirtied up or changed, but it allows less potential for contrast in styling.

It's a great luxury to be able to work outside that system. Quite often practitioners have two portfolios: one of them contains their commercial work, and the other one will be their personal work. Really great creatives, of course they'll want to do projects that aren't just about showing clothes in a studio, and SHOWstudio was very much envisaged as a space where people would want to do that. One of the interesting things is that there aren't as many creatives in the fashion industry that actually want to take advantage of that opportunity as you would think. It's a completely different culture of agreeing to collaborate, especially when things are as freewheeling as they are at SHOWstudio, and you're not being paid, and there are no expenses. It's quite hard to firm up a commitment and to keep it going until something is produced. Things can kind of float away, people have got justifiable excuses for not turning things in: 'Look, I had a commercial job, I had to take it,' and that's the way it goes. Quite often it's difficult to lead those kinds of practitioners into a really abstract area. When we first started we thought that we'd get people to do really audacious anti-fashion work, but actually, if you look at our projects and how it's worked out, that often isn't the case, even though there are some amazing projects that are very abstract. I think that we have become known as a potential container for people's strange and non-fashion-centred projects, but I think that our audience is extremely fascinated with the culture of the industry itself, so naturally we try to get a balance between the two.

ES: Who are your audience?

PM: It's globally based, and we get around 110,000 viewers per month. A good proportion of our audience members work in the industry, and we know that a lot of key industry people are watching and reading, and maybe even posting on the forum. It's amazing how literate our audience are about the fashion industry. People know a lot about the culture of a shoot, and they are very opinionated about it. There is a lot of discussion about whether fashion as a culture is spent, and it's all about exclusivity and the art world now. It is true that your average household knows about how fashion is made, and you could say that to some extent it's been stripped of its mystique, and in some ways maybe we are responsible for that.

ES: The site has undergone several restructures and redesigns since it began.

PM: The first of those was in 2002–3, when we started creating channels of content. That was really to reflect the way that we were trying to think about the commissions. We were aware that we were starting to create projects that were not only constructed in different media, but had different intentions. So we were able to separate 'film', which was a large part of what we were creating around that time, from 'play', which consisted mainly of interactive projects, games and multimedia toys, commissions to do picture message stories and things like that. 'Live' was a very important section to us, and I think it's really become our USP. Because it was live, we were to some extent able to treat the internet like a live broadcasting channel for shoots, real-time projects, anything where we were using live imaging. At that time, we were starting to be able to work out what we were doing, which I was keen on doing, because it was very amorphous when I started. The content was fantastic, but it's very difficult commissioning in that kind of environment. What ultimately happens is that nothing gets done, because you get caught in the headlights of infinite possibility. Following on from that, there were several different redesigns, and then we redesigned so that you could see into the studio in November 2004.

ES: That was when you introduced the live webcam?

PM: That's when we started to realize that we needed to introduce live imaging into our own process, if we were going to purport to be about other people's creative processes, which naturally was what live imaging was starting to throw up. The first example of that was *Sleep* in December 2001. We started to make SHOWstudio – literally, the words 'show studio' – be about showing the studio process, and naturally we had to be part of that, no matter how reluctantly. It was with some trepidation that we turned the webcam on ourselves, because we're not that fascinating, just a bunch of people in a basement commissioning much more interesting people in the industry to make creative things. To turn the lens on ourselves seemed somewhat narcissistic, but it was a necessary evil. The danger is that the focus shifts onto yourself, and you find yourself inextricably linked to it, and that can be problematic. There are cameras on us all day, people correspond with us all day, and the sense of familiarity of us at the centre of it can become quite personal. It can become hard to deal with. People discuss us a lot on the forum, and they want a lot from you, and they try and provoke discussion. But that's what you open up by making yourself contactable.

In April of 2005, we started to answer some of the demands coming from our contributors. They seemed to want to start getting involved in the process of our image-making, and we had a lot of mail asking, 'Why don't you do this, why don't you do that? There was great enthusiasm for projects that we created like *Come as You Are* (December 2002) or *Exquisite Corpse* (November 2002) or the downloadable garment projects, where you can make up garments and style them and post them on the site. We felt that we'd reached a point at which what we're doing had become established enough that people understood what they were participating in, so we wanted to make that explicit. Maintaining the site had also become very time-consuming, and it wasn't always evident, the amount of energy six people had to devote to keeping it going. We thought, well, that's part of our process too, we should turn that out into the open.

We brought in a forum and a blog, so we could give a literal breakdown of what was happening in the studio during the day, and we started structuring our commissioning differently. We'd been creating one or two projects a week, and it had got to that stage where it was just massive, we were taking on far too much. I wanted to slow it down a bit, to try and unpick what we were creating and how we were using it. We decided to produce one big thematic project every one or two months, and incorporate all the different formats that we were known for − our downloadable garments, our live interviews, our live broadcasts, our film, our interactives. It would still be a kind of jumble of formats, but it would be thematically consistent, and we could penetrate an idea a lot deeper than we were. The first of those kinds of projects was *Sittings: Thirty Men* (April 2005), which was a menswear story that Simon Foxton did, which was all about a live portrait sitting.

The second project was *Dress Me Up, Dress Me Down* (June 2005) (Plate 14) which was about that genre of internet pornography where you can access a girl in front of a webcam and direct her. Both projects had a creative at the centre of them who was allowed to create a lot of content, and Liberty Ross was very open to participating in *Dress Me Up*. We wanted her to take control of her representation in the run-up to the project, and then on the day we wanted to flip it around and turn it over to the viewer, so they could dress and style her during a live broadcast, the way that you can over those pornographic sites. I commissioned different texts about photography from various people: the consumer of pornography, the cynical fashion photographer who knows that what they do is quite similar to pornography, people who objected to it, that sort of thing. It's a kind of classic SHOWstudio approach that had lots of different strands under one heading. That's really the way I'm most comfortable working, programming a whole season, rather than just doing one project and then chucking it and doing the next thing. The interactive format also allows the viewers to get much more interested and start commenting, and that can direct the way we decide to take some of the projects. We quite often canvass opinion from our viewers about what they think about something.

ES: The fashion industry is a notoriously closed one, and SHOW is in the unique position of working from within the industry, but at the same time staying slightly on the periphery in terms of being somewhat more objective.

PM: Yes − and none of the people that populate the studio are real 'fashion people'. By that I mean that we're not people that are really led by fashion itself, we're just really interested in it, and we love the process of it. Fashion's currency is gossip and money, and it can be really crass and pretty depressing. But I think when you're on the outside looking in, it opens up many more possibilities. It's a much more nourishing place to be, mentally. In order to know what's interesting to somebody that isn't in the industry, you have to preserve that outsider perspective. Even if you do become an insider you've got to try and remember what it was that you thought was interesting about it before you were in it, so that you can focus the camera on that thing. Fashion's not very good at history, it's just good at seeing everything through the lens of the present, and what's hot this season. It's not really good at working out what would be fascinating about the structure of it, just because people are so busy.

Particularly over the last ten years, and especially over the last five, fashion's got more and more corporate. It's more sophisticated in monitoring its commercial success. Advertising and editorial have become closer, and there's not the same creative space that there once was − not even in the eighties − to innovate. It's unusual to turn open your process, because people are really focused: it's a very tight, fast and intense system. There are so many demands on the key players − there are fewer and fewer photographers, you'll notice at the moment, shooting the campaigns: it's Steven Meisel, Mert and Marcus, and Craig McDean. They are all very fine and accomplished image-makers, but it does point to the fact that the climate at the moment is very anxious, and advertisers really want to make sure that any risk that they take is rewarded. So it's a luxury to be able to indulge in a project where you're trying to throw open your creative ideas. The aesthetic of process, as it were, is becoming very fashionable. 'Behind-the-scenes at the shoot' – that's starting to pepper lots of fashion media. But a genuine commitment to it, and not just the look of it, is unusual – who has the time to do it?

ES: You've mentioned that many of the fashion magazines that are doing really well at the moment are very much engaged with tabloid culture, and quite proudly anti-academic. A lot of the content on SHOW is not what you'd think of as typical fashion editorial. It's very critical, it's very self-reflective, and it asks a lot of questions about fashion and representation.

PM: I guess that's reflective of who Nick and I are as people. Nick's a very clever man, and is very unfashiony, in a lot of ways – he came from a science background, he's very erudite and searching. It's probably no surprise that he chose an editor that was from a museum background, and had studied design history and museum history and had that kind of outlook. I hope it doesn't seem that we're too precious, although I guess that to some people I'm sure we are. We've never really had to toe the line to a market or a commercial paymaster. Hitherto, Nick Knight has paid entirely for SHOW, so it's followed our whims, and it is our natural inclination to have somebody say, 'Right, what is this?' That's what our content is: what is fashion? It's the shoot, it's a live broadcast, it's an interview, this is how it happens and it's no more magical than that on the level of production and describing and intention. But we also know that once it's on a printed page it means something else, and that's the level at which we can be fairly complex in terms of interpretation. We did something on Galliano and his tailoring process: when it came to having a downloadable garment, you got, in very basic terms, 'this is how he cuts, this is how his patterns look, this is how he drapes', but we also asked Caroline Evans to talk about the notion of spectacle in his work, and what happens once it's represented. That's a kind of natural current for me. Somebody who runs a magazine might say that that's all very well when you're running your own website, but when you've got pages to fill and you've got an advertising credit to fulfil, you can't have some whimsical, abstruse and academic slant on it. You're going to have to think about your bottom line, and who your reader is.

In a sense, the 1990s were all about the second wave of the style press, an entrepreneurial, brattish, swaggering bunch of kids taking over the publishing community. That was very much characterized by *SleazeNation*, *Dazed & Confused* and *Raygun*. If I were to follow that to its logical conclusion, SHOWstudio is kind of the third wave of the style press. It throws things back to being about production and intention, as much as they are about product and representation.

ES: SHOWstudio is more engaged with the idea of fashion as performance and process, and less concerned with the idea that 'fashion only exists in representation', which is the opinion of theorists like Ulrich Lehmann.

PM: That's like saying 'fashion is a photograph', which is a quote that Peter Saville uses a lot. It depends what he means – it's a great sound bite, isn't it? I think on one level fashion does exist at the level of representation, and the image is becoming more and more important. People are now able to consume fashion through fashion media and not actually get into contact with the garments themselves. But that's not to deny all sorts of other physical elements to it.

We're showing that the whole notion of fashion image-making can be, literally, a performance. For photographers, there had been a kind of bottoming-out of subject matter, and they have been very keen to put themselves in their own pictures recently. What we've been doing in terms of live broadcasts is giving people an opportunity to kind of stage-manage their own representation, and make their jobs into something that's entertaining for others – the whole culture of the set, which is fascinating. What we've been trying to do through motion and sound and inter-activity, albeit through virtual mechanisms, is to draw attention to the physicality of it, and to try and get away from the way that a lot of fashion websites represent fashion. Our idea was to defy the virtual quality of the internet, and that was the idea behind making it exist in a real space. Turning the webcam on the studio rooted it in a physical context, instead of it happening somewhere, sometime, with strangers, which is the kind of relationship that you tend to have with websites. It doesn't ever feel like the fashion content is very physical, it seems like they're made up of lots of images that have been passed on by press departments, which often they are. So projects like *Shelf Appeal* – which was really a basic front-of-book style magazine picture story, three or four hundred words about a very strange fashion object each week – try and address the objecthood of fashion. For me, that's extremely important.

ES: *More Beautiful Women* (June 2002 onwards) is one of my favourite projects on the site. Getting a professional model to stand still in front of the camera and do nothing for three minutes is an amazing way of thinking through ideas around physicality, agency, identity and performativity.

PM: *More Beautiful Women* comes out of a set of activities that Nick does: he always gets his models to do one of these films, and he gets them to kiss a piece of glass – he's got all these glasses in his archive somewhere. Peter Saville had drawn his attention to Andy Warhol's series *Beautiful Women*, which is women just doing screen tests, just staring at the camera. What it does, of course, is it draws attention to the space between the still and the film, and how uncomfortable a model is when she's undirected – how women, in order to deal with the lens, need to pose or to talk, or do something. Few of them are comfortable when completely undirected, although Kate Moss can zone out, and Gemma Ward's very good at it too. Others, especially the older models, cannot bear it, and need to pull a pose, and then pull back out of it and strike another one. It's totally fascinating, seeing what they're like as moving stills.

ES: Critical writing on fashion photography often tends to present the fashion photographer as an independent creative, and to gloss over or ignore the collaborative culture of the shoot, and the agency of the model.

PM: That can be true, but it rarely is. If you watch Kate Moss with a photographer, you realize how much of a collaboration it is, and that what is achieved is because of everybody else. People don't realize what a big part the stylist can play, or indeed the hairstylist, in directing the photographer. It can be a cast of thousands on a set, but the industry really does perpetuate the idea, especially because of its pay structure, that the photographer is the all-important factor. Over the past five years, people have started to realize there's been a kind of division of labour. Hair and makeup, set-builders, casting agents, those kind of people are all starting to become named, known quantities, and people are starting to realize what role they have.

ES: As well as showcasing the process and industry of fashion photography, SHOW opens up some really interesting lines of critical inquiry into fashion image-making.

PM: I came to SHOW from writing a PhD on fashion photography, which was never completed, so maybe in some ways I'm playing out a lot of my own academic interests when I can. And Nick has probably spent twenty years thinking about what the theoretical potential is – although maybe not in those terms. Before I started at SHOW, I was fascinated by the fact that it was starting to suggest potential for fashion media that would be different, that would be self-referential and explicit about what it was doing. What the multimedia platform, in tandem with what is achievable via the internet, makes possible is kind of breathing life into the still. Traditionally we've understood fashion by the definitive still, where you only see one angle of the garment. SHOW explores the idea that you can see 360 degrees, you can hear the sound of a garment, you can watch it move – that's how fashion was designed to behave. It's in spite of fashion photography rather than because of it that SHOWstudio is progressing.

PART III

Image and Identity

9 Stardom and Fashion: on the Representation of Female Movie Stars and Their Fashion(able) Image in Magazines and Advertising Campaigns

Bärbel Sill

A look at the history of fashion imagery reveals that fashion and stardom are very closely linked. Can fashion simply not live without its most valuable model, the movie star? Truth to tell, Hollywood's stars have always played an important role in fashion magazines as well as in the marketing of fashion and beauty-related products. These stars simply appeal to the masses, certainly as much as Hollywood films do. But no one has ever become a star just because he or she decided to: it's the public who makes the star. In other words, if you want to become a star, you also have to look like one, to seduce and convince the public of your 'star qualities'. As it turns out, star quality can be influenced by fashion and beauty – a fact which makes these two phenomena inseparable from stardom.

The star is an object of visual fascination, and so is the model. But not every model is a star. And not every supermodel with star attitude has necessarily the quality to be a movie star. Claudia Schiffer tried to be one – and failed. Cindy Crawford tried it – and failed too. Diane Heidkrüger also tried it – went to Hollywood, called herself Diane Kruger, did some blockbusters with stars such as Brad Pitt and Orlando Bloom, but became the model-turned-actress with starlet qualities, rather than a genuine movie star. But Cameron Diaz did it: she became one of the biggest stars in contemporary American cinema.

Even though every model does not have the qualities of a movie star, nearly every movie star, it seems, has the qualities of a model. A simple look at the

September 2005 issues of international fashion magazines shows how frequently movie stars appear as cover girls: Nicole Kidman can be admired on the cover of French *Vogue*, Renée Zellweger on the cover of German *Vogue*, Sarah Jessica Parker on the cover of American *Vogue*, Demi Moore on the cover of *Harper's Bazaar*, Jennifer Lopez on the cover of American *Elle*, Kate Hudson on the cover of German *Cosmopolitan*...and so on: the list seems almost endless.

Whereas models *are* models, movie stars *play* the model for fashion magazines. They participate in photo shoots, where they smile for the cover of a magazine or present the latest fashion trends. But they also appear in advertising campaigns and photographs illustrating their own personal look. Whether these are photographs from fashion photographers, paparazzi or any other photographer, movie stars *act* as models the moment they are photographed: everything stars wear seems to deserve the term 'fashion', from jogging pants and flip-flops to maternity clothes and designer gowns. Most models, in contrast, do not have that same effect. They present fashion, make fashion suggestions, rather than fashion statements (Fig. 13).

13. Frédéric Imbert, untitled fashion photograph.

The public identifies differently with movie stars than they do with models. For us, movie stars often function as important role models, affecting our collective consciousness. They can be the personification of everybody's dreams: perfect idols to admire, models to imitate, or simply everyday heroes. Fashion photography supports the identification process between the star and the public, in contributing to the creation of a *fashion image* for the star. In imitating it, the public virtually 'turns into' the star – at least fashion-wise. The fashion image, then, is a crucial aspect of the way the public identifies with the star – and so is fashion photography.

FASHION AND THE STAR SYSTEM:
AN HISTORICAL OVERVIEW

For the American star system and its functioning, the world of fashion and beauty has always been a crucial factor, one whose significance for the success of a star should not be underestimated. Movies and fashion photographs allow the public to discover the latest fashion, haircut and makeup trends, modelled by their favourite stars.

Clothes-horses like Gloria Swanson or Marlene Dietrich knew how to present themselves to their advantage in order to look glamorous, and in doing so they set the standards for future movie stars. During the classical Hollywood era, every studio had its own wardrobe department and costume designer, such as Adrian or Travis Banton.[1] These top talents knew how a movie star had to look: stylish, extravagantly chic, almost unattainably beautiful, and they succeeded in getting the public to associate stardom with style, glamour and divinity (Fig. 14).

Instead of creating a general look that fitted every star, they created individual trademark looks: this way, Joan Crawford became famous for her shoulder pads, whereas Marlene Dietrich seduced men and women equally with her androgynous style. Fashion photographs made possible the distribution of movie stars and their knowledge of fashion on an extra-cinematographic level. At that time, movie stars already appeared not only on the big screen, but also in advertising campaigns and in both fan and fashion magazines. In the June 1939 issue of *Photoplay*, Glenn Walters presents different Hollywood stars wearing the latest 'fashion musts': Jane Wyman shows herself in a swimsuit,

Claudette Colbert wears an evening gown in one picture and a suit in another, Bette Davis presents a shirt with a long skirt, and Lana Turner a weekend wardrobe (Walters 1939: 45–54). In advertising campaigns, Lucille Ball or Lana Turner could be admired as models for Woodbury Powder, and Marlene Dietrich was the face of Woodbury's Cold Cream. Rita Hayworth was the perfect model for Pan-Cake Make-Up by Max Factor (Heimann 2001).

In fashion photography, Hollywood found an important platform for producing stars with a trademark look or signature style, and for creating fashion and beauty icons with which the public was longing to identify. Fashion photography influenced the reception of cinema fashion by the public, in that it presented the star as a fashion reference – a divine creature from the screen worth admiring for her style. As Anne Hollander (1974: 68ff) remarks, particularly in the 1930s and 1940s there was a 'new nationwide desire to look like a movie star'. But when the classic star system reached a crisis at the end of the 1950s, the production system of trademark looks for stars was disrupted – and movie-star style changed.

14. Marlene Dietrich (late 1930s).

With the emergence of the 'straight from the rack look' (LaVine 1980: 137), and as a result of changes in the film industry during the 1960s and 1970s (such as the restructuring of the industry, an increase in the number of televisions and VCRs in private households, and a new generation of spectators), movie stars no longer saw their style either produced or commercialized with the same methodic character. As Patty Fox (2000: 77) puts it, 'the stars of the 1970s would force Oscar to get hip. Self-expression appeared to be every major celebrity's goal as they paraded the stage. No longer would the classic mold of movie star work...Stars were making a statement. Their own.'

Consequently, the influence of their personal fashion and beauty system on the public changed, and the movie star lost his or her reputation as a fashion reference. Soon enough, someone else would function as such: with Faye Dunaway's appearance in *Bonnie & Clyde* in 1967 and Diane Keaton's in *Annie Hall* in 1977, a transfer was happening, from actress-based to character-based influences on popular female fashion. As Epstein (2000: 467) notes, no longer would the on- and off-screen look of a star influence film-inspired fashions, but the look of a film character.

Throughout the 1960s and 1970s, movie stars were not represented in fashion photography in the way that they were throughout the classic Hollywood era. With the star system finding itself in crisis, the distribution of the movie star through magazines and advertising campaigns diminished. Fashion photography started to concentrate more on models than on stars.

Following the New Hollywood era[2] in the 1980s, the star system experienced a renaissance with the emergence of a new movie-star type to worship: the action hero. Although the movie industry and the public were giving most of their attention to Arnold Schwarzenegger, Sylvester Stallone and Bruce Willis, the fashion business wasn't – not even to female movie stars. It was the female model who got all its attention. And the situation for female movie stars would get worse: in the late 1980s, the supermodel appeared in magazines and advertising campaigns as the new female celebrity for the masses. Supermodels like Cindy Crawford, Linda Evangelista and Christy Turlington began to replace the movie star as the ultimate ideal of fashion and beauty. They became the new stars the public worshipped: 'They got the press, the glamour, the cachet, the boyfriend, the exposure, the lifestyle and, in some cases, the money that movie stars are used to' (Ginsberg and Lockwood 1996: 56).

But the supermodel would ultimately not be able to replace either the movie star's popularity or his or her influence on the public. During the early 1990s, the movie star celebrated a comeback as a fashion and beauty reference, and since then the female movie star has retained that role. A comparison between different cover pictures and fashion shoots in American *Vogue* from 1989 (the beginning of the supermodel era), 1993 (when the supermodel was at the height of her success) and 2002 (when the movie star reigns again on the covers of *Vogue*) illustrates this.

After 1995, the female movie star also re-emerged as the queen of fashion and beauty in advertising campaigns – and the male movie star followed. According to Ginsberg and Lockwood (1996: 56), 'suddenly dozens of actors and actresses, from ingénues to Oscar nominees, are angling for and appearing in major fashion and beauty ad campaigns, in print and television'. At the time of writing, this development shows no signs of slowing down: more than ever, beautiful movie stars try to seduce the public, to transform them into faithful disciples of a particular fashion or beauty brand. Julianne Moore, Melanie Griffith and Halle Berry are the 'Revlon Girls', Gwyneth Paltrow did Christian Dior first, now she does Estée Lauder, Winona Ryder still plays the sweet kleptomaniac for Marc Jacobs, Liv Tyler, taking her inspiration from Audrey Hepburn, is the 'very irresistible Givenchy girl', Penélope Cruz does Ralph Lauren, *Sex and the City* star Sarah Jessica Parker does Garnier, Quentin Tarantino's muse Uma Thurman did Lancôme first, before she became one of *the* Louis Vuitton faces – after Jennifer Lopez, Christina Ricci or Scarlett Johansson (who herself did Calvin Klein and then L'Oréal), Demi Moore and Halle Berry are the latest 'Versace ladies'... and this is only the beginning of a very long list.

Contemporary magazines and advertising campaigns attest to the amount of media coverage that is again given to star style since the early years of this century. Nowadays, however, it is not so much the on-screen look that seems to interest the public most, but the star's off-screen look. Gwyneth Paltrow is one example; another is fashion icon Cameron Diaz, who not only has a signature look but a personalized style:

> 'When it comes to what she [Cameron] wears, she's constantly creating,' Lucy Liu, her *Charlie's Angels* costar says. 'For Cameron, it's an art form, and it's all about transformation and change – like turning a skirt into a tube top. Something could cost $10 or $10,000 – either way, if she's

comfortable in it, she makes it work. She defines her own fashion, and people follow it.' (Green 2003: 226)

Consequently, if we speak of an evolution, during the 1960s and 1970s, from actress-based to character-based influence on popular female fashion, we can also speak of a transfer from character-based to off-screen-image-based influences on female fashion during what could be called the era of the 'neo-star system'. In the course of that time, the American star system experienced a renaissance, which ultimately redefined the function of movie stars and models in fashion as well as in fashion photography.

THE ERA OF THE 'NEO-STAR SYSTEM'

These days, movie stars seem to be the magazines' and advertising campaigns' favourite subject. The large number of movie stars on the cover of many international magazines, from *Glamour* to *Vogue*, suggests that stars have a unique quality. According to fashion designer Muccia Prada,

> stars do bring something to fashion photography that models don't: the memory the audience has of them from the big – or little – screen. 'Actors bring so much, they add a narrative from their collective movie images … They add character to the clothes, and an intensity.' (Ginsberg and Lockwood 1996: 58)

In other words, if a movie star is involved in fashion photography, the fashion photograph profits from the multi-dimensional character of the star's persona. In addition, movie stars seem more 'credible' than models. It is easier for the spectator or the reader to recognize him- or herself in the *star* than in the model.

'They [fashion companies] all want to use actors,' says Olga Liriano, head of the celebrity division at Ford Models. 'Photographers find it more interesting. Supermodels are waning and they're spent. Photographers feel actors can give more.' But whether or not that's actually true, it seems that actresses are more believable than supermodels, who, as Liriano puts it, are

> so skinny and almost flawless. Even with a Demi Moore people can relate to her. She's been so open about how she got in shape. [Actresses have] done interviews about their regimes. When you hear Kate Moss say, 'I eat hamburgers,' people say, 'Sure.' (Ginsberg and Lockwood 1996: 59)

A fashion model usually doesn't profit from a relationship of identification relation with the public. A model is admired for his or her beauty; people might want to *look* like a model, but they don't necessarily want to *be* this or that model. A fashion model's function is by definition to present clothes. Most models do not have a particular style; they wear whatever they are told to. Some top models, however, may develop a distinctive personal fashion and/or beauty style. Kate Moss, with her signature look, illustrates this aspect. Still, models with a particular fashion persona are rare, since they appear in fashion photography in too many different clothes for such a persona to develop. As for their public persona, only top models seem to have one.

A star, on the contrary, is a phenomenon that is mostly based on his or her public persona or image. Therefore, when a star appears in fashion photographs, not only are his or her star qualities taken into consideration, but also his or her style. Clothes and the way a star dresses can show to advantage a star's persona. As a consequence, fashion photography influences the star's public image. At the same time, it has the power to enhance the star's signature style.

The fashion photograph of a movie star, then, is more complex than that of a model. In part, this is because the fashion photograph must always respect the continuity within the star's image or persona (though, as we will see below, there is also room for a certain amount of heterogeneity). Continuity represents a central aspect in the conception of a star image. A persona based on continuity guides the expectations of the public, as Faulstich et al. (1997: 13) suggest. It supports the identification process of the public with the star, and therefore can enhance the latter's stardom. Continuity refers not only to fashion photographs of a star presenting the latest designer clothes, but also to photos of the star's 'off-screen fashion look'. Even though items of this 'off-screen fashion look' often consist of clothing that is lent by designers for special occasions, people tend to attribute it to the star's personal fashion system (discussed below). Consequently, on and off screen, fashion statements made by movie stars in fashion photography often show a high level of continuity: Hollywood star Scarlett Johansson, for example, can often be seen in a 'new diva' look with Marilyn Monroe appeal.

Models, in contrast, generally show no continuity at all in fashion photography (the example of the supermodel is the exception), as they simply do their job: to present the latest fashion. For models, modelling means 'working'. As for stars, modelling means 'one way of displaying his or her star qualities, nourishing his or her star persona as well as the public's appetite for the star'. Models are 'trendsetters', whereas movie stars confirm a fashion trend, making it official. Or, to put it differently: whereas in fashion pictures involving a model the clothes are the star, the star in fashion pictures involving a star is…the star herself.

THE FASHION IMAGE

A star's fashion image is the combination of all elements defining a star's personal look: from clothes and accessories to makeup and hairstyle. This look functions as a vital part of his or her star persona or *star image.*

For the movie star, the conception of a fashion and beauty image represents a system, in that the systematic choice of certain pieces of clothing or a particular makeup and hairstyle allows the star to create a personal style. With this personal style, the star has a means to identify him- or herself as such, and to highlight his or her individuality. Hollywood star Catherine Zeta-Jones's fashion image is characterized by elements such as long, lavish hair, cat-eye makeup, red lipstick and tight feminine dresses, often with deep necklines. Combining the qualities of hair, clothing and makeup with elements of her off-screen personality, Zeta-Jones's star persona is that of a sensual, seductive and very feminine woman.

By definition, all movie stars have a fashion image – although some are more distinct than others. It is an important part of the star's persona: it gives it attitude, makes it individual, defines it from the point of view of dress. Both images are inextricably linked to one another: together, they define the movie star as such. Fashion photography, then, is an important means not only to conceive, reflect or develop the star's fashion image, but also to represent the connection between his or her fashion image and his or her star persona – and hence to confirm his or her star status.

THE FASHION PHOTOGRAPH

As a consequence, the fashion photograph can be considered as a vital part of the star's overall fashion image, and thus of his or her star persona. As an object of great visual power, the fashion photograph supports the creation of the star's personal fashion system, in that it displays the look of a star, identifying at the same time the different items that characterize his or her look. In other words, a personal fashion system underlies every star's fashion image as well as his or her star persona.

To give an example: Angelina Jolie's personal fashion system consists primarily of basic single-coloured items with simple cuts and a glamorous look. Her signature style then can best be described as a 'minimalist-but-glamorous style' that she expresses in different ways and with different elements: at the 2004 Academy Awards, for example, she wore a long white satin gown with expensive jewellery, for her visit to the Actors Studio in April 2005 she was dressed in a black blouse and blue jeans, which she combined with a watch and a Louis Vuitton bag (Internet Movie Database, 2006). As for her appearance on the July 2005 cover of *W* next to Brad Pitt, she looks like a real Hollywood diva in a simple white vintage swimsuit, combined with an extra-large cream-coloured cape and Cartier earrings.

Every item a star wears in a fashion photograph becomes an element of his or her fashion image. Thus the relationship between stardom and fashion is not just a matter of a designer giving a star some clothes to wear; it's about the way that the star, as opposed to the model, is able to create a signature look, a fashion image. As a consequence, fashion allows the star to conceive and individualize his or her star image. 'Yes, designers get exposure – but actors get a glamorous image and free clothes. We enhance their image. It's a fair exchange,' says Pamela Barish, who dresses many Hollywood stars (Ginsberg and Lockwood 1996: 58). At the same time, stars 'personalize' the clothes they are wearing in transferring elements of their star image to the clothes. Thus they have a capacity of advertising the clothes, which models on their own may not. Acting is fundamentally different to modelling, in that the model is unable to give the clothes they are wearing the same 'character' as a star does.

When a fashion photograph appears in the media, the star's wardrobe gets media coverage. At the same time, it is accessible to the masses – a basic necessity for the construction and existence of stardom. Fashion photography is therefore an important means for the marketing of movie stars through fashion – and vice versa. Seen through the star's image, clothes are no longer the simple creation of a particular designer, but acquire additional meaning depending on the star presenting them.

For example, Gwyneth Paltrow appears regularly on the covers and pages of magazines, wearing the latest designer clothes from Calvin Klein, Marc Jacobs, Versace to Givenchy – and many others. The March 2002 issue of American *Vogue*, entitled 'Gwyneth, the Power of a Fashion Icon', and the June 2004 issue of *W*, which shows the Hollywood star pregnant, present Paltrow not only as a 'movie star' but as a fashion icon and a role model: the incarnation of the modern Hollywood beauty. Paltrow knows about the effect a well-chosen wardrobe has on her fashion image and, as a consequence, on her star image. Her status as an icon depends not only on the beautiful garments which she is wearing, adapted to her personal fashion system, but also on the fashion pictures that capture every aspect of it. This, in turn, has an effect on the public's perception of the clothes themselves:

> At a certain level, Gwyneth sells clothes like no other actress. To the fashion industry she is a gold mine. 'We have had countless times when Gwyneth has been photographed in things that we may or may not carry in our store, and women come in seeking exactly what it is she is wearing. They are desperately seeking Gwyneth. If she is wearing a particular item, then women want it.' (Sykes 2002: 585)

Movie stars provoke a different way of understanding and thinking about fashion. When regular models present clothes, the public generally reacts to the clothes, whereas when movie stars present clothes, the public generally responds to *the star in the clothes*. In other words, stars can revaluate or devalue fashion, depending on their fashion image and how this interacts with the clothes that they wear.

Participating in fashion shoots is something stars do not only to get media coverage but also to create both continuity and heterogeneity within their image. A varied image is crucial to the star's popularity: by expressing a certain diversity within their fashion image, the star's image is less predictable. Hence it fascinates the public even more, necessarily enhancing the star's bankability.

The fashion photographs of Oscar-winner Hilary Swank in the February 2004 issue of German *Vogue* (Knauf and Albrecht 2004: 202–7) illustrate this.

On the one hand, her style suggests the perfect continuity: Swank wears simple-coloured items, primarily dresses or tops with a deep neckline, with clearly defined cuts: no fancy bits, nothing distracting – a purely minimalist wardrobe. At the same time, her style also suggests heterogeneity: in one picture, Swank wears a jacket on top of a skirt; in another, she can be seen in a dress made out of linen tweed, a material which makes the dress more 'complex' than the other dresses, which are simply black or red, or – as on the cover – purple. But still continuity exists within these items, as they are minimalist ('simple cut') and belong to the same category ('dress') or are simple-coloured ('light colour').

Since fashion photography influences the star's fashion and star image, not every movie star wants to be photographed by any photographer: a bad picture could mean bad publicity. Fashion photographers like Patrick Demarchelier or Mario Testino are just two of the 'lucky ones' to be known to work regularly with stars in front of their camera, from Gwyneth Paltrow to Nicole Kidman. Working with movie stars turns these photographers into so-called 'star photographers'. Thus a relationship of equals develops, one between stars from different areas – a relationship regular models and star photographers do not necessarily share.

Out of the mutual relationship between a star and his or her stardom on the one hand and fashion on the other, a certain interdependence results, which fashion photography not only captures but also makes use of. But what influences the consumer more: the actual clothes? The fashion photograph? The star? Or simply each one of these in their own way?

CONSUMING STARDOM AND FASHION

The spell of movie stars is as powerful as the spell of fashion, and both have the capacity of seducing the masses. When stardom and fashion come together in fashion photography, they form a triangle of elements – star, fashion, fashion photograph – that combine powerfully to seduce the consumer. At the same time, they all have something in common: the clothes, the fashion photograph and the star are *all* objects of consumption. Clothes and fashion magazines, however, are concrete objects of consumption, whereas the star has always been and still is an abstract concept intended for the public's consumption. It is that consumption that ultimately allows the star to exist.

The star system pushes the public to consume not only the star, but also his or her signature style, as presented in film, magazine and advertising. The creation and dissemination of a signature style is a way of marketing both the star and the fashion product. In view of this, a particular meaning is given to fashion photography. It is more than just a picture of a movie star in beautiful clothes: the fashion photograph allows the star's persona (which is itself a combination of the on- and off-screen persona) to be displayed in a fashionable way, giving it media coverage through magazines and advertising campaigns. Fashion photography supports a systematic presence of the movie star and his or her signature style in the media. To the movie star, a fashion photograph then represents an important means of building, reinforcing and maintaining his or her stardom. For the designer, it means effective advertising: 'having the right star wear your clothes at a high-profile event is worth tens of millions of dollars in advertising' (Chun 1997: 56). Fashion, it seems, cannot live without the movie star as its most valuable model. In the 1930s, fashion photography became a key element of the star system – and the fashion photograph the 'ambassador' of star fashion. The present shows that in the end, after years of 'star development' and a 'star crisis' in the 1960s and 1970s, the movie star's attraction is very powerful again, and the star system again at the height of its efficiency. In order to be efficient, the system has used and still uses different media platforms in order to function. One of these platforms certainly remains fashion photography.

NOTES ON CHAPTER 9

1   Gilbert Adrian, known as 'Adrian', worked for over ten years at MGM, dressing stars such as Greta Garbo and Joan Crawford. As for Travis Banton, he was a head designer at Paramount first, and may be best remembered for Marlene Dietrich's costumes.

2   New Hollywood refers to the time between roughly 1967 and 1980 when a new generation of young filmmakers came to prominence in America, changing not only the way Hollywood movies were produced and marketed, but also the kinds of films that were made. It is also called 'post-classical Hollywood'.

WORKS CITED

Chun, R. (1997) 'The Hollywood Style Connection', *Mirabella*, March–April: 56–60

Epstein, Rebecca L. (2000) 'Sharon Stone in a Gap Turtleneck', in David Desser and Garth S. Jowett (eds) *Hollywood Goes Shopping* (Minneapolis and London: University of Minnesota Press)

Faulstich, W., H. Korte, S. Lowry and R. Strobel (1997) '"Kontinuität" – zur Imagefundierung des Film- und Fernsehstars', in Werner Faulstich and Helmut Korte (eds) *Der Star: Geschichte-Rezeption-Bedeutung* (Munich: Wilhelm Fink Verlag)

Fox, P. (2000) *Star Style at the Academy Awards: A Century of Glamour* (Santa Monica: Angel City Press)

Ginsberg, M. and L. Lockwood (1996) 'You Oughta Be in Pictures', *W*, July: 56–59

Green, A. (2003) 'Shooting Star', *Vogue*, May: 214–19

Heimann, J. (2001) *All American Ads of the 40s* (Cologne: Taschen)

Hollander, A. (1974) 'Movie Clothes: More Real Than Life', *New York Times Magazine*, December: 68ff

Knauf, B. and N. Albrecht (2004) 'Der Lieblings-Liebling', *Vogue* (Germany), February: 202–9

LaVine, W.R. (1980) *In a Glamorous Fashion: The Fabulous Years of Hollywood Costume Design* (New York: Charles Scribner's Sons)

Sykes, P. (2002) 'Gwyneth: The Power of a Fashion Icon', *Vogue*, March: 504ff

Walters, G. (1939) 'Photoplay Fashions', *Photoplay*, June: 45–54

10 Developing Images: Race, Language and Perception in Fashion-model Casting

Stephanie Neda Sadre-Orafai

He doesn't look like a David. Maybe he has a Chinese name we could use...You should start telling people that I'm Brazilian...He should get a lot of work especially with that whole Nureyev thing going on in fashion right now...She's very *Black Hair* magazine, not exactly what we do here...So we had a meeting and we're going to start doing that whole 'multicultural' thing...I love her. She's like 90 percent chic and 10 percent trashy. Very European...

Black Hair magazine. Brazilian. Trashy chic. The majority of conversations in modelling agencies revolve around types. From casting breakdowns to the direction of development for new models, types form the grammar of the modelling industry. Despite the focus on visual aesthetics and performances, modelling depends on linguistic elaborations and classifications.[1] Racial, national and regional types are a central way of narrating a model's persona and image. Crafted from more than a model's heritable or visible features, these descriptions exploit models' ambiguous features and selective biographical details, resulting in a highly effective shorthand that frames what the viewer sees, although never in a definitive way.

The purpose of this essay is to explore the processes by which models become intelligible as specific types, and to uncover the unique position of racial, national and regional classifications. I argue that racial, national and regional types are particularly powerful in their affective potential and flexibility as framing devices capable of shaping how models' images – in the dual sense of their personas as well as actual photographs – are read. Through an examination of the casting process, I find that seemingly rigid categories of race and national origin, while assumed to be essential, are nonetheless malleable features of models, attributed to them in different ways at different times by different industry professionals. In addition to this kind of labelling, naming is another important part of the casting process and can performatively transform how models' images are read. Understandings of these images are co-constructed, guided by visual and linguistic cues to both industry-specific and broader culturally based stereotypes, and occur through social interaction. While casting is purportedly a solely visual practice, I find that language heavily shapes its outcomes. I argue that attention to the linguistic dimensions of the processes of producing models' images reveals similarities to racial passing, which likewise centres on the conscious management of perception. That is, both passing and the production of models' images exploit the trust inherent in everyday social interactions while also intensifying its risks. Likewise, as in social interactions, the assessment of a model's persona is a central technique used within the casting process. I foreground the tension between the visual and linguistic as two distinct yet inseparable channels in these practices, each of which has varying tolerances for ambiguity and dissimulation.

Model casting provides a critical site through which to explore the interrelationship of language and vision, especially as it relates to racial classification. A deliberate, time- and money-intensive task, the casting process depends on the ability to convey verbally and visually the concept of a desired image or set of images and then to describe and select corresponding characteristics in a model. There are three primary relationships in the casting process: client–agent, agent–model and model–client. Attention to the relationships and activities that go into the production of fashion imagery allows for a practice-based analysis of fashion photography that goes beyond its public and visible features, yielding a clearer picture of how exactly the everyday work of fashion is accomplished.

For the purposes of this essay, I use the following definitions: *Models* are the human subjects of fashion photography. *Agents*, or bookers, represent models, get work for them, and in return take a percentage of their earnings. *Clients* include a range of people who use a model's services, whether or not they directly pay for it, potentially including photographers, magazine editors, stylists, designers, catalogue houses, advertising agencies, hair and makeup artists, show event producers, art buyers and casting directors. This breakdown centralizes the modelling agency as a key site for understanding the casting process. Neither directly visible nor credited in published work, modelling agents are the least identifiable participants within fashion photography. As such, this essay foregrounds agents so as to demystify their involvement in the production of fashion photography.

My analysis is based on 17 months of combined fieldwork and employment at a boutique fashion modelling agency in New York. During my time at the agency I had the opportunity both to observe and participate in the casting process, primarily through marketing and development. Marketing takes place within the client–agent relationship and is the solicitation of work for models from clients by agents. It includes responding to clients' casting calls, arranging appointments for models with clients, sending model composite cards (cards with models' images and statistics that function like a graphic business card or resumé) to clients, and making cold-call inquiries to clients.

Development primarily occurs between agents and models, and is the direction of the image of new models. It can include the supervision of weight loss or gain, making changes in models' hair and clothing styles, documenting changes with Polaroid images, and scheduling practice or test photo shoots to get models comfortable in front of the camera, and to acquire images for a portfolio and composite card. Development also includes honing a set of linguistic frames to position models in the most lucrative way. This process often proceeds through trial and error, with feedback from clients incorporated into the eventual marketing strategies used to gain work for models.

I begin with a theoretical overview of passing, its similarities with the casting process, and the affective dimensions of each. I then explore these features in an example of a new model in development. I discuss the ways in which language, especially racial, national and regional terms, shapes how models' images are perceived and the role of models, agents and clients in this process. I end with a discussion of why approaching fashion photography from a linguistic perspective gets closer to the circumstances of its actual, everyday production and may be instructive not only for understanding how fashion photographs are produced, but also how our broader conceptions of race and nationality are constructed.

PASSING AND THE AFFECTIVE DIMENSIONS OF THE CASTING PROCESS

Requiring an 'intimate understanding of the mechanism by which society claims to discern difference' (Moriel 2005: 25), passing is an ideal metaphor for the process of managing and producing a model's image. Just as an individual 'who passes will have to be alive to aspects of the social situation which others treat as uncalculated and unattended' (Goffman 1963: 88), so too must models, agents and clients be highly attuned to the ways in which the tiniest details of a model's behaviour and appearance may be interpreted. Their heightened awareness of the routinely observed but infrequently consciously monitored occurs at the level of embodied performance for the model: naming and labelling by the agent during marketing and development, and through a series of evidentiary forms of evaluation used by clients in the casting process.

Like photographs, which function as both an index and distortion of reality (Sontag 1977: 5), models are a contradictory medium. They must simultaneously exhibit an infinite mutability while being faithfully transparent: constantly transforming, constantly themselves. As incongruous as this may seem, this same type of duality can be found in broader conceptions of Western personhood. A stable inner self shrouded by a dynamic surface is well within Western logic's division of inner and outer, surface and interior, mind and body etc. (Besnier 1990: 420). Because the sense of an essential self requires a correspondence between an individual's appearance and actions and how one thinks of oneself, difficulty arises when the seemingly immutable self is subject to dissimulation or transformation (Taylor 2005: 748).

Indeed, in the US the spectre of self-transformation exists both as national fantasy and anxiety. While on the one hand self-transformation is central in meritocratic ideologies of racial uplift, assimilation, religious conversion, class mobility and up-by-the-bootstraps narratives of self-making, it is also keyed as dangerous in its non-socially sanctioned forms of racial and class passing, criminal deception and other ruptures of often unspeakable or disavowed social hierarchies. Relying on 'external verification through the myth of transparency' (Jackson 2005: 68), the idea of a singular, authentic self is firmly anchored within essentialist ideologies, most notably commonly held ideologies of racial difference. Motivated by an urge to reconcile the outer with the inner, attention to appearances relies on a particular kind of trust of vision. Just as reality itself is socially constructed, perception too is a socially, culturally and historically distributed thing (Sacks 1984: 421–42). That appearances should be trusted or approached sceptically, that they should reveal inner motivations or essential identities, are all specific to a particular sociocultural and historical perspective, one in which passing as a phenomenon is possible (Besnier 1990: 430) and racial and other identities are perceived both visually and affectively.

While the possibility of passing generates anxiety about the reliability of surface appearances and contributes to the creation of elaborate mythologies and litmus tests for measuring authentic relationships between inner and outer, it is only possible through social interaction, which itself occurs largely as affective embodied events based on trust rather than proof. As such, individuals use conditional and subjunctive management styles to cope with the uncertainties of social interaction to gain what Giddens calls 'ontological security' or the 'shared – unproven and unprovable – framework of reality' (1991: 36). This takes the form of 'if-can tests' (West and Zimmerman 1987: 133), wherein appearances are taken at face value unless there is specific evidence to doubt it, or through a model of sincerity (Jackson 2005) in which the utterly unknowable subjective qualities of individuals are bracketed and taken on faith.

For individuals passing, however, these processes become conscious management issues, as they do for individuals with reasons to doubt the sincerity of the social interaction. This is similar to the casting process in that casting is all about the management of perception. With clients ultimately interested in controlling the perceptions of their eventual consumers, agents working to influence clients' perceptions of models' images, and models themselves materializing these images through their embodied labour, casting is a series of carefully and consciously managed social interactions intended to produce desired affective responses.

In her study of the New York modelling industry, Wissinger characterizes the model–agent relationship as creating pathways for affective labour, which is 'always already communicative and collaborative…[and which] cannot take place outside of the networks within which affect is made productive' (2004: 107). By referring to modelling as affective labour, Wissinger identifies two points at which affect, or the embodied and sensorial dimensions of experience, is modulated and made productive. In the first instance, the model as embodied agent executes various appearances, expressions and emotions. When captured in specific media and circulated, these images then act on and elicit affective responses from their viewers (Wissinger 2004: 23). While she rightly notes the collaborative nature of models' work and its reliance on the larger fashion system for its coherence and efficacy, Wissinger is less concerned with the ways in which seemingly intractable but no less affectively productive attributes – such as race and national origin – are also modulated by both agent and model (as well as clients) to great effect. Indeed, I would argue that national descriptors and racially inflected colour terms are often used as *the* terms that anchor a model's X-factor, or affective potential. In the following example of a new model in development I explore how this process can play out.

'AFRICAN GIRLS ARE WORKING'

As discussed in the overview, development is a learning experience for both agents and models, and often results in unexpected consequences. Early in my fieldwork at a New York boutique modelling agency, I overheard a debate between the head booker and a new black model named Laura as they finalized the details of her first composite card. After several months of development Laura wanted to change her name. She felt that her own name was too American and that she would get a better response if it sounded more exotic. Specifically, she wanted to take an Ethiopian name. The head booker was hesitant about changing the model's name after several months of marketing, and introducing her under her own name. He was particularly nervous about attempting to pass her off as Ethiopian. While Laura easily could have been Ethiopian – indeed, people had already been misrecognizing her as such – she was born in the US of Caribbean heritage.

Laura persisted, claiming that all of the working black models were from Africa and that the name change was vital for her career. Less than a month earlier, Ethiopian model Liya Kebede had signed a $3 million contract with Esteé Lauder, becoming the first black spokesmodel in the company's more than 57 year history (Trebay 2003: C16). This event brought into focus the dearth of work available for black models, as well as the popularity of 'African' models. Despite Kebede's differences from other African models (e.g. her lighter skin tone compared to Sudanese model Alek Wek's dark colouring), their success contributed to hers, and hers reflected back on them. Model scouts began looking for 'African' models in an attempt to profit from this once-again-popular type.

The agency where I was working was also looking for 'African' models; the head booker, however, was interested in a far darker-skinned model than Kebede. For him, transforming Laura, who was neither African nor dark-skinned, into an 'African' model did not make sense. Laura offered to affect an accent or not to speak at all if it would help. He asked her what she would do if she met with an Ethiopian client. What if they spoke to her in a language she did not understand or asked details about culture or geography that she did not know? He argued that the potential to damage the agency and her own reputation and credibility was too great. He was willing, however, to work with her middle name, Sefaye, which sounded to him vaguely French. Created by her mother, the name could not be traced to a single ethno-cultural source. After working out a respelling, complete with a hyphen and accent mark, they agreed to try the name out first on the website to see clients' response before printing it on the composite cards and marketing her under it.

Client response, however, can be highly unpredictable. The new name occasioned a call from a bookings editor at a national teen magazine. Desperate to find a 'brown-skinned Bollywood' girl for an India-inspired shoot, the editor called to ask about the new girl on the agency's website. Was Se-fé South Asian? The editor could not tell from the name or the images. Rather than being cued to Ethiopia or even Africa, the client's need motivated a different reading. In discussion with the client, I suggested Se-fé's Caribbean heritage as a *possible* source for the South Asian associations of her image and name. This suggestion reinforced what the client needed to see in Se-fé. While the client was initially unsure about Se-fé's suitability for the shoot, my explanation quickly secured the booking.

FRAMING IMAGES WITH LANGUAGE

This example demonstrates the power of linguistic framing in shaping what clients and agents see both in models and their images. It also displays the unstable and co-constructed nature of model development, and the ways in which the disclosure of information about a model is both guarded and staged. While clients tolerate visual ambiguity within the casting process, they will often ask questions about a model's 'real' or 'actual' identity. These types of questions range from the circuitous – 'Where is the model from?', 'What is his or her background?' – to the blunt – 'What *is* he or she?' This suggests that questions of authenticity are vital to the casting process, and that casting may be understood as an evidentiary process concerned with the relationship between outward signs and inner states, and not simply a purely aesthetic or commercial process preoccupied solely with appearances and marketability.

Casting is, after all, about potential and prediction. Will the model chosen be able to collaborate with the other producers – photographers, hair and makeup artists, set designers etc. – to create the desired image? Will the image have the intended effect on its viewers? While it may seem that a model's contribution is solely tied to his or her physical appearance, it is important not to forget that modelling is a performance that draws on skill and experience. This performance, however, is consistently naturalized as a model just being him or herself,[2] wherein 'no matter what the look, if the control of that look is visible, it becomes less attractive, and therefore less valuable' (Wissinger 2004: 213). As such, who the model *is* becomes extremely important. The achievement of a naturalized persona that reads authentically to clients is essential.

Nevertheless, the model's appearance remains an important channel of communication. Visual representations of models – how they appear in person or on film – secure the necessary ambiguity required for the possibility of recognizing the model as a range of types. Indeed, as suggested above, the status of the visual in its broadest sense is itself ambiguous. On the one hand, the visual claims a kind of evidentiary status that suggests a faithfulness to reality and inner states. This is especially evident in the commonplace industry practice of taking Polaroids – which industry professionals claim to be the least forgiving film format – as an immediate reference of what the model 'really looks like'. Simultaneously, however, prevailing industry notions about the transformative and occlusive power of the camera – that is the use of a range of film formats and techniques to create fantastic and non-indexical images – contribute to a distrust of what is seen.

Linguistic framing exploits this ambiguity and the vacillation between trust and distrust of the visual. Framing is needed to instil confidence in what clients see or think that they see, as well as to build consensus between them, grounding the ambiguity of the model's visual identity and assuaging the anxiety that this can generate, as in the case of Laura/Se-fé. This process is mediated by the agent through his or her relationships with both models and clients. In all of this the agent demands full disclosure from the model before generating ambiguous associations through national terms. Conversely, both relationships involving the client are structured around concealment and slow reveals.

In their deployment, racialized colour and national terms not only frame what people see in pictures, but also add wider associations to the overall mood or feeling of an image. National types are used as shorthand primarily for hair colour and type, general facial features and body shape, and skin tone (e.g. German girls are big, Brazilian girls have more body, etc.). Incredibly pithy, national modifiers also make links to other working models that share this national origin. Thus, as a Brazilian model, Giselle is invoked each time another model is described as Brazilian, whether or not they resemble one another. As discussed in the example of African models, contradictory features such as dark and fair skin can be incorporated into a single national or regional term. Using national terms, then, not only saves time communicating a model's look or feel, or affective potential, but also attaches a kind of surplus value. That is, new models described using these terms benefit from the association with more successful models marketed as or known through similar types. Additionally, however, alternative images and ideas are smuggled into these descriptions. National reputations for certain sexual proclivities, attitudes and behaviours abound as much in the modelling world as in everyday conversations. Added to this are broader non-industry-specific culturally based stereotypes. All of these factors weigh on a client's understanding of an agent's terse description of a model as 'X', further solidifying expectations of those models and used as a criteria to judge and 'out' models perceived as inauthentic.

Early in the model's career, agents use these different kinds of terms to make the model's body and features intelligible. That is, agents construct different personas for the model, each of which is easily recognizable to clients as a particular type. Once a model has become successful (for example by gaining high-profile editorial or runway work, securing lucrative, highly visible contracts, etc.), he or she transcends national or ethnic categories and clients begin to ask for him or her by name. Even in these situations, however, racial and national categories remain important, as shown in the case of Kebede and Wek. When a model becomes successful, the categories of identification become public and uncontrollable by the agent, who had, up to that point, been relying on visual ambiguity and complete disclosure from the model to position him or her in multiple ways for different kinds of jobs. Celebrity forfeits this guarded knowledge. This solidification of identity radiates out, affecting other models still under development. Unknown models may now be linked to a newly working model's identification to gain the surplus value of that model's success.

Not all models, however, are framed in these ways. The need and recognition of nationalized shorthand depends on the model's racial background and the market that he or she is working in. For example, in New York national descriptors say very little about Asian models due to the dearth and non-specific nature of castings for Asian models. While I was at the agency, we received only a handful of castings specifically requesting Japanese, Chinese or Korean models. When we did, these were exclusively from either non-US clients or for use in non-US media. Black and white model casting requests, on the other hand, were rife with elaborate colour descriptions and national modifiers bound up in racial hierarchies. Whether it was 'London beat', 'brown-skinned Bollywood', or 'black-black-black', these requests quickly indexed general facial features, skin tone and hair type and colour. In addition to the market and racial background of the model, the client's own identity also determined the use of these terms. While learning to book, I was coached about certain clients' racial and sexual preferences. Agents use this kind of industry gossip – garnered from models' debriefings and other types of buzz – alongside careful study of clients' visual work to match models to clients. In this way the deployment of racial, national and regional types in the casting process is highly contingent, and can shift from one client to the next.

There are limits to the system, however. Just as in passing, there exists the possibility of being 'outed' or exposed. Claims expressed through language, however, are subject to more restrictions than their visual counterparts. Whereas statements about models' features and backgrounds are closely monitored for their truth-value, a great deal of ambiguity is tolerated as far as appearances are concerned. Ways of circumscribing the close attention paid to verbal and written statements include subtle modifications to descriptors, such as adding suffixes like '-type' or '-feel'. These changes, and their lack of direct correspondence with a model's visual appearance, indicate not only the importance of authenticity in the evaluation of models, but also the unacknowledged power of language in these scenarios.

CONCLUSION

Modelling is an image-based industry. People get ahead by seeing what others cannot see, by showing people what they've never seen, and by getting others to see what they see. The use of language builds consensus and eases anxiety around conflicting interpretations of images. It fortifies the visual. Nonetheless, language's transformative power is consistently disavowed in the casting process. Casting choices are allegedly based on the model's appearance and not on verbal descriptions. Attention to naming and typing practices highlights the different ways models are evaluated beyond their aesthetic and commercial potential. Evidentiary forms of evaluation – from the practice of taking Polaroids, to the assessment of models in person with minimal makeup, to the interview process in which models are asked about their ethnic and racial background as well as more phatic questions used to asses their 'personality' – are a central technique used in the casting process, shored up by linguistic frames that draw on and contribute to constantly shifting architectures of racial and national difference. Appeals through language and images must be studied together in order to understand fully not only how fashion photographs are produced, but also how they contribute to and draw from existing stereotypes and structures of racial and national hierarchies. Even before a fashion image circulates, knowledge about race, nation and region has been (re)produced.

ACKNOWLEDGEMENTS

Portions of this research were made possible by funds from the Ford Foundation Predoctoral Fellowship for Minorities. Thanks also to Bambi Schieffelin, Deb Willis, Eugénie Shinkle, Susie Rosenbaum and audiences at the 2005 'Sightlines: An American Studies Conference on the Culture and Science of Vision', sponsored by the New England American Studies Association, and NYU Anthropology Department's 2005 Graduate Research Symposium for comments on earlier drafts of this essay.

NOTES ON CHAPTER 10

1   For related examples on the relationship between linguistic narration and the success of visually based performances in the fields of magic and advertising, see Jones and Shweder 2003 and Mazzarella 2003a and 2003b respectively.

2   See Tyler and Abbott 1998 for a similar example of naturalized labour among flight attendants.

WORKS CITED

Besnier, Niko (1990) 'Language and Affect', *Annual Review of Anthropology* 19: 419–51

Giddens, Anthony (1991) *Modernity and Self-identity: Self and Society in the Late Modern Age* (Stanford: Stanford University Press)

Goffman, Erving (1963) *Stigma: Notes on the Management of Spoiled Identity* (New York: Simon & Schuster)

Jackson, John L., Jr (2005) *Real Black: Adventures in Racial Sincerity* (Chicago: University of Chicago)

Jones, Graham and Lauren Shweder (2003) 'The Performance of Illusion and Illusionary Performatives: Learning the Language of Theatrical Magic', *Journal of Linguistic Anthropology* 13 (1): 51–70

Mazzarella, William (2003a) *Shoveling Smoke: Advertising and Globalization in Contemporary India* (Durham, NC: Duke University Press)

__ (2003b) '"Very Bombay": Contending with the Global in an Indian Advertising Agency', *Cultural Anthropology* 18 (1): 33–71

Moriel, Liora (2005) 'Passing and the Performance of Gender, Race, and Class Acts: A Theoretical Framework', *Women & Performance* 29: 167–210

Sacks, Harvey (1984) 'On Doing "Being Ordinary"', in J.M. Atkinson and J. Heritage (eds) *Structures of Social Action: Studies in Conversation Analysis* (New York: Cambridge University Press): 413–29

Sontag, Susan (1977) *On Photography* (New York: Picador)

Taylor, Janelle S. (2005) 'Surfacing the Body Interior', *Annual Review of Anthropology* 34: 741–56

Trebay, Guy (2003) 'A Black Model Reaches the Top, a Lonely Spot', *New York Times*, 8 April: C16

Tyler, Melissa and Pamela Abbott (1998) 'Chocs Away: Weight Watching in the Contemporary Airline Industry', *Sociology: The Journal of the British Sociological Association* 32 (3): 433–50

West, Candace and Don H. Zimmerman (1987) 'Doing Gender', *Gender & Society* 1 (2): 125–51

Wissinger, Elizabeth Anne (2004) 'The Value of Attention: Affective Labor in the Fashion Modeling Industry', PhD dissertation, City University of New York

11 Sex, Sameness and Desire: Thoughts on Versace and the Clone

Isabelle Loring Wallace

INTRODUCTION

Known to us already as the inventor of heroin and kiddie-porn 'chic', Steven Meisel is routinely linked with images that pack a titillating but uncomfortable punch, and as such the prospect of a millennial media coup was only consistent with everything one might expect of America's most notorious fashion photographer.[1] Indeed, given a decade that had moved from the publication of Madonna's *Sex* in 1992 to the banning of an Opium advertisement in 1999, which is to say, given a decade already framed by scandals born of Meisel's camera, there was every reason to suspect that Meisel would close out both the decade and millennium with a comparably scandalous bang.[2]

Enter here the subject of my essay. In the final months of the year 2000, Steven Meisel did give us something to talk about, yet these photographs would hold little interest for censors and ethical watchdogs. More perplexing than prurient, Meisel's advertising campaign for Versace's Fall 2000 line would win the attention of art journalists and cultural critics instead, and although many of these columnists were quick to note the uncanny appeal of a campaign focused on two credibly adult females in lavish Los Angeles interiors, little more than that was ultimately said about the content of Meisel's descriptively named campaign: *Four Days in LA*.[3]

Comprised of roughly thirty photographs, the majority of which situate the campaign's unsmiling female models together in opulent and imposing domestic settings, Meisel's campaign initially appeared in the context of major fashion magazines and in the shop windows of Versace's own boutiques. As much Las Vegas as Los Angeles, the campaign's gilded, flashy interiors provided a suitable backdrop to Versace's equally glitzy retro couture as modelled by the campaign's impossibly unexpressive, mannequin-like models: Amber Valletta and Georgina Grenville. Coinciding with the appearance of Versace's Fall/Winter collection, the advertisements were destined to disappear after only six months, and yet, for reasons that are, in part, the subject of my essay, *these* advertisements would not fade so quickly from view.

Enlarged and framed behind glass, a selection of Meisel's advertisements underwent a kind of metamorphosis, after which they reappeared *as art* at the prestigious White Cube gallery in London. On exhibit in the summer of 2001, the transubstantiated 4 x 5.25 feet photographs, available in sets of nine, sold quickly, despite both an original un-ownability (as advertisements, everyone and no one could claim to possess them) and their impressive, art-based price range (£12,000–£15,000). Not surprisingly, Meisel's debut at White Cube would generate a second wave of columns and essays about the campaign, and together these articles betray continued interest in the campaign, while also manifesting an enduring reluctance to engage the issue of the campaign's contents.[4] Of course, this reticence is partially a function of who writes and where; yet I'm tempted to say that the tendency of reviewers to avoid analyzing (even determining) their subject is a trend that reflects more than circumstance – indeed, as I see it, this silence is, in some sense, a testament to the fact that Meisel's ads were being engaged at this level, such that it was precisely an awareness of their difficult subject that kept viewers both interested and anxiously silent.

IN EXCESS OF EXCESS

Asked to comment on *Four Days in LA*, Meisel suggests that the series is all about 'extravagance' and 'LA-excess', yet, given the decadent interiors and oversize sunglasses, the tranquilized poodles and turquoise eye-shadow, the rhinestone lighters and four-inch heels, Meisel's observation hardly qualifies as insight, even if it does help us to understand what the ads actually look like.[5] Certainly, no one doubts that 'the look' is terribly important in advertising and fashion photography. Yet I think it is possible to talk about Meisel's series in a different way, one that begins to account for aspects of the campaign not covered in any straightforward sense by recurring rhetoric of excess. Indeed, as we shall see, it is the aspects of the campaign not addressed by Meisel's superficial description which will ultimately reveal a much more ambitious and problematic subject.[6]

First, there is the campaign's considerable investment in the idea of sameness. Not only are the primary models virtually indistinguishable from one another in terms of physiognomy, body type and aesthetic, they are also often positioned in ways that make one the mirror image of the other. In one of the campaign's most visible images, for example, we see Valletta and Grenville on a veranda on either side of a circular table perched atop identical chairs, each echoing the other with the crossing of her couture-clad legs. Wearing matching shiny pants and matching gold necklaces with matching, diamond-shaped pendants, both models wear seventies-styled hair, makeup and nails, all the while betraying through their stiff, mirror-reversed poses and expressions little interest in their matching cups of espresso. Other ads in the series work along similar lines, using both the models and their context to get across the idea of sameness. One, seemingly ubiquitous, image from the campaign features Valletta and Grenville in matching yellow pantsuit-separates, and again sameness dominates. Matching handbags, posture, hairstyles, chairs, makeup, manicures and diamonds are only the most obvious means by which Meisel's photograph insists on sameness. Indeed, a close look at the ad's back-ground reveals, among other things, matching oil paintings of women in profile, themselves a frame for the model on the left, and, playing a similar role *vis-à-vis* the model on the right, a pair of matching, white-shaded lamps. Suffice it to say that here, as elsewhere, there is nothing in the ad that doesn't somehow contribute to the idea of sameness and twinning.

If the sameness of the campaign's female models is the most striking and manipulated aspect of the campaign, it is worth noting that this idea finds expression even when one or both models is absent from the frame. One photograph, for example, features one of the female models dressed in black in the centre of an eclectic but essentially modern white room. As with any of these images, there's a great deal one could say, but for our purposes here what is interesting is the fact that the model is dramatically flanked by two identically sized and styled white poodles. Moreover, if matching white poodles flank her in the foreground, matching black lamps atop matching end-tables flank her in the background – a fact that establishes well not only the interest of the campaign in symmetry, but also its profound commitment to articulating the idea of sameness under necessarily varied circumstance.

Photographs centred around the campaign's lone male model (Lucas Babin) are harder to come by – in fact, they were entirely absent from the exhibition at White Cube. Nevertheless, when they do appear they also express a commitment to the idea of twinning in the absence of twins. One photograph, for example, features Babin in a canary-yellow suit, standing erect between two identical twin beds which are themselves flanked by identical end tables topped with identical lamps. That the accents in this room all have an Asian sensibility – most notably the red silk bedspreads and lacquered screen – is a fact that makes this ad very much like another photograph in Meisel's series in which Babin trades in his yellow pantsuit for a more subdued ensemble in black. Leaving the bedroom for a less personal space within the same home, Asian motifs (two porcelain cranes and two ornamental scrolls) continue to suggest Babin's 'otherness' within a campaign dominated by women, while at the same time returning our attention to the issue of twinning and sameness. For if these motifs can be said to feminize this interior and its inhabitant at the same time they mark him as 'different', they also expose as relentless the focus of Meisel on the double.

Though I've already touched on this point indirectly, here I'll note explicitly a second aspect of the campaign ignored by columnists and reviewers: namely the rigorous segregation of women from men. As strange as it seems in a context obsessively focused on relations between opposite sexes, Meisel's refusal to represent heterosocial contact of any kind is absolute: in this series, men are never shown in the company of women, and women are never shown in the company of men. Because it is tempting to rely on culturally prevalent narratives (wealthy suburban women stay home while their hyper-successful husbands work together outside the home), let me note expressly that all of the campaign's scenarios, whether centred on men or women, are staged at the home during the day. As such, the segregation between men and women, neither of whom seem to work, is one which must be understood as meaningful, and as such the campaign pushes us towards a difficult but compelling possibility:

in the imaginary, pastiched world of Los Angeles, in some unspecified and unspecifiable time, men and women lead distinct lives as a matter of choice.

Related to this is the campaign's indifference to the idea of men's and women's spaces within the home. A quick review of the series shows women in the mahogany panelled study, men in the airy yellow bedroom, and both men and women in the neutral spaces we might call living rooms or dens. Of course, this is not to say that the spaces and accessories aren't gendered: they are, and it escapes no one's attention that the darkened study is a masculine counterpart to the campaign's floral, feminized bedroom. Yet, in Meisel's world terms like 'masculine' and 'feminine' become transparent (and transgressible) stylistic categories, losing in the process much of their potential to damage and police. In other words, in this context it may be possible to speak of a 'feminine space', but in the world constructed by Meisel the signifier is utterly liberated from its biological referent, if indeed that referent can be said to persist.

Of course, what works to destabilize this very possibility is the convincing androgyny of Meisel's models. Again, though little was said about this in the popular press, there is an uncanny indeterminacy at work here, one we might attribute to physiognomy and context in equal measure.[7] Consider by way of description two more images from Meisel's campaign, each of which features a tall, flat-chested model with shoulder-length hair in androgynous attire. The first features the campaign's male model in the airy yellow bedroom, reclining, fully dressed on a bed while wearing black jeans, a black cardigan, a white dress shirt, cufflinks and tie. The second features one of the campaign's female models – though here it might be said that her femaleness is in no way certain, an ambiguity nicely underscored by a name like Georgina – sitting in a living room wearing a spectacular red pantsuit, complete with a red, fur cuffed overcoat which rests regally atop her shoulders.

Given the visual evidence, one would be hard pressed to identify conclusively either of these figures as male or female, let alone, masculine or feminine. Indeed, if anything, advertisements like these subvert essentialist notions of gender through savvy reference to established codes of visual culture; here it is the male model who takes up the recumbent pose of the female nude, while his erect female counterpart adopts the established codes of male portraiture, more specifically in this case codes already deployed by David and Ingres in their neo-classical portraits of Napoleon, a reference secured here by

Meisel's canny inclusion in the ad of two pillows each embroidered with France's signature motif, the *fleur de lis*. Existing as hybrids somewhere between the poles of masculine and feminine, the characters that populate Meisel's world refer openly to the codes of both, even if they conform, in the end, to neither. That said, the question that remains is this: where can the above observations take us, and what, if anything, do my remarks about gender and sex have to do with the idea and image of sameness?

BACK TO THE FUTURE

Writing in the year 2000, Jean Baudrillard observes, 'There is something occulted inside us ... lying in wait for us within each of our cells: the forgetting of death' (5). What Baudrillard is talking about here is the connection each of us has to an earlier state of being in which we were neither mortal nor sexed. Reminding us of this, our universal pre-history, Baudrillard goes on to note that this primordial era came to an end with what he will call the *original* sexual revolution, the one in which organisms evolved from asexual subdivision – a state of guaranteed immortality – to a state of being which entails both sexual difference and death. With this in mind, Baudrillard reads the current interest in cloning as regressive, for what cloning aims, nostalgically, to achieve is our return to a moment in which immortality is once again assured through the infinite and, moreover, the clinical reproduction of the same (Baudrillard 2000: 3–30).[8] Indeed, having evolved from reproduction to pro-creation, we now seem determined to reverse evolutionary history, sacrificing both death and difference for sameness and the promise of eternal life. Contemplating in this way our own point of origin, we in the West thus stand at Eden's threshold, and are now in the process of peering back through its gates in an effort to ascertain and *perhaps picture* what life in paradise might be like.[9]

What would life in paradise be like? And for whom might paradise unfold? It's these questions and more that I see considered in the campaign that has been our subject thus far, and as we turn again to the privileged life of Amber and Georgina, let's do so under the assumption that what's pictured here is the vision of a photographer who finds in the city of Los Angeles and its wealthiest inhabitants a compelling metaphor for life in the era of the clone. After all, Los Angeles has always been associated with paradise and the promise of eternal youth, both of which it claims to have achieved through the miracle of celluloid, which makes of every actress a clone whose immortality is a function of her self-replication in theatres everywhere near you. That this kind of immortality and self-replication goes hand and hand with extraordinary privilege, and that it results in an oppressive and cancerous homogeneity in which an actress begets not only herself exponentially, but also and at the same time a group of imitators, who beget their own imitators and so on *ad infinitum*, is a fact which finds its counterpart in the link these ads make between material privilege and the hellish sameness of Amber and Georgina. Indeed if one actress is rewarded handsomely for her ability to conjure the look of another, in the era of the clone, the reverse obtains: it will be only the wealthy (and perhaps the white) who will be able to purchase the perverse privilege of looking alike, the privilege, we might say, of conformity. Of course, other privileges will also obtain in the era of the clone, not all of which will be comparably perverse, and by way of concluding my discussion of Meisel's campaign, I'll note now a few final implications of cloning's achievement, at least as suggested by *Four Days in LA*.

THE HELL OF THE SAME?

If cloning promises to free us from the fact of mortal finitude while at the same time introducing us to the hell of the same, it may also terminate a culture in no small part determined by the once insurmountable fact of reproduction's (hetero)sexual nature. The final step in a process that began in earnest with the invention of the pill, cloning radically differentiates sexual and reproductive functions, and as such its cultural consequences are sure to be extreme. Returning to Meisel's campaign with this in mind, the segregation of men and women therein acquires new significance. Indeed, when one considers the campaign in light of the topic suggested by the indistinguishability of its main models, one might conclude that if Meisel's men and women maintain their distance from one another in a campaign about twins and twinning, then it is at least in part because cloning will make gratuitous the physical relation of women to men.

As such, some of the campaign's more suggestive photographs should come as no surprise, for what they offer us as visible and paradigmatic is a sexual relation that has always been an index of sexuality's fundamental indifference to the biological task of reproduction. The ad featuring Valletta and Grenville in the bedroom in scanty Versace couture is a case in point. With not a man in sight – save the intrusive one implied by the stern and dismissive gaze of each outwardly facing model – Meisel's photograph, like the series more broadly, suggests a world both frightening and free, for if the uncanny sameness of his models alerts us to the tedium of the same, their proximity to one another in settings such as this at the same time celebrates the irrelevance of biologically bolstered convictions about the 'appropriate' nature of human sexuality. No longer the sole means of reproduction (a fact true since in vitro technology was introduced), the heterosexual act carries less associative weight than it has in the recent (but again, not distant) past, and from my point of view the implied lesbianism of Meisel's 'characters' is but one acknowledgement of this cultural shift.

Also irrelevant in the era of the clone is a woman's biological clock, a fact Meisel's ads seems to suggest, given their much-noted reliance on two models older than most. Though Valletta and Grenville are in truth nowhere near the age of infertility, they are nevertheless well beyond the age of today's typical fashion model, and in this way we might say that Versace's ads are at the forefront of a shift which will entail (among other far more important things) an end to the heterosexist cult of feminine youth. After all, in the era of the clone everyone is equally fertile, as every body part is (at least in theory) equally valuable to the process of reproduction. As such, Meisel's futuristic (but also regressive) fantasy includes not only the suggestion of couples that do not procreate, but also a genuine indifference to the culture's preference for a female body that is visibly fertile.

If cloning will thus retool our notion of parenting (who parents with whom under what circumstances), it may also destabilize an entire ideology and culture based on the idea of essential sexual difference. In other words, if it is possible to say that the liberation of sexuality from reproduction will be one consequence of cloning, then surely the radical liberation of sex from gender will be another. In saying this, I do not mean to suggest that sex and gender haven't always been separable – indeed, the difference between them is as old as hairstyles and make-up. All the same, the advent of cloning would be a conclusive step towards their differentiation – one which would continue to lay bare the theatrical nature of gender, rendering it visible as the ideological performance it's always been.

With this in mind, consider another image from Meisel's campaign. Referencing a traditional kind of portraiture in which wife is seated before standing husband, one image from the campaign shows Valletta and Grenville posed in the dining room in exactly that way, and as such we might say that the ad plays on our knowledge of patriarchal iconography in order to construct a meaning that is at odds with the very referent on which it depends. Once again, we see that traditional codes (this time Western codes of sex-based authority) remain intact, even at the same time that the arbitrary nature of their application, which is also to say the limitlessness of their manipulation, is made visible. In other words, in the world constructed by Meisel someone still assumes the guise of authority (or passivity, or…), but who that someone is will be to an even greater degree a matter of personality rather than sex. Indeed, in the world constructed by Meisel, clothing will tell us something specific about the owner's fantasy of him- or herself, rather than something general and potentially misleading about his or her sex as a whole.

Moreover, and more importantly, the very idea of sex – that is of a biological real to which gender refers – is itself in question, and not only because Judith Butler and others have made a career of its intellectual inter-rogation. Indeed, for Baudrillard, we are on the brink of a major evolutionary crossroad, one that may well render sexual organs and difference gratuitous and ultimately obsolete. Eradicating the very things that distinguish us from our primordial cousins (sex and death), the emergence of cloning thus marks nothing less than the end of man as defined by his essential characteristics. Seen in this light, what ought to be at issue in the current debate is not man's moral constitution, but rather his very existence, for just as bacteria gave way to protozoa, and protozoa gave way to us, so we, of our own volition, may well be giving way to the era of the clone.

IRONIES AND CONCLUSIONS

If cloning is justifiably discussed in apocalyptic terms, here it needs to be said that the image of cloning painted by Versace and Meisel is more glamorous than morbid – a fact that might lead us to reflect on the role fashion may play in the epoch of the clone. As noted, fashion has always been linked with the performative, in the sense that costume has always enabled the individual to falsify or enhance his or her 'natural' appearance, if in truth such a thing exists. In the era of the clone, I suspect fashion's performative dimension will become increasingly important, for as difference becomes a rarity, it will also become valued. So too will the role of the designer and all those associated with the visible dimension of identity. Indeed, for a fashion designer and/or photographer, what better fate than a world in which the theatrics of difference are paramount? A final means of differentiation in a world dominated by the same, fashion may well be our *only* way of constructing difference in the years to come, and as such it seems likely that clothing will be a crucial and highly valued sign of individuality once the individual has been rendered genetically obsolete.[10]

With that in mind, we can better understand the tenor of Versace's perplexing campaign. Indicative of the industry's perverse fascination with a world in which fashion will be king, Meisel's meditation on the prospect of cloning openly concedes the appeal of this phenomenon for those who are in the business – a fact which helps us to explain the sheer number of fashion advertisements which have recently taken the double as their primary motif. More sardonic and explicit in approach, Diesel's *Successful Living* campaign, the ironic theme of which is strategies for self-preservation, includes an ad which stresses the uncanny perversity of the clone, while at the same time openly probing the role fashion will play in a world devoid of real difference.[11] Featuring four inanimate-looking versions of the same teenager dressed in different Diesel outfits, the copy reads as follows: 'I thought my youth was over, but then I discovered cloning. Now I can enjoy being young and attractive again and again. And if I discover a wrinkle, I'll just clone another me: Louise Kemp-Welch (the 1st), born 1893.'

Though Versace and Diesel each address the tiresome cult of feminine youth, Diesel's ad is ironically focused on the psychology from which cloning has stemmed, rather than on the potential consequences of its development. In this way, Diesel's ad is also linked to the several visual artists who have taken up this subject matter, most provocatively Jake and Dinos Chapman, whose mannequin sculptures feature clusters of identical, young bodies, unnaturally attached in ways that draw attention to both sameness and sex, whether through the proximity of identical bodies to each other or through the transformation of noses and mouths into exaggerated versions of male and female genitalia.

Exemplary of the Chapmans' work in this area, the cryptically titled *Zygotic acceleration, Biogenetic, desublimated libidinal model (enlarged x 1000)* (1995)

(Fig. 15) joins with Diesel in stressing the perversity of genetic manipulation, and lines up with Baudrillard and Meisel in its insistence that sex, and more specifically the *act* of heterosexual sex is irrelevant (if not also physically impossible) in a world of cloning and clones.[12] Of course, where the Chapman brothers predictably depart from Meisel is in their pointed indictment of fashion. Decorating the feet of each of these otherwise naked figures is a conspicuously identical pair of name-brand sneakers – a detail I take to suggest not only our long-standing desire for sameness but also the exploitation of that desire by those who sell the commodities that were (until recently) our best means of achieving that illusion.

A pointed acknowledgement that the fashion industry is intimately linked to our desire for sameness, a work like *Zygotic acceleration* leads us to consider the irony, and perhaps also the perversity of advertising campaigns which aim

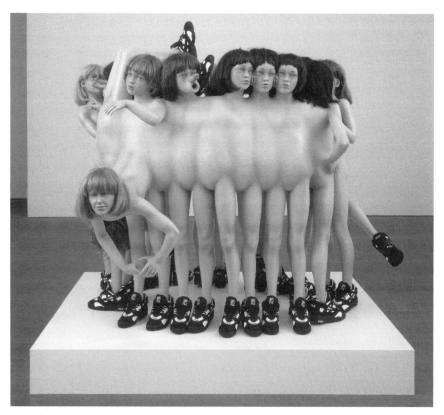

15. Jake and Dinos Chapman, *Zygotic acceleration, Biogenetic, desublimated libidinal model (enlarged x 1000)*, 1995.

to thematize sameness's realization at the hands of genetic engineering. After all, there was fashion long before there was cloning, and what is fashion if not a crude form of cloning predicated on our desire to look alike? Seen in this light, fashion emerges as the original manifestation of a desire science is now capable of gratifying, and in that sense a campaign like Meisel's can be seen as perverted and redundant in its conflation of fashion and the phenomenon of the clone.

If the Chapman brothers can be credited with alerting us to the perversity of this conjunction, we might conclude by considering the possibility that Versace and Meisel are in on the humourless joke. Returning one final time to Meisel's campaign, I direct your attention to the subtle form of the Versace logo worn in these advertisements as both brooch and belt. Here we find an explicit acknowledgment of the morbid connection between fashion and the phenomenon of the clone. For, if the Medusa's head is, in the first instance, the label that marks the clothes and advertisement as Versace, then it is in the second instance an emblem of fashion's self-conscious alignment with a culture that is aggressively courting the possibility of its own extinction.

That said, I end with a discussion of this modest detail because our relation to it is in some ways emblematic of the choice we now face with respect to emerging technology. On the one hand, embracing the culture of clone means avoiding the mortifying gaze of Medusa, who nevertheless resides within its borders. On the other hand, rejecting the culture of clone means resisting the lure of Meisel's identical models and facing the deadly gaze of the Medusa head-on. If the latter seems the less appealing of the two, in conclusion, consider this: if the Medusa's head is emblematic of the terrible consequences that sight can bring, here let us also remember that she is equally emblematic of the consequence of refusing to look, even if only at an advertising campaign that may or may not have been a mortifying glimpse into our future.

NOTES ON CHAPTER 11

1   This essay owes a significant debt to my colleagues and students in the Fine Arts Department at the University of New Orleans. Their response to this campaign sharpened my thinking while validating my sense that the campaign exerts an uncanny fascination among those who look. Thanks are also owed to Jennifer Hirsh for her friendship and flawless Italian.

2   Highly reminiscent of Bronzino's sixteenth-century allegory *Venus, Cupid, Folly and Time*, the banned Opium advertisement was contemporaneous with the Versace campaign under discussion here, and shares its interest in the rhetoric of Mannerist painting.

3   Exceptions to this are the comments of Bruce Hainley, who postulated that the campaign's appeal stemmed from its foregrounding of adult females at a moment when the media is dominated by images of teenagers. Since Hainley's essay first appeared in *Artforum*, many commentators have simply repeated his insight. Hainley has himself expanded on his original insights in the essay written to accompany the subsequent exhibition at the White Cube gallery, London. See Hainley (2000) 'Oh, grow up', *Artforum*, November: 35, and (2001) 'Sunny von Bülow-like' in *Steven Meisel* (exhibition catalogue) (London: White Cube).

4   These essays focused on the legitimacy of the campaign as art. My own remarks will not engage this issue – both because for me absolute definitions of art are, post-Duchamp, untenable, and because from my perspective it will be far more important to consider the issue of the series' elusive content. For a discussion of the campaign's relation to the history of art, see Mark Currah (2001) 'Steven Meisel', *Time Out*, 15–22 August: 50; Rachel Campbell-Johnston (2001) 'On-the-wall-fashion', *Times*, 25 July: 15; Jonathan Jones (2001) 'Steven Meisel', *Guardian*, 30 July: 14; Lynn MacRitchie (2001) 'Dedicated followers of fashion', *Financial Times*, 24 July: 16; Karen Lehrman (2001) 'Bronzino in the valley of the dolls', *Art and Auction*, June: 96–105.

5   Though I use Meisel's remarks as a foil, I am ultimately unconcerned with his account of the series. My interest is not what Meisel wanted to do, or even what he thinks he has achieved. Instead, I am interested in the way the images function as indices of a particular moment, for which Meisel is a talented medium.

6   Unfortunately, Meisel refused permission to reprint his photographs in this essay; the largest collection of plates can be found in the White Cube gallery exhibition catalogue.

7   Meisel's original conception included a still more effeminate male model, one that might have levelled entirely the notion of sexual difference. See Steven Meisel (2001) 'Steven Meisel in conversation with Vince Aletti' (London: White Cube).

8   The fantasy of the double is as old as recorded history. However, as Baudrillard notes, 'Ours is the only period ever to have sought to exorcize this fantasy (along with others) – that is, to turn it into flesh and blood, to

transform the operation of the double from a subtle interplay involving death and the other into a bland eternity of the same'. See Jean Baudrillard (1993) *Transparency of Evil: Essays on Extreme Phenomena*, trans. James Benedict (London: Verso): 114.

9   It is worth noting that cloning became a reality in the shadow of the year 2000, if only because cloning's regressiveness shares with the millennium phenomenon this temporal backwardness, as evidenced by the fact that we counted down the years, months and minutes to the millennium's end. On the peculiar temporality of the millennium, see Baudrillard 2000: 33–57.

10 What an 'individual' is, and whether or not one ever existed is an issue I leave open to debate. Here, suffice it to say that we will feel nostalgically about the individual's absence in any case.

11 At the time of writing, the entire *Successful Living* campaign was available on Diesel's website: www.diesel.com.

12 Since a zygote is a fertilized egg, the title of the Chapman brothers' work refers explicitly to genetic engineering, since in cloning no such fertilization takes place. Nevertheless, I would suggest that the work is visually relevant to both of these related technologies.

WORKS CITED

Baudrillard, Jean (2000) *The Vital Illusion* (New York: Columbia University Press)

12 Beyond Perfection: the Fashion Model in the Age of Digital Manipulation

Karen de Perthuis

Nature, as well as man, was already perfected from the moment of creation. Therefore it had always been possible to imitate this perfection. However, the greater task for any artist lay in inventing images for which nature had not provided a model. (Lehmann 2000: 144)

AN ARTIFICIAL HUMANITY

Artifice lies at the very core of fashion's existence. At every appearance, fashion throws down the gauntlet to nature, mocking its claim over the aesthetic and moral high ground, goading it into submission. With its intimate relationship to clothing, the human body has long been the battlefield where this struggle is played out. Throughout history, the body appears as a malleable form, bowing to fashion's superior armoury, surrendering to its often extreme vision of beauty – padded out, pulled in, shortened, extended in almost unimaginable ways. Meanwhile, fashion's inability (or refusal) to settle on one absolute form of beauty has earned it the vitriolic condemnation of its critics. Its attempt to create and re-create over and over its shifting image of beauty on the canvas of the human body, it is charged, is responsible for manipulating the physical structure of the body by methods that are, at the very least, ugly and, at the worst, mortally dangerous. However, fashion, which has been credited with a power and an aesthetic logic that operates independently of any one individual, can also wear, along with its reputation as a despot, the mantle of an artist. Viewed in this light, its determination to ignore the precedents set by nature can be characterized as a creative impulse. Unable to find, as J.C. Flügel has put it, 'complete satisfaction with reality', it creates a new world 'nearer to the heart's desire' (Flügel 1933: 237).

Of course, at times fashion may respect or expose the natural proportions of the body, but, according to the French art historian Henri Focillon, it is more often the case that the body is required to submit to fashion's whims, undergoing 'incredible transmutations', becoming 'the pretext, the support and sometimes only the material for utterly gratuitous combinations'. In such a way, he writes, 'fashion invents an artificial humanity' (Focillon 1989: 85). Writing in the early 1930s, Focillon's use of this term is not a reference to the woman of fashion who, in the current era of the lunchtime facelift, regards herself as a photographic image, 'unpublishable until retouched and perfected at the hands of surgeons' (Fraser 1992: 6). Nor is he simply describing the appearance of the human being, transformed only superficially by fashion's ornamentations, leaving the integrity of the body – and clothing – still intact. Rather, the suggestion is of a more profound transformation, one where the body and fashion are the same thing – fashion *is* the body. 'Such a humanity,' he continues, 'obeys much less the rule of rational propriety than the poetry of ornament, and what fashion calls line or style is perhaps but a subtle compromise between a certain physiological canon…and a pure fantasy of shapes' (Focillon 1989: 87).

As much as Focillon's observation grants fashion powers of invention, it is worth noting that he does not consider these powers to be absolute. In speaking of 'a subtle compromise' he touches upon an aspect of fashion that is often underplayed – the limitations imposed on *it* by the body. For despite having, over centuries, successfully altered, restricted and manipulated the natural form and surface of the human body, in life and to a lesser extent on the catwalk, fashion's authority has been tempered by the raw materials of a human physiology that continues to put up a degree of resistance to its aesthetic whims. This is less the case in representation. First in illustration, where the fashionable ideal was formed in ink and paper, and then in photography, which had to contend with the more troublesome medium of flesh and bone, the faults of nature have been modified. In many regards, digital manipulation of the image is a continuation of this tendency. In everyday fashion images, it is both ubiquitous and imperceptible, its application little more than a sophisticated version of older techniques that airbrushed the image of a model into the state of perfection that is usually required in fashion's world of a sleek, wrinkle-free humanity.

However, at the conceptual cutting edge of fashion photography, the fundamental principle of digital technology and the process involved in its application is integral to the final result. In the digitally manipulated image there is no original. Instead, the solid elements of the conventional photograph are dissolved into a kaleidoscope of pixels that can, writes Robin Derrick, be 'seamlessly altered, blended and mixed together', making 'anything possible' (Sanders et al. 2000: 2). It is a process that mirrors the operations of imagination or, at least what Coleridge in his famous definition of the modalities of imagination termed 'secondary imagination'. This he described as a process that 'dissolves, diffuses, dissipates, in order to recreate; or where this process is rendered impossible, yet still at all events it struggles to idealize and unify' (Coleridge 1965: 167). For human beings, imagination helps us make sense of the world, essentially by 're-making' the natural, given world. Fashion, sartorial art, is but one way we do this. But for the poet and conscientious advocate of artifice Charles Baudelaire, fashion could be considered not only as an antidote to nature but as 'a symptom of the taste for the ideal…[and] every fashion…a new and more or less happy effort in the direction of Beauty' (Baudelaire 1995: 33).

In the following pages, I explore a type of fashion image that might be the end point of this search for a superior ideal of beauty – a synthetic ideal. In images that, as Derrick puts it, 'wear their artifice openly' the fashioned body of the nineteenth-century modernist vision is realized (Sanders et al. 2000: 2). Fashion, having completed its effort in the direction of Beauty, thus sheds light on aspirations that, in the conventional fashion image, remain hidden. In the schema of the synthetic ideal, which has a metaphysical parallel with imagination, fashion is no longer required to compromise with reality. Finally left free to tailor a humanity according to the precepts of its own aesthetic, it invents something that does not already exist.

THE SYNTHETIC IDEAL

A common charge against the fashion image is that it normalizes artifice, perfection and glamour, thereby imposing unrealistic aesthetic standards upon women and encouraging acts of imitation. Models have long inhabited a homogeneous world of youthful, flawless complexions and toned, fat-free bodies, an artificial situation that is not repeated outside the fashion media, even by models themselves. But with the development of relatively simple procedures that can be undertaken without the inconvenience and pain involved with major surgery, the possibility of achieving the fashionable ideal is brought a little closer. It could be then that, as the 'real' body approaches the ideal of airbrushed humanity, the influence works in the opposite direction, giving fashion representation the impetus to extend the limits of artifice in order to maintain an unattainable level of perfection.

In 'Joanna' (1995), Inez van Lamsweerde and Vinoodh Matadin make these undercurrents of the fashion image their subject, parodying the imitation engendered by fashion, its unrealistic portrayal of women and its determin-ation to maintain an aesthetic beyond the reach of the corporeal world.[1] In this photograph, two models wear elasticized dresses that accentuate and reveal their impossibly perfect bodies. Following a tradition often seen on the catwalk, where the individuality of the models is erased by carbon-copy styling, they are indistinguishable. Both have flaxen hair, golden skin and stand confidently, their arms around each other, like two Nordic goddesses. The only distinguishing feature is the colour of their dress and shoes – one is in red, the other blue. By any measure, but especially compared to the prevailing realist aesthetic of the mid-nineties, the image is one of heightened artifice. There is nothing aleatory or natural about the elements in the frame; every-thing in the environment is controlled and artificial, including the appearance of the models themselves, who float like cardboard cut-outs in a *trompe l'oeil* setting of chequerboard tiles, a columned balcony and a Mediterranean sky. The models themselves seem as artificial as their environment, beyond human in their flawless beauty. Their hair falls in the carefully sculpted waves of a child's doll in its plastic packaging, their eyes glint like diamonds, and the glossy lips of one are frozen in the open-mouthed emptiness of a sex toy while those of the other smile with the vapid artificiality of a Hollywood star. The most striking feature, however, is that on closer inspection these two models turn out to be just one model or, more to the point, two versions of the same model who has been 'remade' and paired with herself on the computer. Once this becomes apparent, the layers of artifice fold back on themselves and the fiction of the conventional fashion photograph is exposed. In this world of exaggerated perfection, there is no original, nothing 'real' to copy. As van Lamsweerde has commented, 'You could never find this girl once, much less twice' (Brubach 1997: 28). Rather than a fashionable ideal, she is a synthetic ideal – an artificial humanity, cloned according to the DNA of fashion.

In 'Joanna' there is an intimation of an eternally renewable body, one which, like fashion, performs the endless repetition of 'the new as the always-the-same' (Buck-Morss 1989: 201). This is a body that has taken on the properties of fashion. Such a body was already anticipated in Focillon's form-ulation of an artificial humanity 'that is not the passive decoration of a formal environment, but that very environment itself' (Focillon 1989: 85, 87). Roland Barthes makes a similar point in *The Fashion System*, suggesting that this is a feature of fashion representation in general. Once the fashion image is considered as a site where everything natural is dissolved into the artifice of fashion, we can view the relationship between clothing and the body in the manipulated image as an exaggeration of something that is already present in the con-ventional fashion image.

In *The Fashion System*, Barthes identified the distinction between the garment that is manufactured and/or worn and the garment that exists only as representation and meaning. Put simply, a picture of a dress is not a dress. What this means is that represented (or in his terminology 'image') clothing does not have the other potential modalities contained in those garments that circulate in the lived world ('real' and 'used' clothing). Represented clothing cannot serve the functions of protection, modesty or adornment. At best, it can only signify these practical considerations. Representation then allows fashion to appear in a more undiluted form (albeit, not as undiluted as 'written' clothing), filtering out the practical functions that threaten fashion with becoming a material (as opposed to idealized) mode of being. A similar process of ideal-ization occurs with the body of the fashion model, which is drained of any biological realities. As Elizabeth Wilson puts it, 'this is the body as an idea rather than as an organism' (Wilson 1985: 58). Collapsed into the sign system of fashion, it cannot signify as itself; it cannot signify as 'body'. Like the manufactured bodies of van Lamsweerde and Matadin's 'Joanna', the body of the model is, writes Barthes, 'no one's body'; it does not refer back to a living, breathing entity; rather, 'it is pure form' and 'by a sort of tautology' it refers only to the garment (1985: 259). In other words, the fashion-model body does not introduce anything new, anything biological, into the image, but can only be a reiteration of that which is already present – 'fashion'. The model appears in this framework, this setting, but does not belong to it; her reality is only in reference to fashion. 'By making its signified unreal,' explains Barthes, 'Fashion makes all the more real its signifier, i.e., the garment'. Thus, he writes, 'the world, *everything which is not the garment*, is exorcized, rid of all naturalism: nothing plausible remains but the garment' (1985: 303; emphasis in original).

BODY AS GARMENT

Barthes's analysis of the fashion model (or, to use his term, 'the cover girl') is limited, but what little he does say challenges the notion that the essential function of the fashion model is aesthetic – rather, she is an absolute body, which signifies only as fashion. He writes, 'it is not a question of delivering a "beautiful body", subject to the canonic rules of plastic success, but a "deformed" body with a view to achieving a certain formal generality' (1985: 259). That this body belongs to an individual as well as having 'the value of an abstract institution' represents a rare structural paradox: between these two conditions there is no 'drift' (258–59). That is, there can be no empirical instance of this 'ideal, incarnate body' – it exists only in the image. In 'It's a Jungle Out There', created by Nick Knight in collaboration with Alexander McQueen, what goes unacknowledged in the conventional fashion image is made transparent (Plate 15). In this image (which appeared as the invitation for the designer's Autumn/Winter 1997–98 couture collection), a beautiful model with glistening, black skin and short, spiked hair is shown naked against a featureless white background. Her arms are distorted and unbalanced in width, one preternaturally long, sinewy leg tapers down to a furred hoof. From her left collar-bone, a sharp, corrugated horn seamlessly extends out towards her elbow and, from her right rib-cage, a smaller horn points menacingly upwards like a dagger. As if further to remove any biological reality, the pubic region, fully exposed and dominating the centre of the frame, is hairless and moulded closed into a smooth, featureless surface, assertively denying the sexual possibility that is implicit (or explicit) in conventional fashion images.

The clothes worn on the catwalk for the *It's a Jungle Out There* show included jackets that featured animal horns emerging from the shoulders and models who wore finger horns designed by jeweller Sarah Harmanee. So although extreme in appearance, the body of the model in the invitation could be considered as the perfect 'accessory' to this collection. But the idea of the body as something fabricated (like the clothes in the show) is more than analogous. The beautiful but freakish creature of *It's a Jungle Out There* is not a product of nature. Rather, fashion which, as Barthes puts it, can 'convert any sentience into the sign it has chosen' (1985: 260) has ignored the corporeal realities of the model to create an utterly imaginary form, in much the same way as it would go about creating a garment. Crucially, this body – woven from pixels – is underwritten by the idea of metamorphosis. In other words, it contains the possibility, inherent to fashion, of reinventing itself in a constantly changing form. By a process of transubstantiation the fleshy, organic substance of the body is transformed into the artificial, synthetic substance of the fashion garment, and the separate ontological states of what is possibly 'clothing' and what is possibly 'body' no longer signify. Instead, they have merged into one thing, and in the new entity that emerges from this alchemical process we witness Baudelaire's description of fashion as 'a sublime deformation of Nature, or rather, as a permanent and repeated attempt at her renewed reformation' taken to the extreme (Baudelaire 1995: 33).

As a designer, McQueen, more than most, has made the relationship between the body and clothing the subject of his collections. In *La Poupée*, his Spring/Summer 1997 collection, this focus brought the designer under intense scrutiny for his decision to stage a scene where the black model Debra Shaw waded through water wearing a skimpy, netted dress and a metal brace that manacled her arms and legs, causing her to move in uneven, mechanical movements. By all accounts, it was an unsettling performance, not least because of the obvious connotations of slavery it evoked. But if, as reported, McQueen had been oblivious to the possibility of such connotations, the element of cruelty inherent in such an image apparently *was* intentional, representing, writes Caroline Evans, the designer's 'wider vision of the cruelty of the world' (Evans 2003: 145). In her book *Fashion at the Edge* she points out that the inspiration for the show, as the title suggests, came from Hans Bellmer's photographs of fragmented and reassembled dolls. In this context, Shaw's appearance can be understood as reproducing the restrictive movements of a doll or a puppet. Nonetheless, it is impossible to ignore Shaw's humanity, her visible discomfort serving as a reminder of her corporeal vulnerability. If, by her movements, she reminds the viewer of a doll, she is 'a doll with a soul', a doll such as those constructed by Bellmer, whose interiors are invaded and exposed.

In her discussion of McQueen, Evans writes,

> Going beneath the skin of conventional fashion, McQueen's first collections explored the taboo area of interiority, breaching the boundaries between inside and out. The fantasy of exploring and probing the interior of the body, although commonplace in contemporary art, is habitually disavowed in fashion by its emphasis on surface, perfection and polish. (2003: 144–45)

Coinciding with its appearance on the catwalk, McQueen (again in collaboration with Knight) also used the same metal brace in a shoot for *Visionaire*. Without collapsing into the realm of conventional fashion, the magazine image shifts the emphasis back to 'surface, perfection and polish'. The theme of *La Poupée* is continued, but here the connotations of a mechanical marionette are replaced by those of a passive sex doll. In 'Laura de Palma', a blonde, blue-eyed model is shown supine in a nondescript void, her legs held open by the metal frame and manacles, which also fix her arms in a welcoming gesture of embrace (Plate 16). Her eyes are open, but, like the rest of her face, they have no expression. Her skin has a yellowish tone and is plasticky with a waxy sheen. In contrast to the catwalk show, where the humanity, the flesh and blood presence of the model is inescapable, this image successfully denies interiority. Despite the sexual explicitness of the pose, this is not a carnal, sexual body. Like the figure in 'It's a Jungle Out There', she is unavailable for sex, her pubic area pixeled into Barbie-doll impenetrability. However, if her purpose as a sex object is thwarted, her purpose as a fashion object remains unquestioned. Although completely 'naked', she is 'dressed' in a fashionably svelte size 8, which is strikingly accessorized by feet that taper down to form a ten-centimetre stiletto heel. The fashion object has now become an inseparable part of her body.

Created around a collection called *La Poupée*, it is not surprising that the model in 'Laura de Palma' resembles the store mannequin or a doll, both of

which belong to an order of 'humanity' that betoken the deep core of artificiality that is the model in the synthetic ideal.[2] However, whereas the unclothed
doll or mannequin is considered 'naked', the unclothed synthetic ideal is not
waiting to be dressed. Rather she comes as a self-contained unit, pre-packaged
as an entity where the body and garment are synthesized into one. The
alterations to the human form in the images described constitute the ultimate
in fashion statements; the infiltration of the body by fashion is permanent.
Even when the fashion object as such is absent – in both 'It's a Jungle Out
There' and 'Laura de Palma' the models are ostensibly unclothed – fashion
remains. This is not only because the body is 'wearing the ghosts of absent
clothes' (Hollander 1975: 86) but because fashion has replaced the very
substance of the body. Fashion no longer requires clothing in order to alter the
body, as the body has itself become the fashion object. In the synthetic ideal
the idea, inherent to digital manipulation, of endless possibilities is applied to
the human body, which is treated as if it is made from the same material as
clothing and can henceforth be cut, shaped, pasted and stitched in any
imaginable way. Such a body no longer carries the characteristics or signs of
the biological human; rather its qualities have become indistinguishable from
those of fashion. If it were possible to go 'beneath the skin' of this body, one
would not find the fragile mechanisms of the organic body but only more of
that which appears on the fashionable surface.

This confounds the way in which the relationship between clothing and
the body has traditionally been characterized. In answer to the question
'Should dress be regarded as part of the body, or merely as an extension of,
or supplement to it?', the authors of *Fashioning the Frame*, Dani Cavallaro
and Alexandra Warwick, suggest there is no definitive answer (1998: iv).
Rather the boundaries between the 'self and other, subject and object,
inside and outside' are permeable and unfixed, always under a relentless
process of review. Body and clothing are not separated or sealed off by
some inviolable barrier, but are 'regions to be playfully traversed', so that
each 'is continually in the process of becoming otherwise' (xviii). However,
in the synthetic ideal, the process of playful interaction between clothing
and body described by Warwick and Cavallaro is arrested, and the uncertainty
over the demarcation of a constantly fluctuating border is removed. In its
place the (provisional) boundary, ostensibly dividing body and clothing, is
permanently dissolved, and the fusion of self and other, subject and object,

inside and outside, animate and inanimate, organic and inorganic becomes complete.

This process of dissolving self and non-self, body and garment, into one occurs in a sequence by Rankin, 'A Little Bit of Gary'. Here, the model, more than wearing the garment, is constituted by it (Fig. 16). The garment itself – a maillot encrusted with onyx crystal beads – consists of little more than two jewelled pieces held together with eight fine ribbons, but the *fabric* of the garment does not stop at its borders. Rather, it extends beyond its edges to invade the entire surface of the model's body – torso, limbs, face and hair sparkle and glow with the glittering, faceted substance of the fashion garment.[3]

Considered in the context of the history of fashion images, 'A Little Bit of Gary' recalls Guy Bourdin's cover for Paris *Vogue* (December 1969) in which two models were meticulously coated in tiny black pearls, attached by hand with glue. In this image the entire surface of the models' bodies (including the face) is also transformed by fashion. However, the semiotic of the two images is quite different. The jewel-encrusted bodies of Bourdin's photograph have a deeply unsettling quality, the colour, sheen and texture of the charcoal-tinted pearls creating the effect of two charred corpses. The morbid atmosphere is also underscored by the inanimate pose of the models (propped up in a bed of fine linen) and the garish painting of their lips, nipples and eyelids in red and

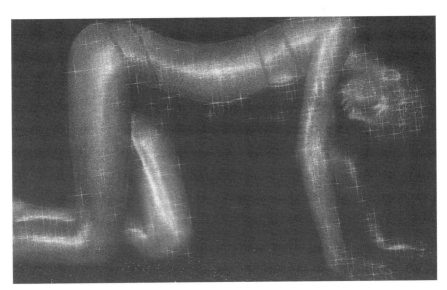

16. Rankin, 'A Little Bit of Gary'.

gold, which makes them look carefully made-up and laid out for view by a mortician. This effect may be more than coincidental. Apparently, during the shoot, the glue covering the models' bodies threatened to suffocate them and they passed out. Bourdin's black-humoured comment was, 'Oh, it would be beautiful – to have them dead in bed!' (Haden-Guest 1994: 136). Whether apocryphal or not, the image lends itself to such a story. Even without any knowledge of the circumstance of the shoot, these bodies appear fragile, vulnerable and, hence, mortal.

No such threat hovers over the body of the model in 'A Little Bit of Gary'. Transformed into a jewelled substance by a computer, she does not register as a sentient being but as an invulnerable and impervious entity. The substance of the garment has seeped into the very core of the body, replacing organic life with deep layers of artifice. With this synthesis of garment and body, the categories of surface and depth, exterior and interior no longer apply. This body, from the core out, is fabricated from the material of fashion; scratch the surface and nothing organic or corporeal will be found. All signs of life – flesh, blood, air etc. have been excised. There is no longer any referent. This body exists only as multiple layers of image – there is nothing 'underneath' to expire.

BEYOND PERFECTION

The clothing/body combinations of 'A Little Bit of Gary', 'It's a Jungle Out There', 'Laura de Palma' and 'Joanna' represent what fashion can do when it is finally able to divest itself of the constraints imposed by the biological body. No longer required to compromise with reality, it uses its absolute reign over the body to invent something for which nature has not provided the model. Here it is following the dream, already familiar to humanity, of 'increased plasticity, an ur-state in which the world becomes totally malleable' (Carter 1997: 3). Thus, fashion turns this impulse back on a humanity that considered itself as *homo faber* – a maker of things – and there is a reversal in the 'natural' order of creation. In the normal scheme of things, humans make objects, specifically, for the present discussion, fashion garments. But in the synthetic ideal, it is 'humanity' that is being made by fashion and it represents a body that has no use, no function, outside of the fashion photograph. As we have seen, this tendency is already present in fashion – plasticity, metamorphosis having always been fashion's ideal. Indeed, it is only through subjection to the principle of metamorphosis that fashion can be perpetually renewed and thus survive as a system. In the conventional fashion photograph we are given an ideal – the fashionable ideal – made from the combination of clothes and body. But in the synthetic ideal, created with the endless possibilities of digitally manipulated photography, this combination is extrapolated or intensified, and fashion reaches a point that it has always been straining towards, without being able fully to realize. This point is not a completion of something 'perfect' in the usual sense of the word; it is not final; the synthetic ideal has no end point, it is not something that has reached, or can ever reach, its goal. (To do so would be the end of fashion.) Rather, what we are given is the inherent possibility of constant change, an ideal where the body/clothing combination, with its pixel-threads, can be, like cloth, woven in countless ways to create the only sort of beauty that fashion understands – endless transformation.

Predictably perhaps, this body – even when radically manipulated – does not stray far from the raw materials of youth, thinness and beauty that the model has always supplied and the fashion industry nearly always demanded. But, given that the fashion image is apparently content to turn the body of the model into 'a fantasy of shapes', it seems fair to ask why is it so resistant to the multitude of actual bodily forms that exist beyond the parameters of its image world. Why does it not respond to its critics and observers who ask where is the representation of those who are not young, thin and beautiful? Certainly, in part, the answer lies in fashion's industrial base, the realities of the market-place and an economy of desire. But it is also the case that fashion cannot incorporate all body shapes in a gesture of aesthetic egalitarianism. If fashion were to allow the body to take over, to be just anything, any shape, any age, it would have no power. The sign of its authority – artifice – would fade. The point here is that fashion does not supplant the natural body with an ideal body but with an imagined one. As with the fashion object, the goal is not the creation of a final, perfect form but rather a form that announces the idea of a continual becoming. In the crucible of the digitally manipulated image, fashion 'dissolves, diffuses, dissipates, in order to recreate'. The traces of its alterations, its re-creations, are invisible, seamless; there is no 'Frankenstein effect' (Carter 2000: 53). Nonetheless, our familiarity with the body – the original, 'natural' body – is such that these alterations do not go unperceived, and therefore carry the idea or possibility of a process of continual metamorphosis.

There can be no doubt as to the narcissism of fashion's project: this is an image of fashion incarnate; that is, fashion presumes a 'bodily' form even as it rejects the material biological substance of that body as irrelevant. By replacing the characteristics that make the body belong to the sign system of the natural order with those of fashion, the synthetic ideal in the fashion photograph is the apotheosis of fashion, and from its deified position it creates an avatar of itself. Having rejected the model provided by nature, it turns to itself as the ideal and creates something 'nearer to its heart desire'. Something that is beyond perfection.

NOTES ON CHAPTER 12

1   It is worth noting, however, that parody does not always achieve its ends. Images that may intend to critique the cosmetic or fashion industry can also encourage either an established ideal or, as one creator of the realist look of the nineties lamented, replace it with another equally unattainable ideal. It could also be said that a critique of fashion via the method of exaggerated artifice is inevitably doomed, as artifice is inherent to fashion's mode of being.

2   The idea of creating confusion around the flesh-and-blood model and the inanimate dummy has been a recurring theme in fashion photography since the 1920s.

3   The rather obscure title is perhaps a reference to the seventies glam-rocker Gary Glitter.

WORKS CITED

Barthes, Roland (1985) *The Fashion System* (Berkeley and Los Angeles: University of California Press)

Baudelaire, Charles (1995) *The Painter of Modern Life and Other Essays*, 2nd edn (London: Phaidon)

Brubach, Holly (1997) 'Beyond Shocking', *New York Times*, 18 May

Buck-Morss, Susan (1989) *The Dialectics of Seeing: Walter Benjamin and the Arcades Project* (Cambridge, MA and London: MIT Press)

Carter, Michael (1997) *Putting a Face on Things: Studies in Imaginary Materials* (Sydney: Power)

— (2000) 'Notes on Imagination, Fantasy and the Imaginary', in John Macarthur (ed.) *Imaginary Materials: A Seminar with Michael Carter* (Brisbane: IMA)

Cavallaro, Dani and Alexandra Warwick (1998) *Fashioning the Frame* (Oxford and New York: Berg)

Coleridge, Samuel Taylor (1965) *Biographia Litteraria* (London: Dent)

Evans, Caroline (2003) *Fashion at the Edge: Spectacle, Modernity and Deathliness* (New Haven and London: Yale University Press)

Flügel, J.C. (1933) *The Psychology of Clothes* (London: Hogarth)

Focillon, Henri (1989 [1934]) *The Life of Forms in Art* (New York: Zone)

Fraser, Kennedy (1992) *On the Edge: Images from 100 Years of* Vogue (New York: Random House)

Haden-Guest, Anthony (1994) 'The Return of Guy Bourdin', *New Yorker*, 7 November

Hollander, Anne (1975) *Seeing Through Clothes* (Berkeley and London: University of California Press)

Kearney, Richard (1988) *The Wake of Imagination: Toward a Postmodern Culture* (Minneapolis: University of Minnesota Press)

Lehmann, Ulrich (2000) *Tigersprung: Fashion in Modernity* (Cambridge, MA and London: MIT Press)

Sanders, Mark, Phil Poynter and Robin Derrick (eds) (2000) *The Impossible Image: Fashion Photography in the Digital Age* (London: Phaidon Press)

Wilson, Elizabeth (1985) *Adorned in Dreams: Fashion and Modernity* (Berkeley: University of California Press)

PART IV

Reassessing the Real

13 Fashioning the Street: Images of the Street in the Fashion Media

Agnès Rocamora and Alistair O'Neill

INTRODUCTION

In the media, the street has become as conspicuous a context for fashion as the space of the photographer's studio or that of the catwalk. No longer simply occupied, in fashion images, by the glamorous figures of professional models, it is the everyday setting of ordinary people whose fashionable looks feed the content of numerous fashion reports. The status of the street as a setting for the articulation of fashion in the contemporary media is the focus of this chapter.

Taking the consecration of the 'straight-up' fashion portrait in 1980 in *i-D* magazine as a starting point, we first chart the appearance of street fashion photography, from the emergence of the street as a visual background to fashion shoots, to the institutionalization of vox-pop fashion images, on which the present paper focuses. We interrogate the values conveyed by such images, looking at the idea of the street as a site for the creative performance of 'real' people. Commenting on the role of journalists in the selection of ordinary subjects and city streets, we then question the status of straight-up images as evidencing what is 'real' about ordinary people. Finally we argue that in many fashion images, detached from the representation of actual cityscapes, 'the street' has lost its characteristic as a situated place to become a blank canvas ready to be filled by the imagination of the reader.

FASHION AND THE STREET

Representations of fashion within the context of the street can be charted across the twentieth-century history of the fashion media. However, the head-to-toe documentary portrait of a fashionable individual captured in the street – known as the straight-up – remains the central definition of this visual reporting on fashion.

In early issues of *i-D* (Fig. 17) the straight-up was established as the magazine's visual signature: a style of dress worn by ordinary people as opposed to professional models, combined in apparent disregard of dominant fashion codes and celebrated in the streets rather than in the rarefied spaces in which fashion was usually found (see also Smedley 2000: 147). The straight-up style of photography deployed by London-based Derek Ridgers and Steve Johnson in *i-D* typically captured fashionable subjects against a brick wall in the street rather than in front of the white backdrop of the studio, lending an immediacy and vitality to what was then becoming known as 'street fashion'. Twenty years on, street-fashion photography has become so commonplace that representational

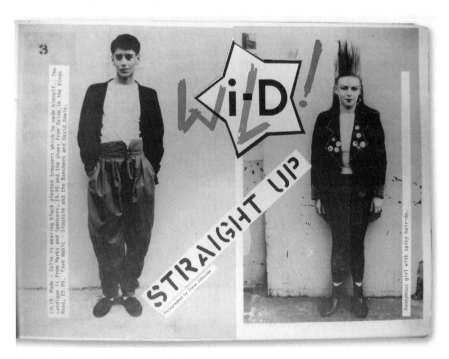

17. 'Straight-up', *i-D* 1, August 1980.

strategies now involve bringing the subjects back into the studio. Furthering this air of unmediated integrity was the inclusion of snatches of conversation with the subject and a detailed list of each item of apparel worn, where it was purchased and how much it cost. This approach documented street style as formed from incongruous juxtapositions – the cheap and the expensive, the old and the new, the beautiful and the vulgar.

The pairing of style and the street has earlier precedents in twentieth-century fashion magazines, where the street was used as a transgressive foil to the representation of fashionable women in cityscapes. However, many of these photographs re-created such spaces in the photographer's studio, often so that the dirt of the street would not soil the clothes, or in order that everything could remain still enough for it to be captured. An example of this is a 1926 photograph by Edward Steichen for American *Vogue*, which depicts the details of a women's outfit centring upon the base of her evening coat, her legs and shoes (see Devlin 1979: 39 for a reproduction of the photograph). With an usher's spotlight casting a circular frame around the shoes, and a theatre programme held by a male companion, the image suggests late arrivals being shown to their seats. What is foremost though, is the purpose of the women's outfit in making an entrance and exit, in defining those moments being whisked between streetcar and theatre stalls, in momentarily being seen as a feature of the street.

Although the unaccompanied figure of the woman in the street was seen increasingly frequently in fashion photographs in the first half of the twentieth century, she often remained bound by the feminine pursuits of a bourgeois existence, with the reality of the street a beautifying prop to the unreal fantasy of high-end fashion. As an object of the gaze, her position contrasted with that of the *flâneur* and the male privileged code of visual spectatorship.

It was not until the post-war period, with the emergence of style-conscious magazines aimed at men that the image of the *flâneur*, somewhat melded with the more modern notion of the 'man about town', began to be visualized in fashion photography. Metropolitan masculinity was shown to be influenced by the industrial atmosphere of the metropolis. This is well illustrated by Terence Donovan's grainy black-and-white photographs of sharply suited men in 'Spy Drama' for the October 1962 issue of *Town*, which became famous as the visual influence for the filmic interpretation of James Bond. In this same period, the representation of the woman in the street was radicalized by the emergence of youth as a social category and its claiming of street culture as its primary context.

Many of the British fashion photographers who in the 1960s would go on to offer a new and confident definition of a woman in the street, which Radner (2000) identified in the figure of 'the single girl' or the 'dolly bird' in new magazines such as *Nova*, are an interesting case in point. As Harrison (1998) argues, much of the fashion photography that made them famous then was predicated on the social-documentary photography of youth cultures and street life they published in the 1950s, with much of it appearing in the new men's titles of the period. David Bailey's photograph of Jean Shrimpton for a *Vogue* 'Young Ideas' story in 1962 is an iconic image of the 1960s single girl. It draws upon a number of visual tropes: in its pop-art use of signs and street furniture to indicate a navigation of the city it injects movement into the image, in its inclusion of passers-by and street traffic it sets vitality into the image, and in the confident but androgynous figure of Shrimpton, who carries a teddy bear in her hand, youth is valorized.

The newly identified social category of youth, and its claim of the street as its terrain, marked a new development in fashion photography's use of this urban space, forcing it to modify its own practices. It was no longer enough to claim the street as the site where fashionable commodities were radicalized, rather it was now the site where style was constructed prior to the processes of commodification. The straight-up allowed the fashion media to document the fashionable styles displayed on city streets in a format informed by the tradition of the vox pop – documenting the opinion of 'the man on the street'. Such an approach informed *Nova* magazine's innovative fashion stories in the late 1960s and early 1970s (see also Williams 1998) before it was more systematically capitalized on by Terry Jones in *i-D* in the 1980s with the magazine's consecration of the straight-up as a legitimate form of fashion photography.

The straight-up is now a staple of fashion journalism from the British *Independent on Sunday* to the French *Jalouse* or the aptly titled Japanese *Street* (Plate 17). Until March 2004, for instance, the *Independent on Sunday* featured a section called 'You've Got the Look' – then renamed 'On the Street'. It read, 'Our experts take to the streets to find out what real people are wearing, and show you how to recreate their style'. Featuring a large straight-up of a 'real' person in a format reminiscent of *i-D*'s fashion portraits, on the right-hand side of the picture is a visual breakdown of items similar to those in the photograph, with their price and a stockist's phone number. In the bottom left-hand corner a small column quotes the subject on their own style. Readers are shown 'how to recreate their style' in a departure from the media's many pages devoted to emulating the style of celebrities and catwalk models. Similarly, *Elle* announces that for its London Street Style Look competition it will be 'starring the hippest girls on the high street. And where better,' the magazine asks, 'to look for inspiration than on the streets of dear Blighty?' (August 2003). 'British street style,' *Elle* continues, 'is renowned for its influence on the catwalk... We'll be looking for real girls' (August 2003).

The unabated popularity of the straight-up is due to its supposed ability to evidence the 'real' and the 'ordinary' in the context of written and visual speculation about the nature of metropolitan fashion. As Smedley observes, images of street fashion in *i-D* in the 1980s 'took as their point of reference and basis of style the notion of the "ordinary person"' (2000: 147), an idea we now turn to.

THE SPATIALIZATION OF FASHION

Straight-up fashion images draw attention to the idea of fashion as a situated practice of consumption, but also as a situated practice of production informed by two main sites – the street and the catwalk. Whereas the latter is the realm of designers, models and other stars, the former is the realm of ordinary people. In visual and written fashion the idea of the reality of the street cannot be comprehended outside the differential relation that unites this term to the catwalk and its associated realm of high fashion. These two spaces are meaningful in relation to each other, both part of the signifying practices of fashion. 'The only legitimacy of the street,' Kostof argues, 'is as public space' (1992: 194): the public space of ordinary people, which contrasts with the enclosed and exclusive space of the fashion show and its extraordinary audience of celebrities and other fashion insiders.

In the media, catwalk fashion and the creations of designers are frequently privileged, suggesting that fashion originates in the mind of designers as its sole producers. The catwalk is the high point of fashion, the space where the extraordinary 'heavenly bodies' (Dyer 1987) of models are paraded. But in street-fashion images, ordinary individuals, 'normal people... with a bit of wit and flair and style about them' as *The Face* (September 2003) calls them, are consecrated as creators in their own right. At once models and designers, their style is celebrated alongside that invented by famous designers and worn by professional models. As *Vogue* (October 2003) tells its readers, 'we love your style', adding, 'you don't need a stylist to have your own distinctive look'. 'Real' people are praised like celebrities. On the street, the 'style star[s]', as *Elle* calls them, are 'real girls' (October 2003), 'heroes' according to *Fashion Weekly*'s headline 'Low Slung Heroes' (Autumn–Winter 1999–2000), which sets the theme for a report on young people's outfits during a skateboarding festival. The 'anonymous law' of the street (Certeau 1988: 92) is bypassed through sartorial style, allowing individuals in the crowd to stand out and affirm themselves as stars or heroes.

The reference to a heroic figure recalls Certeau's (1988: 1, xxii) 'common heroes', 'the ordinary man', who, he argues, is a producer in his own right, an everyday artist. Thus a *Fashion Weekly* editorial celebrates 'the self as hero, as artist, as designer, as architect of an ongoing project called 'me'. 'Self-expression,' the magazine continues, 'has become the only true arbiter of style' (Autumn–Winter 2000–1). In their first issue *i-D* also celebrated the people's everyday creativity, their 'know-how'. 'Style,' the magazine wrote, 'isn't what but how you wear clothes' (cited in Williams 1998: 112). The many pages devoted to straight-up fashion images testify to the title's belief that fashion also originates away from the catwalk, in the ordinary space of the street, as displayed on the body of city-dwellers.

Thus if the catwalk is a space where new fashions are introduced, the street, following fashion discourse, is also a legitimate site of creativity. *The Face* notes in its 'Fashion Futures' feature: 'From bad-boy (and girl) Brit designers in baroque Paris ateliers to 14-year-old logo junkies in Hackney, the ideas are flowing fast and strong' (September 2003). The future of fashion, they argue, belongs not only to designers in the comfort of their studios, but also to the people in the less orderly city streets, 'real people' such as 'students, teachers, architects, shop assistants, hairdressers, chefs, carpenters', who 'represent…that we've still got the most vibrant street culture in the world, sucking in people, looks and ideas from all over the world, and giving them a stage to live on'. Drawing on the metaphor of the theatre, *The Face* highlights what is often perceived to be the 'vitality of street theatre' (Kostof 1992: 196) and its status as a stage for the display of the sartorial creations of ordinary people and 'the performance of fashionability' (Gilbert 2000: 12).

However, if the media celebrate the creativity of ordinary people, it is often as representatives of metropolitan life, of the city they incarnate, as if the city had been styled by the people's inventive power, whose source, in turn, lies in the street itself, the true origin of fashionable creativity. Gilbert (2000: 20, see also Rocamora, forthcoming) draws attention to this 'almost organic sense of fashionability growing out of the rich culture of metropolitan life', which, he argues, informs the rhetoric of fashion culture. The organic metaphor is particularly resonant in discourses on street fashion where pictures of real people on city streets are often captioned by the name of the city where they have been snapped. Nameless, their identity is reduced to that of the city they stand for, itself captured in a sartorial style. A *Vogue* January 2005 'Street Style' feature, for instance, shows straight-up portraits of various women, with the name of the city they live in the sole signifier of identity. The women are Antwerp, Moscow or Berlin, their creativity the creativity of the city they embody. The city that Certeau terms a 'universal and anonymous subject' (1988: 94) is now attributed a face, a body and a style, while 'the practices organizing a bustling city' are no longer 'characterized by their blindness' (93) but by their style-consciousness. The 'certain strangeness' of the everyday, normally hidden to the crowd, is here given a 'surface' (93), that of fashionable city dwellers, offered in the media to the contemplating gaze of the reader. Rendered visible, what *The Face* calls the 'vitality' of the street is materialized, as if tamed and ordered.

Pike (1998: 245), citing Bloom, notes that the city is 'incomprehensible to its inhabitants; as a whole "it is inaccessible to the imagination unless it can be reduced and simplified"'. Street-fashion reports simplify the complexity of city life, making it accessible to the readers' imagination through its visualization as a series of fashionable styles. If in urban spaces people's styles are performed for 'the mixed admiring crowds of public streets' (Kostof 1992: 192), in the fashion media they are performed for the gaze of the readers, who are thus given a snapshot of city life. London, New York or Paris life can be experienced through the vicarious appropriation of the cities' visual identities as epitomized on the bodies of their inhabitants. Translated into sartorial fashions, the city is 'organised and commodified' into a spectacle (Edensor 1998: 217) that readers can partake in by consuming fashion images and the goods they depict.

In street-fashion images, then, journalists attempt to make sense of the city and its streets, their anonymity, their chaotic and disorderly crowds. Such images, to borrow from Certeau (1988: 92), provide a vantage point or prospect from which city life can be captured and comprehended. Gazing at the crowd from the top of the World Trade Centre, Certeau notes how the city can be 'controlled' from this point. One 'is no longer clasped by the streets'. Images of street fashion offer readers a similar vantage point from which city life can be made sense of. In Certeau's example, it is achieved through the pleasurable experience of 'seeing the whole'; in fashion images, it is achieved by seeing the particular – the fashionable city dweller – as an instance and representative of a larger whole, namely street life and the ordinary world of real people.

VOX-POP FASHION

However, like 'the people', 'the street' and 'the real' are vague terms, encompassing generic notions which leave aside the diverse realities they can refer to. This vagueness allows these terms to be constantly appropriated by fashion journalists to convey the value of the ordinary consumers as authors and performers, fashion experts in their own right. The selective process of construction of the street and its 'real' people is hidden behind the 'naturalized' characteristic of street-fashion photographs, which lies in strict contrast to the staged quality of studio shoots where the names of photographers, makeup artists, hairdressers and stylists are captioned. In straight-up images, vox-pop fashion appears unmediated; a direct record of street life.

Often cited as an influence on the straight-up (see Williams 1998), the British national press's earlier documentation of urban punks points to the staged quality of 'reality'. This is underlined in *Not Another Punk Book*, which notes that '[reporters] wanted stories and pictures of vile-looking punks and the kids gave them what they wanted. They had no objections to posing. They'd seen the papers; they knew what was required' (Williams 1998: 111). The pose in this instance was the 'derelict' pose, a threatening swagger often affected by punks. Partly transgressive, partly theatrical, it was only ever performed for the camera, because it was implicitly understood by those who deployed it that it functioned best as a mediatized image. 'Reality,' Lumby (1997: 21) notes, is often 'a code word for a preordained point of view', here, the point of view of the punks photographed but also, in contemporary fashion straight-ups, that of the journalists and photographers involved in selecting 'real people'. *i-D*'s early documenting of street fashion was similarly clearly informed by such a preordained point of view. As Williams (1998: 110) observes:

> While *i-D* magazine, in its first issue (in 1980) took as its identifying style the notion of 'the ordinary', this was overlaid with concerns about fashionability. Democratic as it may have seemed for a generation which had been raised on memories of Sixties glamour and sexuality, waif supermodels and mouthy East End photographers, it was no more 'authentic' than *Nova*. But equally effective, and just as influential.

Thus in the first *i-D* straight-up story, although the price range of style varied, 'all the people in the photographs look similar' (111).

Romantic projections of the city often depict the street as a space open to all (Jackson 1998) and a site for deviance and disturbances (Barthes 1985: 269; Cresswell 1998), but in fashion journalism, the street is not an open space. The multiplicity of the people, the diversity of the street and the complexity of the real are brushed aside, reduced to a fashionable ideal without dissonances. As in most media texts, fashion in images of street styles is generally represented as a feminine domain, the preserve of youth and beauty, the straight-up giving a rather skewed picture of urban life.

This representation is often commissioned prior to a photographer leaving the magazine office. Commenting on a feature about ra-ra skirts, a newspaper journalist says that 'we brief a photographer really clearly about what we want ... I'll just say "Find me 10 girls who are wearing rara skirts", and obviously the pretties get in the paper'.[1] About the criteria for the selection of pictures, she says, 'Usually it comes down to, "Her legs look good in this", if it's a miniskirt'. For a 'ra-ra skirt vox pop' story, for instance, she asked the photographer to 'find me the prettiest girl that you can find with a short skirt', and then show her the pictures: 'The less attractive girls will go out'. Similarly another fashion journalist observes, 'There's no irony in what we do. All the people have to look good ... then we go to Ascot ... what we have to do is they have to be young, they have to be pretty, they have to be titled ... I mean it's narrowed down to such a kind of ridiculous ideal.'

Discussing French journalists' practice of 'le micro-trottoir' – literally 'pavement-microphone' – Le Bohec notes that, 'The man of the street is supposed to reflect common opinion without questioning the different social uses of the street, of the social discrimination of the time slot and exact place where one is, of the social structuring of space' (2000: 116). The fashion media rarely identifies the locations where its subjects have been found. However, there are significant discrepancies between city streets, between the types of people who occupy them and between the fashions they wear. A prime example is offered by Bourdieu in 'Le Couturier et sa Griffe' (1975). The French sociologist draws attention to the distinction that existed in the 1970s French field of fashion between the two banks of the Seine in Paris, which corresponded to a distinction between social spaces. The right bank was the conservative one of established designers and their elite customers, while the left bank was that of avant-garde designers and their younger more adventurous customers. Saint Laurent famously exploited this geographical distinction in the marketing of his couture and prêt-à-porter lines, the latter named Saint Laurent Rive Gauche.

Different areas of a city provide different goods and services to a variety of social groups. The real people of London's Bond Street are different from the real people of Camden, who are different from the real people of Hoxton. To these different realities correspond different fashionable styles. Fashion writer Andrew Tucker (1998) illustrates this idea in *The London Fashion Book*, where he splits the cities into different quarters, which he associates with different styles: for example the East End with 'The New Generation', Notting Hill Gate with the 'Haute Hippie', and Knightsbridge with the 'Thorough-breds'. This mapping is itself a simplification of the diverse realities one might encounter in each of those areas, but it draws attention to the idea that cities are made of streets where a wide variety of real people from different social backgrounds and with different visual identities can be found.

Moreover, through the documentation of street styles not only do journalists offer selective definitions of the fashionable city subject, but they simultaneously construct and define their own roles. Although concessions are made to the creative style and the authorship of the people, readers are reminded that true expertise remains the attribute of fashion journalists. As the *Independent on Sunday* signals, '*Our experts* take to the streets to find out what real people are wearing, *and show you how to recreate their style*' (21 September 2003, our emphasis). Although real people are given a voice, as Le Bohec notes '"to give a voice" is only another way, for journalists, of taking the best role, in part because it is their criteria of quality which will prevail' (2000: 121).

The selected styles are sanctioned by fashion journalists to whom the elective power of good taste is ultimately conferred. Fashion journalists are 'gatekeepers...After they have completed their difficult and often mistaken process of winnowing, they engage in a process of dissemination with which they make their choices known' (McCracken 1990: 82). What is fashionable is what journalists *say* is fashionable. As Bourdieu notes in a sentence where the word 'writer' could be replaced by 'fashion expert', 'the consecrated writer is the one who has the power to consecrate and to win assent when he or she consecrates an author or a work' (1993: 42). The ultimate fashion expertise lies in the power to attribute fashion expertise, in 'the power to consecrate producers or products' (42).

In street-fashion images, then, the people, the real and the street are emptied of their complexity and diversity to the point where, stripped of its many layers, the street, in many fashion photographs, is also stripped of its identity as a situated physical place to become a blank abstract canvas.

THE BLANK CANVAS OF THE STREET

This article began with the identification of the straight-up style of street-fashion photography cemented by *i-D*. In August 2003 (the straight-up issue) the magazine revisited its heritage with a 34-page spread featuring 'straight-ups from the streets of London, Paris, New York, LA and Hong Kong'. It begins with a mock dictionary definition, stating 'Straight-up: n. Documentary style of photography that uses head-to-toe street portraits to capture people in both real and imaginary situations and to ask them a series of questions defining their lives, loves and beliefs. Invented in 1980 by *i-D*.' In claiming that the straight-up can comprise both real and imaginary situations, the definition contradicts the origin of this kind of fashion photography and its status in contemporary fashion media as evidencing all that is genuine and authentic about fashionable metropolitan cultures.

An imaginary situation for the straight-up is the shelter of the photographer's studio, where the chosen subjects might be photographed against the clinical quality of white background paper to isolate and illuminate them better. The claim also refers to the advent of digital technologies within fashion photography and the possibilities they have heralded in terms of image manipulation and the fabrication of imaginary contexts. This is very much underlined by the feature spread itself, which, when read as a fully fashioned statement, demonstrates how far the contemporary homage has shifted away from the original form. Rather than the simplicity of a wall in the street as a backdrop, we are shown the spaces of the catwalk show, the photographic studio and the 'non-place' (Augé 1992) of urban wasteland as evidencing street portraiture informed by contemporary fashion. The figures they depict are far from ordinary – a model at a fashion show, some more dressed as New York vigilante law enforcers the Guardian Angels, singers, actors – while the settings are confined to fashionable districts such as London's Westbourne Park, Bethnal Green and Shoreditch.

Epitomizing such a shift away from the reality of city walls as visual signifiers of the street is *The Face*'s September 2003 spread 'Fashion Futures' (Fig. 18). The white background of the studio, which magazines such as *i-D* had moved away from, is now reinstalled, this time as part of the magazine's endeavour to represent street fashion. Young 'real people' wearing their own outfits are photographed to illustrate the idea that Britain has 'still got the

18. 'Real People', *The Face*, September 2003.

most vibrant street culture in the world'. No street is shown, only the white background of the studio, a blank canvas for the readers to fill 'the street' with their own images and meanings. In an age of digital-image-alteration technologies, the photographs look not unlike a single layer of a Photoshop file, showing only the subjects, dislocated from their context. In fashion magazines that regularly use these kinds of digital software for image alteration, the word 'street' has come to speak for itself; unencumbered by the representation of its actual referent, a white background is now enough to represent 'the street'.

In a 14-page photo spread for *Vogue* Paris (March 2001) entitled 'Street Couture', photographer Terry Richardson uses a similar white canvas to act as a background for the outfits presented. On three occasions, two pictures are presented side-by-side, one in which the background is the white studio wall, the other an actual city street, the two melting into one another as the gaze of the reader looks from one image to the other, imprinting on the white canvas the urban landscape it is juxtaposed against. In *Elle's* section 'Streetstyle', a white canvas is also used as a background for the fashionable items photographed as still life. Again, no street is shown. The 'vitality' of the street is here reduced to a collection of inanimate objects. Detached from any actual referent the street is now immaterial, a virtual 'non-place' readers can appropriate and fill with meaning, in the same way they would the objects photographed.

In the examples mentioned above, the white background of the studio and its representation on the magazine page assumes the state of a ghost in the way it evokes the street in the mind of the reader. The use of a white background to evoke a notion of the street suggests that the contemporary condition of metropolitan fashion is indeed haunted by a prior vision of fashionable street culture as credible, actual and real. One could claim that the contemporary fashion media are haunted by these visions as they are unable to extend representations of fashionable street styles beyond the type of fashion photography defined as straight-up. The apparent uninterest in visually locating the production of fashion and style in the geographical referents of the city's streets suggests that the street is no longer a site that can radicalize the documentation and dissemination of fashion. Perhaps the only space that remains as a legitimate site for the radicalization of street fashion is the terrain that the mind of the fashionable subject cognitively supplies as it turns the pages of a fashion magazine.

ACKNOWLEDGEMENTS

The authors would like to thank Becky Conekin and Marketa Uhlirova for their invaluable comments on an early draft of this chapter.

NOTES ON CHAPTER 13

1   The journalists' quotes in this paper are from interviews for Agnès Rocamora's ongoing study of fashion journalism.

WORKS CITED

Augé, Mark (1992) *Non-Lieux* (Paris: Seuil)

Barthes, Roland (1985) *L'Aventure Sémiologique* (Paris: Seuil)

Bourdieu, Pierre with Y. Delsaut (1975) 'Le Couturier et sa Griffe', *Actes de la Recherche en Sciences Sociales* 1: 7–36

Bourdieu, Pierre (1993) *The Field of Cultural Production* (Cambridge: Polity Press)

Certeau, Michel de (1988) *The Practice of Everyday Life* (Berkeley: University of California Press)

Cresswell, T. (1998) 'Night Discourse: Producing/Consuming Meaning on the Street', in N.D. Fyfe (ed.) *Images of the Street* (London: Routledge)

Devlin, P. (ed.) (1979) *The Vogue Book of Fashion Photography* (London: Thames & Hudson)

Dyer, R. (1987) *Heavenly Bodies* (London: Macmillan)

Edensor, T. (1998) 'Culture of the Indian Street', in N.D. Fyfe (ed.) *Images of the Street* (London: Routledge)

Gilbert, David (2000) 'Urban Outfitting: The City and the Spaces of Fashion Culture', in Stella Bruzzi and Pamela Church Gibson (eds) *Fashion Cultures: Theories, Explorations and Analysis* (London: Routledge): 7–24

Harrison, M. (1998) *Young Meteors: British Photojournalism 1957–1965* (London: Jonathan Cape)

Jackson, P. (1998) 'Domesticating the Street: The Contested Spaces of the High Street', in N.D. Fyfe (ed.) *Images of the Street* (London: Routledge)

Kostof, S. (1992) *The City Assembled* (London: Thames & Hudson)

Le Bohec, J. (2000) *Les Mythes Professionnels des Journalistes* (Paris: l'Harmattan)

Lumby, C. (1997) *Bad girls: The Media, Sex and Feminism in the 90s* (St Leonards: Allen and Unwin)

McCracken, G. (1990) *Culture and Consumption* (Bloomington: Indiana University Press)

Pike, B. (1998) 'The City as Image', in R. LeGates and F. Stout (eds) *The City Reader* (London: Routledge)

Radner, Hilary (2000) 'On the Move: Fashion Photography and the Single Girl in the 1960s', in Stella Bruzzi and Pamela Church Gibson (eds) *Fashion Cultures: Theories, Explorations and Analysis* (London: Routledge): 128–42

Rocamora, A. (forthcoming) 'Paris Capitale de la Mode: Representing Fashion in the Media', in C. Breward and D. Gilbert (eds) *Fashion's World Cities* (Oxford: Berg)

Smedley, Elliott (2000) 'Escaping to Reality: Fashion Photography in the 1990s', in Stella Bruzzi and Pamela Church Gibson (eds) *Fashion Cultures: Theories, Explorations and Analysis* (London: Routledge)

Tucker, Andrew (1998) *The London Fashion Book* (New York: Rizzoli)

Williams, Val (1998) *Look at Me: Fashion and Photography in Britain, 1960 to the Present* (London: British Council)

14 The Elegance of the Everyday: Nobodies in Contemporary Fashion Photography

Kate Rhodes

Ordinary people are largely absent from fashion photography. Historically, it is the beautiful, the wealthy or the famous who sell the designer garments promoted by fashion magazines and mass-market advertising. But since the late 1980s, the central figure of the fashion photograph – the model – has become fragmented. A number of the best-known contemporary fashion photographers have chosen to use non-professional models, 'real' people either found on the street, enlisted through flyers or called on to volunteer themselves and lend their 'ordinary' looks to fashion photographs. These amateur models typically grace the so-called 'alternative' fashion press, magazines such as *Tank*, *Purple*, *i-D*, *Dazed & Confused*, *W* and *The Face*, that emerged in the 1980s and 1990s. The effect is significant and two-fold, at least. These new faces simultaneously signify an unconventional snub to the idealized form of the fashion model while forming a unique marketing strategy designed to appeal to a sophisticated, image-savvy demographic.

The appearance of average and unusual looks in advertisements for domestic goods and services is commonplace. The very ordinariness of these people stands for reliability in the products they market, while quirky or quaint looks provide the memorable twist to a new product size, flavour or deal. Fashion advertising, however, is generally not concerned with the register of the everyday or with facts; instead it 'hides the origins of things' (Finkelstein 1994: 116). Julian Stallabrass suggests the unlikely nature of the effect when he writes,

'Advertisements may deal sometimes with disturbing or even horrific imagery, but it is more difficult to imagine them dealing with something which is their precise obverse: with the fragmented, aged, dirty…with the discarded' (1996: 184). But in a radical development that flies in the face of fashion's obsession with fantasy, fabulous nobodies – the old, the plump, the poor – are redirecting consumer desire through the medium of the 'ordinary person'.

Historically, fashion photographers have introduced aspects of 'the real' into their images via gritty, emotional or shocking locations such as war-ravaged streets, foul living rooms, toilet blocks or abattoirs. In the shift described here, fashion photographers introduce the everyday and imperfect into their images by way of the model. Think of Nick Knight's 1996 western-movie-inspired advertisements for Levi Strauss, combining the biography and image of elderly men and women. Think too of Juergen Teller's carbon-copy, flash-saturated portraits of wealthy couture clients with access to the most expensive garments in the world but lacking the poise of the professional model, published in *W* magazine in 1999. By the time of Anders Edström's images of dumpy models in ill-fitting garments and with wind-mussed hair, recruited via an advertisement posted at a Swedish supermarket for *Purple*, 2001, such imagery was forming a movement.

These are but a few of the numerous examples of contemporary fashion photographers, including Corinne Day, Mario Sorrenti and Terry Richardson, who have employed friends, lovers and other non-professionals as models. In a parallel development, art photographers who make forays into fashion photography, such as Nan Goldin and Martin Parr, have at times used non-professional models, in keeping with the documentary style of their non-fashion work. In 1985 Goldin photographed her girlfriends at a local Russian bathhouse for a *View* lingerie shoot, while in 2005 Parr published *Fashion Magazine*, a portable artwork in the guise of a fashion magazine, its pages dominated by non-professional models.

The figure of the amateur model signals a productive tension in fashion imagery, between the refreshingly transformative effects of 'real' people in contrast to relentlessly similar beauty icons on the one hand, and the coloniz-ation and commodification of private lives in order to grab attention on the other. In a more generalized discussion around advertising, Robert Goldman also debates the use of imperfection as part of an effort to signify the real and suggests that 'alternative' forms, though they may initially be seen as radical, are inevitably 'instrumentalized into another marketing ploy aimed at extending the commodification of desire' (Goldman 1992: 171).

HISTORY

Historically, the use of non-professional models dates back to the early years of fashion photography. During the late nineteenth and early twentieth centuries, the non-professional model was generally an aristocrat or actress, captured in their own up-to-the minute fashions or paid to lend their fame to the latest creations before the profession of 'model' was formalized. Fashion photographs at this time resembled portraiture – as they arguably do once again today – and their intentions were similar, as the genres overlapped without a great deal of distinction.

Swiss-born photographer Edward Steichen created some of the earliest examples of realist fashion imagery. In the mid-1920s, editor-in-chief and publisher of *Vogue*, Condé Nast, told Steichen, his latest prodigy, 'Every woman [Baron Adolf] de Meyer photographs looks like a model. You make every model look like a woman' (Hall-Duncan 1979: 54). In opposition to the Pictorialist approach of his famous predecessor de Meyer, Steichen redefined fashion photography using the avant-garde framework of sharp focus modernism: directional lighting, graphic effects, unusual angles, an interest in geometry and a desire to inject a sense of contemporary life into his images. In Steichen's shots for *Vogue*, fashion models incarnated a sense of assertiveness and through his 'signature' model, the socialite Marion Morehouse, he was thought to have captured the modern woman of the day: 'elegant without romanticism and feminine without sentimentality' (Hall-Duncan 1979: 54).

However, it was Martin Munkacsi's snapshot-like photographs of models outdoors and in motion – playing tennis, golfing, running – that revolution-ized the look of women in fashion photography in the early to mid-1930s. Munkascsi, a news and sports photographer, initiated a new casualness in fashion photography and slowly made room for the appearance of more everyday situations and everyday activities as the backdrop to fashion. Fashion models were shedding their status as the human embodiment of the dress-maker's dummy, and fashion photographers began to move away from rarefied and statuesque poses in grandiose settings that heavy camera equipment, and equally weighty social mores, demanded in the 1910s and 1920s. This shift away from the simple description of fashion took place alongside perceived changes in women's relationship to the world beyond home, the relaxation of dress codes and the rise of prêt-à-porter.

While the 1950s saw a wave of 'anti-establishment' photographers such as William Klein capture the model as a living force in realistic situations, sixties London was the birthplace of a 'far-out' fashion photography that ushered in a dynamism and theatricality, reflecting interests in the extremes of the everyday to space-age fantasy. Brian Duffy – who along with Terence Donovan and David Bailey was one of the 'Terrible Three' – described the working-class trio's photographs as ones that began to make models 'look real'. Their images evoked spontaneity, youthfulness and sexual liberation, qualities widely sought-after by the post-war generation. Model Jean Shrimpton sums up the look to which so many responded when she says, 'I looked like every other young girl my age … all I did with any degree of success was to embody ordinariness – which is, of course, a hugely marketable quality' (Craik 1993: 105).

From its first issue in 1980, Terry Jones's *i-D* magazine published 'Straight-up', a section which took the guise of a street-based fashion shoot, including amateur-type images of 'found' people and an outline of their ensembles, listing where they had purchased their clothes, or noting if they were self-designed. As stylist Elliott Smedley has noted, 'these images took as their point of reference and basis of style the notion of the "ordinary person" and reinforced the credo that fashion was "lifestyle"' (Smedley 2000: 147). They represent a contemporary extension of the social pages that once functioned as fashion photography in the nineteenth century and which is today characterized by the anonymous Tokyo street fashion featured in Shoichi Aoki's *Fruits* series, or the numerous street-fashion websites such as HEL LOOKS from Helsinki, Finland (www.hel-looks.com). The 'Straight-up' pages also sought to promote the ideal *i-D* reader: youthful, creative, street-smart. Especially in the case of younger readers, *i-D* recognized that identity is often fragile and fragmented, and that we seek to define ourselves through the eyes of others, a social dynamic at the heart of lifestyle marketing. The cumulative effect is dissatisfaction on a treadmill: constantly evolving hunger for a slippery, shape-shifting image.

The most notorious example of a realist approach to fashion photography at the end of the twentieth century was so-called 'heroin chic', an 'anti-fashion' style of imagery dwelling upon the androgynous, the too-skinny and the deathly looking. It was a look that flirted with grunge music, squatting and drugs. Rebecca Arnold's comments distil the attitude of many fashion photographers during this period. On Juergen Teller's fashion work she writes, 'they express the 1990s obsession with images that are "real", that are harshly lit, exposing the skin as mottled and tired, showing up bruises and flaws rather than smoothing away any sign of the living/dying flesh' (Arnold 2001: 82). These photographs have been widely understood as symptomatic of a late-twentieth-century malaise, and reflect the banalities, anxieties and feelings of alienation associated with everyday life at the turn of the millennium.

Much fashion photography over the 1990s was created in tandem with the work of fashion designers whose explicitly deconstructed garments helped give form to this new, often harsh realism in fashion imagery. Caroline Evans captured this moment when she wrote, 'In the 1990s the perfect body of mainstream fashion was progressively challenged by the abject, fissured and traumatized body of more cutting-edge fashion, another form of the return of the repressed...' (Evans 2000: 94). For example, during the late 1980s and into the 1990s, Belgian designer Martin Margiela re-fashioned second-hand clothes for his collections, left unfinished seams exposed or sprayed his garments with mould. He staged fashion parades in a Salvation Army thrift store and a car park, and became the catalyst for other designers to host their runway shows in unadorned and non-exclusive locations. Fashion historian Elizabeth Wilson described this style of design as the 'aestheticization of dystopia' (2003: 137). A certain contemporary cultural instability was reiterated within fashion photography from society itself, as it was in contemporary art and cinema over the same period via the work of artists and directors such as Mike Kelley, Thomas Hirschhorn and Gus Van Sant.

While based on a kind of realism, heroin chic and other 'anti-fashion' fashion trends were in part a backlash against society's stereotypes, an excessiveness characterized by the 1980s and the dominance of the supermodel. From around 1990, a surge of interest in Christy Turlington, Naomi Campbell, Linda Evangelista, Claudia Schiffer and Cindy Crawford promoted the women into a superior class that expressed a club-like mentality, a business drive and a 'born to rule' attitude. While distinguishable as different women, the group epitomized 'techniques of wearing the body', that is they promoted a formulaic recipe for a 'technical beauty' with a Darwinian undertone: tall, thin, rich (Craik 1993: 91). Later that decade, the inclusion of Kate Moss – the unknown waif with crooked features – signalled a thirst for variety in the face of fashion and brought a sense of performativity to fashion photography. Like Twiggy and Jean Shrimpton before her, Moss embodied the fairytale switch from 'found' woman-child into professional model before the eyes of magazine readers seduced by the possibility of continuous self-transformation.

In a now famous quip from 1938, British photographer Cecil Beaton stated, 'I want to make photographs of very elegant women taking grit out of their eyes, or blowing their noses, or taking lipstick off their teeth. Behaving like human beings in other words ... But naturally that would be forbidden' (Hall-Duncan 1979: 202). Today, models are regularly shown doing just those things, and much more. In Juergen Teller's infamous Versace images of Kristen McMenamy from 1996, she is shown naked, bruised and scarred. What might have seemed wholly taboo to Beaton has become reality, and models have been photographed in what look like post-rape and abuse scenarios. A number of photographers, including Teller and notably Izima Kaoru, have pictured models and celebrities as if they are dead.

RE-ROUTING DESIRE, DODGING NOVELTY

Fashion photography that traffics with the truly everyday, the unflattering and the flawed, and which engages non-professionals, would seem to be a reflexive and historically significant 'intervention' in fashion photography, a sign of life that eclipses the alienation and anxieties associated with the aspirations for perfection promoted by a capitalist ethos. Such imagery posits everyday people and their plain, clumsy, chubby, wrinkly or dysmorphic bodies against the commodity ideal. As a result, their appearance prompts a range of psychic, voyeuristic and fetishistic effects that re-route the intricately orchestrated spectatorial desire associated with the expected subjects of fashion photography. Evolving social dynamics can help us to understand the changing appearance of fashion photography, as fashion historian Gilles Lipovetsky suggests:

> To be sure, the dynamic of postmodern, individualistic culture has not eliminated the artificiality of the fashion photo, but it has freed it from the old imperative of ostentatious aestheticism by allowing greater openness to intimate sensations, inner feelings, unusual fantasies, physical suffering, and individual imperfections. (2002: 9)

But is the injection of 'physical suffering and individual imperfections' into the fashion photograph a convincing alternative to 'ostentatious aestheticism', as Lipovetsky suggests? Arguably, images that lack professional models may still be incorporated by a desire for innovative marketing precisely because of fashion photography's commercially driven imperative for novelty. The amateur becomes a signifier of their own instability and innate artificiality, rather than a figure of intimacy and individuality, as their role is reduced to one of transparent shock or subversion. Non-professionals speak the truth of the lie: eschewing reality, paradoxically, is the reality of fashion photography. Models do not resemble real men and women, they resemble each other. Fashion photographers' use of non-professionals – their friends, street kids, the disabled, the elderly, overweight teens and the poor – are at the core of the metastructure of referent systems designed for the savvy alternative press subscription. That is, the non-model tends to appear in the context of the deliberately opaque 'non-ad', a 'minority method of advertising' designed 'to sell us a commodity-sign' (Goldman 1992: 157).

The wave of imagery involving amateur models might also be considered in relation to another current cultural context, that of reality television and other 'reality' portraiture facilitated by new technologies: camera phones, personalized websites, webcams and blogs. Like reality television, the appearance of non-professional models reflects a simultaneous obsession with manufacturing celebrities out of ordinary people, or with celebrities caught out doing ordinary things that supposedly render them more 'real' or 'human'. A recent example of an attempt to undermine the promotion of unattainable beauty in this way can be found in Rankin's shoot for the 2005 Dove 'Campaign for Real Beauty', which focused on six 'real' women, sending the message that overweight or older bodies are no longer to be feared or shunned. Simultaneously, however, the Dove advertisements fetishize common traits – grey hair, freckles, scars – as a sign of their commitment to the 'average' woman without venturing towards the complete spectrum of 'normality' that includes obesity, disability and deformity. The advertisements signal how mutability itself has become charged with meaning when it embodies shifts in current social concerns.

There is, however, a difference between the 'warts and all', 'dirty realist' fashion photography so significant to the 1990s (epitomized by photographers such as Nigel Shafran and David Sims and Corrine Day's images of the as-yet-unheard-of Kate Moss in her London flat) and the use of non-professional models. As Smedley laments, 'realist fashion imagery did not, and does not, go as far as it might' (2000: 155). The power of the typical fashion model derives from the gap that exists, that must exist, between professional models and average readers in order to propagate desire. The professional model is an object, human flesh turned into an image. The non-model can be understood as yet another facet of an innovative photographer's oeuvre and a marketing tool that seeks to subvert the mainstream but in fact relies on the same drive for novelty and the same appeal to commodity fetishism at the level of the sign. Indeed, the non-professional may actually represent a kind of hyper-conformism: he or she underlines the fact that the power of appearances, whether typical or not, rests in their ability to fascinate and dazzle.

NEW OR NOVEL? EXAMPLES FROM NICK KNIGHT AND MARTIN PARR

Nick Knight and Martin Parr are consciously driven by reflexive assessments of fashion imagery and the way that it modulates consumer desire. Knight has worked as a fashion photographer for more than twenty years, while Parr has only begun to take fashion images following a successful career as an art and documentary photographer. Knight has been contracted to British *Vogue*, while also photographing for magazines such as *Dazed & Confused*, *i-D*, *The Face* and *Visionaire*, as well as for fashion and advertising projects for clients including Alexander McQueen, Calvin Klein, Christian Dior, Levi Strauss, Yohji Yamamoto and Yves St Laurent. Since 2000 he has also headed up his own influential fashion website, SHOWstudio. Parr is widely regarded as the pre-eminent documentary photographer of Britain's social mores. He is currently one of the most visible members of Magnum photo agency, a well-established cluster of predominately traditional documentary image-makers and photojournalists. Parr has been taking photographs for magazines such as *Amica* and *Citizen K* since 1999, and now produces up to five fashion shoots a year. For both photographers, their use of non-professionals co-exists with their work using agency-based models. While Parr's documentary-style images differ formally from Knight's studio-based practice and often heavy use of computer manipulation, both regularly use strategies of shock and irony, and occupy a parallel position with concept-based contemporary art photography.

To a large degree, Knight's subversiveness involves a repositioning of the dictates of beauty embodied by the traditional supermodel at an institutional level, that is within the traditional context of fashion photography, the magazine. As will be discussed in detail, his photographs offer a formal intervention into fashion photography's claims over perfected body image and lifestyle marketing, while Parr, on the other hand, might be seen to make structural inroads into the debates around idealized image construction and its relationship to sociality. For both Knight and Parr, the non-model is a tool in the trick box of the photographer to lift the veil from the real, seeking to act as an opponent to the false desires and illusions woven into the 'hyper-reality' of fashion's image. Perhaps the distinction in their varying desires to use non-models is as simple as their positions inside (Knight) and outside (Parr) fashion.

Knight's shoot in collaboration with fashion designer Alexander McQueen used disabled athletes for a fashion spread in the street-smart style magazine *Dazed & Confused* in 1998, and it remains his most notorious (Fig. 19). The cover story, entitled 'Fashion-Able' includes garments by Hussein Chalayan, Rei Kawakubo for Comme des Garçons, and McQueen, who tailored their clothes to the models' individual specifications (Church Gibson 2000: 361). The men and women are directed in characteristic mannequin poses, but their severe disabilities create a shocking disruption within the images, the glossy surface and tasteful styling at odds with the atypical subject. Conventional models' attributes − young, slim, flawless − make them a focus of desire. Knight's subjects, however, re-direct the usual relationship produced by the model, creating a complex dialectic of attraction and repulsion that characterizes all of the images in this series.

In recent times, as Lipovetsky sees it, 'the body has become an obsession, a primary concern', which, among other phenomena, has 'liberated fashion photography from the need to promote clothing as its central focus' (2002: 9). Certainly magazines such as *Dazed & Confused* have found success in not just selling products, but rather selling their sophisticated readership themselves as they consume their own knowingness. Photographs such as Knight's reveal a desire to promote and enjoy the unconventional. As he argues, '*Vogue* talks to me about photographing the modern urban woman...Well, the modern urban woman has breast cancer, or is in a car crash. But that's not the woman

19. Nick Knight, cover image for *Dazed & Confused* 46, September 1998 (guest edited by Alexander McQueen).

I'm photographing for *Vogue*. So there's a balance that needs redressing' (Knight 2002). In Knight's images, the flawed body of the non-professional is a form of positive differentiation signalling agency, power and risk. These models display a confidence and individuality that wrestles with the pursuit of the perceived ideal body while highlighting the cyclic effect of a quest predicated on a mixture of narcissism and self-loathing (Craik 1993: 85).

The non-professional is an interloper, a part-timer in the world of fashion. They are defined by more than their image, where the professional model has *become* their image. As one model states, 'You exist through others' eyes. When they stop looking at you, there's nothing left' (Rudolph 1991: 40). Rather than strict imitation, the non-professional's explicit lack of perfection and their novelty, a fact heightened in Knight's images, can be relished as a mode of knowing parody apparently beyond morality and politics. His images of athlete and model Aimee Mullins, most particularly, forge a strange and emotional condition of attraction to her good looks and bare torso, repulsion at her limbless stumps and shame at how the gaze, while conditioned not to stare, is in fact invited to the scopophilic comfort zone that is fashion photography.

Presenting novelty as a form of seduction is a significant element of Martin Parr's *Fashion Magazine*. While resembling a conventional publication, Parr's magazine has been entirely constructed by the artist. All the illustrations are his, including the advertisements, travel and food photographs, and the look and feel of the magazine reflects Parr's well-established photographic language: snapshot-style, social commentary often constructed through humorous juxta-positions drawn from everyday life and printed in saturated colour. The models in Parr's fashion photographs are mainly 'found' subjects whom he asks to pose as an interruption to their daily activities. Parr states, 'I started out working with models. Then I wanted to photograph real people more and more. I wanted to go into the street, with a designer and a pile of clothes, and find someone, dress them and take photos…I love doing that' (Parr 2005: 34). For Parr, the non-model offers a detour around the glamour of the expected model subject. Like the people that feature in his art practice, their simple – and importantly instantaneous – transformation from 'everyday' figures on the street to image subjects is thus tantalizingly authentic.

In a shoot from 2003, republished in *Fashion Magazine*, Parr captures shoppers at the Somerfield supermarket chain wearing Karen Walker, Playboy and Nike while they fill their plastic baskets with bran flakes or minced beef and onion pies (Plate 18). The clothing credit lines at the bottom of each page are the only element that drags the photograph into the realm of fashion from the world of documentary. The subjects, who continue their everyday activities with only a change in clothing to indicate their new role as models, sour the untouchability and allure of the designer garment. They neither pose for Parr nor address his camera, creating images that reveal the mutant qualities of fashion as it seamlessly moves from commodity to image and then to sign before the lens. Once a sign – a cultural marker, an intangible symbol – the fashion photograph, as Parr reveals, may operate alternately as a brand tool and artwork, simultaneously attracting seduction and repugnance as a discordant unpleasure.

Fashion photographers like Guy Bourdin made their fame by adopting a surrealist-inspired aesthetic of juxtapositions and a central strategy of combining unrelated elements in a single image context. In Parr's fashion photographs, not only is the setting unexpected, but so are the models themselves. In the 'Accessories' section of *Fashion Magazine*, a spread on Spring 2005 shoes features brand-name footwear modelled by non-professionals, cropped so that only their feet appear on the page. Chanel's 'Elephant' sandals are sported by women with rough heels, stumpy toenails and sun-spotted skin; over-sized veins poke through the gaps in printed cotton Alaïa wedges; a hairy foot models the latest pair from Marni, and images of shoes by Kenzo and Louis Vuitton are blurry and out of focus.

Settings at odds with the usual depiction of fashionable garments were pioneered by photographers such as Beaton, who in the 1940s posed beautiful women in London's bomb-scarred ruins. However, by placing the product on *someone* unexpected, novelty becomes a force at work within the image, consumed with a delicious sense of irony by a knowing clientele. Parr plays on the stylistic differences between genres and, in turn, on the viewer's expectations of them. He makes fashion photographs look like documentary photographs and his documentary photographs look like pages from *i-D* or *Purple*. He toys with the codes of advertising and the way designer products, particularly fashion, perpetuate social divisions. Parr's long-term interest has been focused on the visible signs of England's class structure, as highlighted in series such as *The Last Resort* (1983–86), *Signs of the Times: A Portrait of the Nation's Tastes* (1992) and *Think of England* (1999). These books deal in often scathing observations of the things that ordinary people do when in search of a life less ordinary. Even Parr is not immune from the desire for self-transformation. Humorously, the face of *Fashion Magazine* is his own, and it is one that fulfils the novelty value of the non-professional. This time Parr is laid bare as the middle-aged, ordinary-looking, unsmiling subject posed as cover model in an anachronistically hand-coloured, old-fashioned studio portrait.

CONCLUSION

While 'difference' may be central to a politically and aesthetically provocative style of fashion photography, it is also a commodifiable spectacle. In the context of the fashion magazine, where perfection is a supreme and repetitious ideology, the non-professional is an anomaly, a scrambling of the code. Importantly, this style rarely penetrates the big-circulation magazines, and remains the province of independent publications which cultivate a clever 'anti-fashion', even 'anti-model', rhetoric. These magazines form a triumvirate with photographers (who often move freely between the fashion and art worlds) and designers (who make garments refusing perfection through an aesthetics of ruination). As Caroline Evans notes 'in apparent revulsion against the Beautiful, recent generations of photographers prefer to show disorder, prefer to distil an anecdote, more often than not a disturbing one, rather than an ultimately reassuring, "simplified form"' (2003: 194). As might be expected, an enduring interest in the aesthetic of the repressed only reiterates the notion that there will never be any one quantifiable ideal of beauty, only views onto it. The project that is picturing beauty – arguably the project of fashion photography – is therefore splintered into simulacral shards which see but which cannot be entirely seen.

Masquerading as a fashion model before the reader, the non-professional plays out many of the fantasies and desires that constitute fashion photography itself, creating a relay of effects and a dissolution of the non-model's subjectivity through reflections – much like the experience of watching the pseudo-famous participants of reality television who *act* themselves for an audience. Perhaps this was to be expected as the latest vampiric act in an avant-garde advertising that seeks to confuse the borders of art and life. With strangely ordinary, discordantly normal people inside the fashion we have been led to believe is so desirable, contemporary fashion photography makes the real a complex and potentially shadowy ideal.

WORKS CITED

Arnold, Rebecca (2001) *Fashion, Desire and Anxiety: Image and Morality in the Twentieth Century* (London and New York: I.B.Tauris)

Church Gibson, Pamela (2000) 'Redressing the Balance', in Stella Bruzzi and Pamela Church Gibson (eds) *Fashion Cultures: Theories, Explorations and Analysis* (London and New York: Routledge)

Craik, Jennifer (1993) *The Face of Fashion: Cultural Studies in Fashion* (London and New York: Routledge)

Evans, Caroline (2000) 'The Return of the Repressed', in Stella Bruzzi and Pamela Church Gibson (eds) *Fashion Cultures: Theories, Explorations and Analysis* (London and New York: Routledge)

— (2003) *Fashion at the Edge: Spectacle, Modernity and Deathliness* (New Haven and London: Yale University Press)

Finkelstein, Joanne (1994) *Slaves of Chic: An A–Z of Consumer Pleasures* (Melbourne: Minerva)

Goldman, Robert (1992) *Reading Ads Socially* (London and New York: Routledge)

Hall-Duncan, Nancy (1979) *The History of Fashion Photography* (New York: H.N. Abrams)

Knight, Nick (2002) 'Fashion: Show Stoppers', *Independent on Sunday*, 29 September

Lipovetsky, Gilles (2002) 'More than fashion', in Ulrich Lehmann (ed.) *Chic Clicks: Creativity and Commerce in Contemporary Fashion Photography* (Boston and New York: Institute of Contemporary Art with Hatje Cantz)

Parr, Martin (2005) *Fashion Magazine* (Paris: Magnum)

Rudolph, Barbara (1991) 'Marketing Beauty and the Bucks', *Time*, 138/14, 7 October: 38–40

Smedley, Elliott (2000) 'Escaping to Reality: Fashion Photography in the 1990s', in Stella Bruzzi and Pamela Church Gibson (eds) *Fashion Cultures: Theories, Explorations and Analysis* (London and New York: Routledge)

Stallabrass, Julian (1996) *Gargantua: Manufactured Mass Culture* (London and New York: Verso)

Wilson, Elizabeth (2003 [1985]) *Adorned in Dreams: Fashion and Modernity* (New Jersey: Rutgers University Press)

15 The Line Between the Wall and the Floor: Reality and Affect in Contemporary Fashion Photography

Eugénie Shinkle

At the back of the Fall–Winter 2005–6 fashion issue of *Purple* is a visual essay by Juergen Teller. Fourteen of the sixteen photographs, part of Marc Jacobs' Fall–Winter 2005 advertising campaign, feature model Kristen McMenamy in evening wear. McMenamy is made up like a porcelain doll in a horror film. Her face is covered in white foundation, her hair is bleached, crimped and brushed out poker-straight, and her eyes are ringed with black eyeliner. Her poses are awkward, at times grotesque, and in several of the images she appears semi-clothed. None of this is especially shocking in itself – indeed, this sort of disturbing content has become something of a commonplace in recent fashion imagery. Nonetheless, there's something strangely unsettling about this spread, something that left me feeling a bit queasy, but unable to say exactly why. The unnerving effect of these images, and the failure of language to fully describe it, is the subject of this chapter.

Shot against the white-painted wall of a raw industrial space, Teller's images call attention to a visual trope that has become commonplace in recent fashion photography: the line between the wall and the floor. The alternative fashion press, in particular, delights in this dirty little detail: mucky skirting boards, rubbish and forgotten objects, tumbleweeds of dust and hair gathered in the angle between the wall and the bare concrete or dirty carpet beneath it. But this small environmental detail points to something much larger. The line is the apotheosis of fashion photography's fascination with the abject, and an emblem of its penchant for 'realism' (Arnold 1999; Evans 2000). It is an index of the street and of the gritty, transient world – complete with dirty flats, dirty clothes, blemished skin and lank hair – that lies beyond the fantasy realm of the designer's studio and the couture boutique. From 1980 onwards, the line was the stock-in-trade of magazines like *i-D*, *The Face*, *SleazeNation* and *Raygun*. Primly avoided, until recently, by more mainstream publications like *Vogue*, most of the 'alternative' lifestyles emblematized by the line are, these days, thoroughly complicit in the system of global capitalism that they set out to challenge three decades ago.

In what follows, however, I'd like to consider reality from a slightly different angle, and to explore the line between the wall and the floor as something more than a rhetorical figure. Too often, it is assumed that 'reading' a fashion image is the best (if not the only) way of working through its meaning. However, as Brian Massumi notes, 'approaches to the image in its relation to language are incomplete if they operate only on the semantic or semiotic level, however that level is defined (linguistically, logically, narratologically, ideologically, or all of these in combination…)' (2002: 27). The meaning of a fashion image (or any image, for that matter) is never purely rhetorical, never completely determined by linguistic codes – not 'logically connected to [its] content in any straightforward way' (24). Indeed Massumi understands such codes as sets of 'invariant generative rules' that *restrict* possible meanings rather than creating space for them to emerge. The meaning of an image, in other words, consists of far more than just what we read into it or what we are able to *say* about it. Looking also comprises a visceral dimension, and in Teller's images this dimension ruptures the circuit of desire that is typically understood as the ultimate goal of fashion imagery.

Just as dress and fashion are situated bodily practices (Entwistle 2000), so too is image perception. The act of perceiving an image involves *affective* responses on the part of the viewer, most of them involuntary. Affective responses are 'experiential [representations] of the personal significance of situations' (Clore and Gasper 2000: 14). Broadly speaking, they consist of emotional and physiological reactions which function in concert, beneath the level of conscious awareness, to shape our experience of an image and the way we feel about it. We do not simply 'see' images, in other words, we are *touched* by them in ways that structurally based critical approaches cannot adequately explain. More than just a text to be read, the image is also a site of affective labour.

This is true of all images, but fashion images, which address the body explicitly, bring the notion of affective response into sharp focus.

The body is a key term in the following discussion. Though many discussions of fashion photography focus closely on the body of the model (often casting it as passive and superficial, shaped by language and by a culturally determined repertoire of poses), the body of the photographer is only occasionally mentioned, and the body of the viewer is rarely, if ever, taken into account. Yet meaning takes shape via the traffic that goes on between all three of these bodies. The following discussion will concentrate on the affective exchanges that go on between two of these bodies: the represented body of the model in the image, and the real-world body of the viewer. As I will show, both of these bodies are also situated bodies, and both are active terms in the formation of meaning.

Art forms such as sculpture have always traded on tactility and affect, but these perceptual dimensions don't often play a part in the analysis of fashion imagery. Yet tempering the perceptual dimensions of touch and visceral response with desire has long been part of fashion photography's *modus operandi*. And when fashion photography takes on the guise of performance art, as it does here, the affective dimensions of perception are brought into close and productive contact with the aesthetic and signifying conventions in the image. We'll begin by examining the latter conventions, and the way that they operate to construct reality and the 'real' in fashion images. Aesthetically, Teller's images are among those that suggest a privileged relation to the real by borrowing from other photographic forms, such as the snapshot. On the level of signification, we will examine the way that the conventional fashion pose works to conceal or disavow the model's physical body: here, the real is framed as an outside or exterior, an unruly quality that representation can't quite come to terms with. While Teller's series presents a clear challenge to conventional aesthetic and signifying codes, it is the complex relationship between coded meaning and affective response that gives them their peculiar intensity. The third section of the paper details some of the key elements of affective response. Taking a brief detour into the unlikely field of cognitive neuroscience, we will explore how this discourse understands the interface between the image and the real – focusing closely on what it means to experience an image in an embodied way in a real-world context – before turning to Teller's images.

REALISM IN FASHION PHOTOGRAPHY

Since it first appeared in the alternative fashion press at the beginning of the 1980s, the line between the wall and the floor has become the emblem of a kind of banal realism in fashion imagery, representing a rejection not only of the public values of capitalist culture, but of its private ones as well. Though the tactics of documentary photography have been used by fashion photographers since the 1930s, fashion images have not often risked confusion with other forms of reportage. The 1980s, however, saw the emergence of the 'straight-up', which, at least initially, functioned as both fashion photograph and social document. In the straight-up, which was typically shot against the wall of a building or club rather than in a photographer's studio, the line features prominently as an emblem of the vibrant authenticity of the street, and as a defiant refusal of the exclusivity and superficiality that typified the world of commercial fashion.

Teller, along with contemporaries like Corinne Day, Glen Luchford, Davide Sorrenti, David Sims, Nigel Shafran and Wolfgang Tillmanns, was an early champion of the naive realist aesthetic, which dominated the editorial pages of the alternative fashion press for much of the nineties. The 'snapshot' style of such images lends them an air of authenticity that fashion photography is generally thought to lack. Approaching reality 'through the realm of the low-tech' (Poschardt 2003), the work of Teller and his contemporaries traded on the unstudied credibility of personal photography and on the close relationship that it suggests between photographer and model. For Teller in particular, this intimacy – and the mutual trust that goes with it – is a vital part of his work. We see it in his 1996 collaboration with McMenamy, who poses naked in a shabby flat, with bruised, blotchy skin and 'Versace' scrawled on her torso in lipstick. In this raw and intense series, Teller rejects both the formal conventions of fashion photography and the superficiality of the fashion world with its narrow definitions of beauty, creating a space for the model 'to find some authentic form of conveying herself' (Poschardt 2003).

To the more cynical eye, however, realism in fashion photography is just another marketing ploy. As Ulrich Lehmann understands it, realism is simply one rhetoric among many others, an artificially limited language projecting 'a cultural and commercial universality through a shared interest in [clothes]' (2002: np). Under this argument, the realist fashion photograph is nothing more than an attempt by the world of fashion to shed its commercial image by co-opting the codes of 'legitimate' forms of artistic photography (Smedley 2000). The suggestion that this courtship is ephemeral and motivated largely by fashion's obsession with novelty casts the fashion image as a quintessentially postmodern form of representation, one in which aesthetic concerns are necessarily subordinate to the logic of capital.

This approach makes no distinction between fashion photographs and advertisements – both are 'social texts motivated by competition for market shares' (Goldman 1992: 9). It claims that images that appear to have dispensed with commercial agendas have, in fact, done no such thing. Though realist fashion photographs may challenge conventional codes, they are simply coded differently, designed to appeal to a market that eschews the conventions of more traditional imagery. Rather than being a radically different kind of image, they simply require a different kind of interpretive labour, and the identity of their market is based, in part, on its ability to perform this labour. As Rocamora and O'Neill note elsewhere in this volume, the 'reality' emblematized by the street has long been emptied of any actual social significance. This compromised realism is a form peculiar to fashion – a pseudo-documentary aesthetic that gestures outside of the realm of fashion, but that derives its logic from within this realm.

SIGNIFICATION AND THE POSE

Posing, for most of us, is a social game fraught with anxiety and internal contradiction: 'I pose, I know I am posing, I want you to know that I am posing, but … this additional message must in no way alter the precious essence of my individuality…' (Barthes 1981: 12). For Barthes, posing is about making oneself into an image, becoming an object for the camera. Because this image never coincides with the self, however, posing is a kind of death, a loss of self. The anxiety of posing is less of an issue for the professional model, for whom individuality is a marketable, rather than an essential, quality. The professional model knows how to work on her or his skin from within, to avoid sacrificing the self by ensuring that it is never fully revealed to the camera. The failure of the posed self to coincide with the 'real' self is less of a concern here, because the pose is not about identity, but about representation – it is part of a lexicon of poses, and as such it is not intended to represent anything personal or essential about the individual who assumes it.

Up until the 1950s, this lexicon consisted primarily of formal gestures copied from other art forms. A 1911 issue of *Les Modes* features the actress Mistinguet in a variety of self-consciously sculptural 'attitudes' as she models winter ensembles. As a young model in the 1930s, Lisa Fonssagrives used arrested dance movements – 'still-dancing', as she termed it – in front of the camera, and studied portraits in the Louvre to learn 'how to sit, hold her hands, and smile' (Gross 1996: 47). In the 1960s Richard Avedon juxtaposed the formal studio tradition with the vitality of outdoor realism to create a signature style that has gone on to become a commonplace in fashion photography (Hall-Duncan 1979). Framing his models against a seamless white studio backdrop, Avedon put them through a range of abstracted 'real-world' gestures and poses – a rhetoric intended, as Barthes remarks, 'to give a spectacularly empirical version of the body…' (1985: 259). The quintessence of the fashion pose is its difference from the gestural repertoire of real, situated bodies. The fashion pose signifies 'fashion' before anything else. Its sole context is that of the fashion image, and this self-referentiality often makes it difficult to read the fashion pose in a conventional way.

The narcissistic character of the fashion pose has also led to claims that it masks the actual body beneath it, reducing the latter to a 'pure form which possesses no attribute' (Barthes 1985: 259) or a mannequin that 'bears no relation to the sensual body' (Lehmann 2002: np). 'Taken "in charge" by an intelligible system of signs, [its] sentience…dissolved in the signifier' (Barthes 1985: 260), the body of the model, we are told, can only ever communicate with the consumer in the language of fashion and the fashionable. Here, the real (to which the body belongs) is cast as an existential register that needs shaping by signification in order to be available to experience. At the same time, however, the posing body is always, necessarily, a situated body, part of a wider material environment – and as such, it is available to the viewer as both a signifying form and as a potential site of affective exchange.

IMAGE PERCEPTION AND AFFECTIVE LABOUR

Though image perception is typically associated with vision, it is not restricted to this one sense. In fact, the human sensory apparatus integrates information from several different sensory channels in order to create a single coherent sensation. What we think of as a simple visual impression actually involves a combination of sensory modalities.

Vision and touch are particularly closely linked, and the traffic between them is especially relevant to this discussion. As Yi-Fu Tuan points out, 'our visual environment feels ineluctably tactile even though we touch only a small part of it' (2005: 76). We have long thought of things as diverse as human expressions, colours and artworks in terms of tactile values. More recently, research in the field of cognitive neuroscience has found that vision and touch share the same neural substrate: both senses are processed in the same area of the brain, rather than in separate areas, as was formerly thought (James et al. 2004). The phenomenon of visuo-affective mapping makes use of this crossover between vision and touch. So-called 'mirror neurons' in the brain fire not only when we perform a particular action ourselves, but when we witness someone else performing it (Buccino et al. 2004). Seeing pain and feeling pain, for example, activates the same area in the brain. During social interactions, this phenomenon enables us to 'transform visual information about someone else's emotional state (on the basis of facial expressions or other relevant cues) into similar emotional dispositions of our own' (Morrison and Ziemke 2005). Visuo-affective mapping thus plays an important role in human features like empathy.

Emotional response is also an important part of image perception. Emotions, however, consist of more than the manifest feelings that we recognize as anger, happiness etc. Though emotions are often described as 'states of mind', it is more accurate to describe them as 'states of body'. They involve not only expressive behaviour, but physiological changes as well: a change in pulse rate, the dilation or contraction of blood vessels, and the release of various hormones and neurotransmitters (Damasio 1994). Such responses take place, on average, half a second *before* we become aware of the emotion in our conscious mind (Massumi 2002: 28). This presents a significant challenge to the notion of a rational self in control of its emotions.

In short, what we think of as a visual experience is in fact a complex response involving both the mind and the body. The full extent of this response is neither fully available to consciousness, nor fully describable by language. We don't simply see and read images, we *feel* them, and this introduces some complications into semiotic or aesthetically based distinctions between the image and the real. Examining the image as a site of affective labour means considering perception as an embodied exchange, and the real as a dimension of perception that exists alongside, rather than exterior or prior to, the image's sociolinguistic context.

Affective response should not, however, be confused with 'natural' or 'primitive' behaviour. Though it may begin before language kicks in to describe it, affective response is also shaped by its cultural context. The embodied self is a feedback system that belongs to an historically specific time and place – a world that furnishes both the context and the possibility of subjectivity. Affective response includes both social and historical elements, but it 'mixes them with elements belonging to other levels of functioning and combines them according to a different logic' (Massumi 2002: 30). Historical meaning is embedded in gestures, postures and actions as well as language; cultural memory is not simply 'retained' in the mind but *incorporated* in, and by, the body. The relationship between affect and signification is thus not one of *before* or *after*, but one of simultaneity. The rhetorical codes in the image work in concert (though not always, as we'll see, in perfect harmony) with the affective dimensions of perception to shape our experience of an image, to make it meaningful. Here, the real is neither an aesthetic category nor an 'outside', but a perceptual dimension. With this in mind, let's turn to Teller's unsettling spread.

TELLER AND MCMENAMY: VISION, TOUCH AND ABJECTION

No longer bound to ideals of beauty, fashion imagery has come to serve equally as a platform for the exploration of the grotesque and the disturbing. Teller and McMenamy's collaboration plays with the boundary between the two. McMenamy's androgynous, 'jolie-laide' persona and Teller's stripped-down style with its use of harsh direct flash lend the images a raw and confrontational air. Shot through with references to bondage, the series plays strongly on the power relations between photographer and model. But the potency of the *Purple* spread goes deeper than this. Equally compelling is the ambiguity of feeling that the images evoke. On this level, what they deliver is 'not so much a specific message, but rather contemplation without meaning' (Bate 2004: 33) This is not to suggest that the images aren't meaningful – far from it – only that what is meaningful about them is not easily put into words. Considered alongside the more obvious content of the series, these affective responses allow us to examine the images not just in terms of their manifest cultural meaning, but phenomenologically, in terms of their effect on the individual viewer.

When we look at a representation of the body, we perceive it in terms of our own experience of embodiedness. We don't simply 'read' the postures and gestures that a body assumes, we map these postures and gestures onto our own body, feeling them in our own skin and bones, muscles and viscera. Although the conventional fashion pose may have little to do with real-world actions, it is nonetheless part of a lexicon which provides a context and gives it identity as a pose. McMenamy and Teller parody or refuse this lexicon. In several of the images, Teller's flash captures her in jerky motion, her face contorted, neck stretched and eyes bulging as she snaps her head back. In others, she flops forward from the waist like a weirdly hinged mannequin, or stands stiffly, her feet sticking out at odd angles and her arms held awkwardly. Her postures bear little relation to real-world actions or to other fashion images. Indeed, many of the attitudes in which Teller has captured his model don't make sense in any context, except perhaps that of modern dance. Even here, the impression is less of a body captured in motion, than of one caught in an unsteady state *between* gestures. McMenamy lacks the physical grace and control that we expect of either a model or a dancer. Instead, hers is a distorted, uncomfortable, poorly-managed body, tossed about wildly like a crash-test dummy. Viewing these images, we make McMenamy's discomfort into our own, mapping her strangely contorted limbs onto our own body, feeling the same kind of dis-ease and distress that we feel when looking at a broken limb.

Though we are invited to empathize with McMenamy on a bodily level, her facial expressions provide little in the way of emotional cues. Her gaze vacillates between passive and confrontational, settling most often on bland neutrality or semi-consciousness. Her eyes, heavy-lidded in some images, rolled back into her head in others, are alternately glazed and glaring. Even when she meets the eyes of the viewer, as she does in several of the shots, there is no clear intention in her look – at times it displays the vague inwardness of a trance. Emotions are designed to provide information and guide our attention; while a strong emotion can direct our attention, a vague one can let it wander. McMenamy's ambiguous or neutral facial expressions are difficult to read in concert with her postures. Rather than shedding light on her interior state, lending some sort of meaning to her contortions, they merely make it, and them, more opaque. McMenamy doesn't let us in, and her zombie-like state (like that of a body animated by a will that is not its own) parodies the model's conventional role.

There are still more conflicting sensory memories embedded in these images. Dress, as Joanne Entwistle has noted, is both an 'intimate experience of the body and a public presentation of it' (2000: 7). Clothing is more than a sign worn on the surface of the body, it is an interface that operates on the boundary between self and other, where the individual's experience of their own flesh comes into contact with the public realm. The wearing of clothes has both tactile and sociocultural memories embedded in it, and fashion photography trades on this link between the sensual and the social, using the drape and texture of fabric to evoke its touch on the body. In Teller's images, however, this touch is awkward and slightly repellent. McMenamy is swathed and smothered by her outfits, many of which appear ill-fitting or simply too big. A red velvet strapless dress sits precariously low on her small bust; an electric-blue silk tunic hangs from her shoulders like a wet dishrag. Clad in an unbecomingly high-waisted, puff-sleeved black dress, hands clasped nervously at her waist, she seems upholstered, imprisoned in her frock. Set back from the picture plane, with an expanse of concrete floor in front of her and a brick wall at her back, the latter image combines the uncomfortable touch of cold satin and concrete against the skin with the withering shame of turning up at a formal event in a hand-me-down dress two sizes two large. Silks, satins and velvet – materials that should drape softly, caressing the skin – appear heavy, cumbersome and too thick. Some of the dresses stand away from her body like over-starched doll's costumes. Teller's flash reflects harshly off the surface of others, giving them a hard, metallic sheen or a gun-metal opacity that obscures the shape of both dress and model. Even McMenamy's hair is peculiarly textured. Dark brown at the roots, bleached white at the crown, and brassy yellow at the ends, it has been crimped, straightened and brushed until it hangs bristling. In one double-page close-up, her features are almost obscured by the gutter, while her hair reaches out across both pages like filaments of wire. Like the dresses she models, it is stiff and unyielding, unwelcoming to the touch.

McMenamy's wild contortions stand in sharp contrast to other images in which she sits or stands passively, looking straight into the camera, her body slack and her arms hanging limply at her sides. In two of the photographs, she appears semi-clothed, the straps of her outfit pulled down to reveal her breasts as she leans back against the brick wall. In one particularly strong image, she lifts her skirt, parting it like theatre curtains, to reveal her crotch. Her gaze is open and direct, calmly acquiescent as she performs this incongruously intimate gesture (Plate 19). This is not the carefully crafted semi-nudity (or total nudity) of the conventional fashion image. Here, not only do we share the discomfort (tempered, perhaps, with the erotic charge) of appearing in public partially clothed, but we glimpse the relationship of trust that forms the core of this performance. Facing the camera with an open gaze, self-consciously posing, with all of the vulnerability that this involves, McMenamy invites Teller to peel away the layers of artifice that form the model's pictured (picturable) identity. Quite simply, she exposes herself.

CONCLUSION

Jean Arnaud, discussing the work of Canadian artist Michael Snow, comments on his use of the photograph as an 'active interface between its referent (before) and the viewer's space (after)' (2005: 14). Fashion photography operates in a similar way: its power lies, in part, in its ability to link seeing and meaning to *feeling*. Teller's images play on this indirect and equivocal form of address, stirring up emotions but refusing to let these feelings settle out into verbal form. They are meaningful to us not just because they speak languages (of dress, gesture etc.) that we understand, but because they link us affectively to the bodies that they re-present. In this, they are no different from any other image of a body. However, a good fashion image, or at least a memorable one, always brings the viewer back to the body, always comprises this fragile balance of the spoken and the unspeakable, this frustration of rational, legible vision.

We map our bodies onto other seen bodies, and it is partly through this intuitive mapping of our own perceptions onto the corporeality of others that we form our sense of self. Mapping one's own self-image onto an image of oneself – modelling, posing for the camera – is quite a different thing. The conscious and able management of this performance – the awareness, on the part of the professional model, of the delicacy of skin between self and persona – is an acquired skill. This is something that McMenamy knows and deliberately forgets, just as Teller has dispensed with the formal attributes of fashion photography. It is this knowing and forgetting which allows their collaborative performance to engage with the real as an aesthetic, an unknowable quality, and a link to embodied agents – and thus to challenge and redeploy the cultural codes of fashion, to break away from the ideological strictures that pull the body away from the self and banish it from the image.

WORKS CITED

Arnaud, Jean (2005) 'Touching to See', *October* 114 (Fall 2005): 5–16

Arnold, Rebecca (1999) 'The Brutalized Body', *Fashion Theory* 3 (4): 487–502

Barthes, Roland (1981) *Camera Lucida: Reflections on Photography*, trans. Richard Howard (New York: Noonday Press)

— (1985) *The Fashion System*, trans. Matthew Ward and Richard Howard (London: Jonathan Cape)

Bate, David (2004) 'After Thought Part II: Neo Realism and Postmodern Realism', *Source* 41 (Winter 2004): 34–39

Buccino, F., N. Lui, I. Canessa, G. Patteri, F. Lagravinese, C. Benuzzi, A. Porro and G. Rizzolatti (2004) 'Neural Circuits Involved in the Recognition of Action Performed by Nonspecifics: An fMRI Study', *Journal of Cognitive Neuroscience* 16 (1): 114–26

Clore, Gerald L. and Karen Gasper (2000) 'Feeling is Believing: Some Affective Influences on Belief', in Frijda et al. (eds) *Emotions and Beliefs: How Feelings Influence Thoughts* (Cambridge: Cambridge University Press): 10–44

Damasio, Antonio (1994) *Descartes' Error: Emotion, Reason, and the Human Brain* (New York: Penguin)

Entwistle, Joanne (2000) *The Fashioned Body: Fashion, Dress, and Modern Social Theory* (Cambridge: Polity Press)

Evans, Caroline (2000) 'Yesterday's Emblems and Tomorrow's Commodities: The Return of the Repressed in Fashion Imagery Today', in Stella Bruzzi and Pamela Church Gibson (eds) *Fashion Cultures: Theories, Explanations and Analysis* (London and New York: Routledge): 93–109

Goldman, Robert (1992) *Reading Ads Socially* (London and New York: Routledge)

Gross, Michael (1996) *Model: The Ugly Business of Beautiful Women* (New York: Warner Books)

Hall-Duncan, Nancy (1979) *The History of Fashion Photography* (New York: H.N. Abrams)

James, T.W., K.H. James, G.K. Humphrey and M.A. Goodale (2004) 'Do Visual and Tactile Object Representations Share the Same Neural Substrate?', in M.A. Heller and S. Ballesteros (eds) *Touch and Blindness: Psychology and Neuroscience* (Mahwah: Lawrence Erlbaum)

Lehmann, Ulrich (2002) 'Fashion Photography', in Ulrich Lehmann (ed.) *Chic Clicks: Creativity and Commerce in Contemporary Fashion Photography* (Boston and New York: Institute of Contemporary Art with Hatje Cantz)

Massumi, Brian (2002) *Parables for the Virtual: Movement, Affect, Sensation* (Durham, NC and London: Duke University Press)

Morrison, India and Tom Ziemke (2005) 'Empathy with Computer Game Characters: A Cognitive Neuroscience Perspective', in *AISB '05: Proceedings of the Joint Symposium on Virtual Social Agents* (UK: Society for the Study of Artificial Intelligence and Simulation of Behaviour): 73–79

Poschardt, Ulf (2003) 'Feeling What You See', in Ute Eskildsen (ed.) *Juergen Teller: Märchenstüberl* (London: Stiedl)

Smedley, Elliott (2000) 'Escaping to Reality: Fashion Photography in the 1990s', in Stella Bruzzi and Pamela Church Gibson (eds) *Fashion Cultures: Theories, Explorations and Analysis* (London and New York: Routledge): 143–56

Tuan, Yi-Fu (2005) 'The Pleasures of Touch', in Constance Classen (ed.) *The Book of Touch* (London: Berg): 74–79

Contributors

Sascha Behrendt has been involved in the fashion industry since the early eighties, when she worked as a model in Paris. Since 2002 she has worked with Peter Saville at Saville Associates as freelance art director for various clients, including Stella McCartney. From 2003 until 2005 Sascha art directed all of Stella McCartney's fashion campaigns, as well as consulting for Greys advertising agency on their hair and beauty clients. Sascha now lives in Berlin with her young son and partner, photographer Ernst Fischer, where they are working on separate creative projects.

Dr Becky E. Conekin is Principal Lecturer and Senior Research Fellow in Historical and Cultural Studies at the London College of Fashion, the University of the Arts, London, and Course Director of its MA in the History and Culture of Fashion. She holds a PhD in History from the University of Michigan, Ann Arbor. She is the author of *The Autobiography of a Nation: The 1951 Festival of Britain* (Manchester University Press, 2003). In the Spring of 2006, she co-edited and contributed to the special tenth anniversary double issue of *Fashion Theory* on *Vogue* magazine. She is the co-editor of *The Englishness of English Dress* (Berg, 2002) and *Moments of Modernity: Reconstructing Britain 1945–1964* (Rivers Oram Press, 1999). She is currently working on a variety of topics, including Lee Miller, fashion modelling in the 1950s, and the English cottage garden as a symbol of Englishness in the twentieth century.

Caroline Evans is Professor of Fashion History and Theory at Central Saint Martins College of Art and Design, University of the Arts, London. Her recent books are *Fashion at the Edge: Spectacle, Modernity and Deathliness* (Yale University Press, 2003), the co-authored *The London Look: Fashion from Street to Catwalk* (Yale University Press, 2004), the co-edited *Fashion and Modernity* (Berg, 2005) and the co-written *Hussein Chalayan* (NAI Publishers, 2005).

Philippe Garner is International Specialist in Twentieth Century Decorative Art and Design at Christie's London. His career spans over thirty years; he was instrumental in introducing photographs to auction, and he has played a key role in expanding the field of twentieth-century decorative arts and design. Philippe Garner has published numerous books, articles and essays on decorative arts, design and photography, and has curated a number of museum exhibitions at locations such as the Hôtel de Sully in Paris and the V&A museum in London.

Susan Kismaric is Curator in the Department of Photography at the Museum of Modern Art in New York. She has organized numerous exhibitions, including *Path of Resistance* (2000), *David Goldblatt: Photographs from South Africa* (1998) and *William Klein* (1981). She has authored numerous exhibition catalogues and has also contributed essays to a variety of major books published by the museum, including *Modern Starts* (2000) and *People, Places and Things* (1999). Before joining the museum, she attended Pennsylvania State University and worked for five years in the picture collection at Time & Life Corporation. She has been a visiting Senior Critic of Photography at the Yale School of Art since the early 1980s, most recently in the spring of 2006.

Margaret Maynard is Associate Professor and an Honorary Research Consultant in the School of English, Media Studies and Art History at the University of Queensland. She is an acknowledged expert on fashion and dress studies in Australia. Her most recent book is *Dress and Globalisation* (Manchester University Press, 2004). She is currently working on a cultural history of twentieth-century Australian fashion photography, funded by an ARC Discovery Grant. She is editor of volume 7 (*Australia and the Pacific Islands*) of *The Encyclopaedia of World Dress and Fashion* (Berg, forthcoming 2010).

Alistair O'Neill is a Research Fellow and Senior Lecturer in Cultural and Historical Studies at London College of Fashion, University of the Arts, London. Recent projects include curating the exhibition *Fashion Lives* (British Library, London, 2005) and the publication of *London: After a Fashion* (Reaktion Books, 2007).

Karen de Perthuis has worked as a fashion stylist and costume designer in the film, advertising and fashion industries for many years, as well as teaching and writing on fashion. She has a PhD in Art History and Theory from the University of Sydney for her thesis 'Dying to be Born Again: Mortality, Immortality and the Fashion Model'. In 2006 she was awarded a scholarship under the 'Thesis to Book' linkage project between the University of Sydney and Pan Macmillan Australia, and is currently reworking her doctoral thesis into a book titled *The Idea of Fashion*.

Eva Respini is Assistant Curator in the Department of Photography at the museum of Modern Art, New York. Exhibitions that she has organized at the Museum include *Fashioning Fiction in Photography Since 1990*, *Out of Time: A Contemporary View*, *New Photography '05: Carlos Garaicoa, Bertien van Manen, Phillip Pisciotta, Robin Rhode* and *Projects 81: Jean Shin*. She is the co-author of *Fashioning Fiction in Photography Since 1990* (Museum of Modern Art, 2004), and has contributed to MoMA publications on contemporary art, including *Greater New York 2005* and *Contemporary Highlights*. She is also an instructor at the School of Visual Arts, New York. She holds an MA in Modern Art and Critical Theory and a BA in Art History from Columbia University.

Kate Rhodes is Curator at the National Design Centre Melbourne and Cultural Program Manager at the L'Oréal Melbourne Fashion Festival 2007–8. She was formerly Curator at Craft Victoria and Assistant Curator of Photography and Contemporary Art at the National Gallery of Victoria. She completed a masters thesis on the cinematic impulse in contemporary photography at the University of Melbourne in 2002, and is currently completing an MA by Research at the Royal Melbourne Institute of Technology on the aesthetics of poverty in fashion.

Dr Agnès Rocamora is a Senior Research Fellow and Senior Lecturer in Cultural and Historical Studies at the London College of Fashion, University of the Arts, London. Her writing on the field of fashion and on fashion journalism has appeared in various journals, including *Fashion Theory* and the *Journal of Consumer Culture*. She is a contributor to *Fashion's World Cities*, edited by C. Breward and D. Gilbert (Berg, 2006), and is currently working on a monograph entitled *Fashioning the City: Paris, Fashion and the Media*, to be published by I.B. Tauris.

Stephanie Neda Sadre-Orafai is a doctoral candidate in the Department of Anthropology at New York University. Her dissertation research explores the production of commercial multicultural iconography through an analysis of the casting process – specifically the linguistic, visual and embodied practices of and interactions between models and casting professionals – in the New York fashion industry. She is the recipient of a Ford Predoctoral Fellowship for Minorities and a Wenner-Gren Foundation for Anthropological Research Dissertation Fieldwork Grant.

Eugénie Shinkle is a photographer and Senior Lecturer in Photographic Theory and Criticism in the School of Media, Arts and Design at the University of Westminster, London. As well as fashion photography, she has a special interest in digital games and the haptic and embodied dimensions of image perception, and lectures and publishes widely in these fields. She is also a regular contributor to photographic journals such as *Source*, and has been exhibiting her photographic work internationally since 1992.

Bärbel Sill was born in Germany in 1972. She studied French and English Literature as well as Media Studies at the University of Cologne before obtaining her doctorate in Film and Media Studies at the University of Sorbonne Nouvelle in Paris. Specializing in movie stars, her doctoral thesis dealt with the star system in American Cinema. In 1996, she also started working as a fashion and beauty assistant for international fashion magazines like *Marie Claire*, *Elle* and *Vogue*, before becoming an editor herself. Since 2004, she has worked as a freelance TV journalist, reporting on international news, fashion and film.

Isabelle Loring Wallace is Assistant Professor of Contemporary Art at the Lamar Dodd School of Art at the University of Georgia in Athens. She has published widely in the field of modern and contemporary art on topics ranging from Edouard Manet to Jenny Saville, and is currently at work on a book entitled *Signification and the Subject: The Art of Jasper Johns*.

Index

Figures in *italics* refer to illustrations, figures in **bold** refer to essays.